Keep Your Dog Healthy
the Natural Way

Also by Pat Lazarus

Keep Your Cat Healthy the Natural Way
Healing the Mind the Natural Way
Keep Your Pet Healthy the Natural Way

Keep Your Dog Healthy
the Natural Way

Pat Lazarus

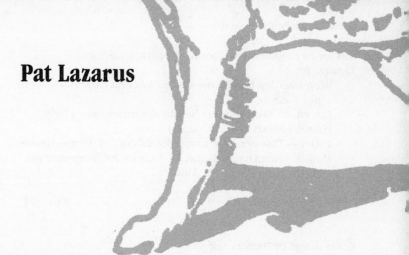

Fawcett Books
The Ballantine Publishing Group • New York

A Fawcett Book
Published by The Ballantine Publishing Group

Copyright © 1999 by Pat Lazarus

All rights reserved under International and Pan-American Copyright Conventions. Published in the United States by Ballantine Books, a division of Random House, Inc., New York, and simultaneously in Canada by Random House of Canada Limited, Toronto.

Fawcett is a registered trademark and the Fawcett colophon is a trademark of Random House, Inc.

A portion of this book was published in *Keep Your Pet Healthy the Natural Way* by Pat Lazarus, Macmillan, 1983. Copyright © 1983 by Pat Lazarus.

www.randomhouse.com/BB/

LIBRARY OF CONGRESS CATALOGING-IN-PUBLICATION DATA
Lazarus, Pat.
    Keep your dog healthy the natural way / Pat Lazarus. —1st ed.
      p.   cm.
    Rev. ed. of: Keep your pet healthy the natural way. c1983.
    ISBN 0-449-00514-3 (alk. paper)
      1. Dogs—Diseases—Alternative treatment. 2. Dogs—Health.
  3. Holistic veterinary medicine. I. Lazarus, Pat. Keep your pet healthy the natural way. II. Title.
SF991.L33   1999
636.7'0893—dc21   99-10801
                                        CIP

Cover design by Barbara Leff
Cover photo © Steve Solum/WestStock

Manufactured in the United States of America

First Edition: July 1999

10 9 8 7 6 5 4 3 2

Dedication

This book is dedicated to the people who shared my strong desire to give to the public new information that can give shiny, healthy, and long lives to our dog companions— and who worked with me to make this book possible.

Obviously, I owe the very existence of this book to the many holistic veterinarians who freely gave of their time and expertise in interviews with me, in sending published material, and in checking the manuscript word for word for accuracy.

Those veterinarians are, in alphabetical order, Nino Aloro, D.V.M., of Virginia; Sheldon Altman, D.V.M., California; Ihor John Basko, D.V.M., Hawaii; John Fudens, D.V.M., Florida; Robert Goldstein, V.M.D., Connecticut; Michael W. Lemmon, D.V.M., Washington; John B. Limehouse, D.V.M., California; Jack Long, V.M.D., California; S. Allen Price, D.V.M., Alabama; Phillip Racyln, D.V.M., New York; Norman C. Ralston, D.V.M., Texas; Robert J. Silver, D.V.M., Colorado; Priscilla A. Taylor, D.V.M., California; Carvel G. Tiekert, D.V.M., Maryland; and Neal K. Weiner, D.V.M., California.

I owe gratitude to my husband, Joe, also a medical writer, who helped me with many of the mechanical aspects of this compilation and who gave me strong psychological support, as he has throughout our marriage.

And I must thank Brendan Robinson, who stepped in and rescued the manuscript after a computer breakdown. Perhaps fittingly, it was Brendan's inspired work in devising a successful healing diet for his pet scheduled for euthanasia that started my interest in holistic veterinary medicine some two decades ago.

Contents

Foreword

*I invite you to read this book and begin an adventure of a
lifetime, one that I believe may dramatically change not
only your dog's life, but also your own.*

*It is with great pride that I have written this foreword
for Pat Lazarus' book,* Keep Your Dog Healthy the Natural
Way. *When the author contacted me approximately a year
ago to contribute, along with many other holistic
veterinarians, information for this book and its companion*
(Keep Your Cat Healthy the Natural Way), *I thought, Sure, why
not? I had contributed to other authors' books, and I had
done radio and television appearances, given lectures, and
written articles on holistic veterinary medicine.*

*Everyone I have helped has been sincerely dedicated to
providing the public information that can help suffering
animals and improve not only the length but also the
quality of their lives. What I didn't expect was the unusual
professionalism, intense determination for detail and
accuracy, intelligence, and thoroughness with which
Lazarus has compiled these two books.*

*None of this would have surprised me if I had known
when Lazarus first contacted me that she was the author of*
Keep Your Pet Healthy the Natural Way, *a similar
compilation of many holistic veterinarians with expertise
in treating various disorders. That earlier book was hailed*

*as a breakthrough in veterinary medical literature and
became what is known in publishing as a classic: that is, it
remained in print for some seventeen years. Even then, the
book went out of print only because the author recalled the
rights in order to compile her newest books, which greatly
expand and completely update the first one.*

*The breadth of knowledge Lazarus has reported on here
gives readers a broad range of viewpoints, expertise, and
therapies—including natural diet (which is definitely not
the packaged and canned foods you may be feeding your
dog), nutritional supplements, acupuncture, herbs,
homeopathy, chiropractic, and glandular extracts—from
which each reader can choose what is best for the
individual animal companion. She also covers many
disorders, getting her information not only from cutting-
edge research but directly from holistic veterinarians with
expertise in treating the individual disorders. This broad
range of practical information is unique in the array of
books available to the public.*

*In reading this book you will find, if you are newly
discovering alternative therapies for dogs, that there are
countless noninvasive, nontoxic, and gentler ways to cure
your sick companion than what I personally call the "cut,
burn, and poison" approaches of surgery and drugs. You'll
find that these techniques, which truly live up to the
Hippocratic oath taken by doctors ("first, do no harm"),
tend to be less expensive than drugs and surgery. And, as
Lazarus points out with holistic veterinarians' clinical
statistics and with numerous inspiring case histories from
their files of "doomed" dogs (including her own miniature
poodle), alternative techniques often restore animals to
radiant good health even after they've been diagnosed as
"hopeless" or "terminal" by veterinarians practicing only
conventional medicine.*

As Lazarus is careful to point out, very often the same therapies are used successfully by holistic M.D.s to treat similar disorders in humans. So as you read about how holistic veterinarians successfully treat arthritis, glaucoma, diabetes, cancer, etc., you will also be gaining new hope and suggestions for rebuilding your own health and that of your human loved ones.

As detailed as Lazarus' research and information are, she presents everything in a style that is always interesting and easy to understand for lay readers. (Her patience, gentleness, and understanding as she takes readers on a journey that may be relatively—or even completely—new to them has often reminded me of the spiritual qualities of my beloved grandmother.)

In giving readers knowledge of the full range of holistic choices open to them and their canine companions, Lazarus includes the expertise of the full spectrum of veterinarians using natural therapies: beginning with the most conservative holistic veterinarian, whom I personally consider mainly a conventional doctor who provides some holistic therapies, and progressing through to a radical like myself.

Actually, I didn't become a radical overnight: I have been in practice for over thirty-four years. For the first eight years, I practiced only the conventional therapies that I had been taught earning my D.V.M. degree. For the next seventeen years, I used both conventional and holistic medicine. As I added to my expertise in natural techniques, I found I had to rely less and less on potentially toxic therapies. Now I am a completely holistic practitioner who has rejected conventional veterinary medicine to the point of returning my New York and Florida licenses to practice drugs and surgery. I now practice under an H.M.C. (homeopathic master clinician) certification, which *allows me to use homeopathy to treat animals as well as people. But my first love is still the animals.*

Like Lazarus and the other veterinarians whose work she covers in this book, though, I realize that nutrients and homeopathy often cannot work alone in an intense emergency situation. When someone contacts me about a dog or cat who truly needs surgery or a drug, I refer the person to a conventional veterinarian, and then try to maintain control over the animal's total recovery, and reduce harmful side effects, by working with that doctor to add appropriate natural treatments.

As Lazarus stresses, many holistic veterinarians will directly use drugs and surgery in emergency situations. Yet if your dog has symptoms of, say, one of the acute infectious diseases that can overwhelm his body within hours, she urges you to rush him to the nearest available veterinarian, orthodox or holistic. ("It would be a shame to waste valuable time getting your companion to a holistic veterinarian," Lazarus writes, "when that doctor would probably start with the same treatment as the orthodox doctor.") Then, like me, she recommends that a holistic veterinarian be consulted by phone to add natural therapy to bring your dog to a real recovery and to offset the harmful effects of conventional treatment. Antibiotics, for instance, can help fight an infectious disease; but in destroying harmful bacteria, they also destroy "friendly" bacteria, which are crucial for overall good health. To offset this destruction, a holistic veterinarian may suggest a natural therapy of probiotics. These contain, in the proper balance, all the friendly bacteria and other microorganisms naturally present in a healthy body.

The bottom line is that I urge people to use drugs and surgery only for emergency, acute, life-threatening situations. These situations are those in which

conventional (orthodox) medicine triumphs. Natural
therapies take longer because they don't just cover up the
symptoms; they work biochemically within the body to get
at the actual cause of the symptoms and alleviate that.

   While conventional veterinary medicine is most helpful
in emergencies, especially if used along with natural
therapy, it can do nothing to prevent *disease. (And, as*
Lazarus details in this book, conventional medicine is
actually a major contributor to disease.) Holistic
veterinary medicine reigns supreme in prevention.
Lazarus devotes several chapters to details of how it is
almost completely within your power to prevent *your dog*
from ever becoming sick in the first place. She gives very
persuasive facts detailing exactly why holistic
veterinarians have always stated that the so-called
"nutritionally complete" commercial dog foods are a major
cause of disease and premature death in dogs. And she
lays open for your investigation the facts behind why
veterinarians specializing in natural care state that the
overuse of standard vaccinations is another major cause
of disease in our smaller friends. She also explains how
the misuse of these vaccinations is becoming an
increasing concern even among conventional
veterinarians and M.D.s.

   The author gives specific information on what you
should feed your dog to treat him to a long and disease-
free life, and she tells how you can make his natural diet
less expensive than the embalmed commercial pet foods.
(If you think "embalmed" is an overly dramatic word,
consider that formalin, a chemical commonly used in
preparing the dead for burial, is added as a preservative to
some pet foods.) The author also gives you very specific
information on how not to overuse standard vaccinations,
when to use homeopathic nosodes instead, and what

nutrients to give your dog to offset the dangerous effects of standard vaccinations when these may be the best way to protect your companion from a specific disorder.

Lazarus even gives details of how you should modify the basic preventative natural diet for what she calls "special times in your dog's life": pregnancy, lactation, puppyhood, and senior years. She even includes sections on how best to start orphaned puppies and stray adult dogs on the road to natural good health.

When my "right-hand" assistant, Barbara Foster, read the prevention section of this book, she commented that "this is the best—most complete—information on prevention that I've ever seen in a book." I agree.

Lazarus does not shortchange another basic difference between conventional veterinarians and holistic veterinarians: the latter doctors' tendency to make healing the animal's unique spirit a much more integral part of the therapy to heal the animal's body. Although Lazarus states she never knew an orthodox veterinarian who ignored an animal's psyche, she gives examples from holistic veterinarians such as: "We try not to treat a dog with, for instance, parvo, as if he were just 'a case of' parvo. Is he a frightened dog with parvo? Is he an angry dog with parvo? Is he a dog with parvo who feels lonely?"

That striving to treat the animal as an individual entity also is shown, as the author stresses, in the fact that holistic veterinarians don't tend to treat animals basically according to the disease label that best fits their symptoms. Our concern is more with what, exactly, is biochemically off base within the individual dog's or cat's body that is causing the symptoms that fit those of disease x or disease y. The author gives many examples of this, one of the most poignant being the case of her own small poodle, Shiki, who had been diagnosed by a major orthodox *veterinary center as having terminal cancer. Of course, the disease label of terminal cancer is an automatic death sentence in the world of conventional medicine. When she took little Shiki to holistic veterinarian Marty Goldstein, D.V.M., he said that he wouldn't consider Shiki as "a case of terminal cancer" but would scientifically test to see what nutrients were unbalanced in her body, which glands were functioning poorly, etc. You'll see more medical details, and the happy outcome, in "Shiki's Journey" in this book's introduction.*

In short, Lazarus has compiled, working closely with many holistic veterinarians, another unique book that can be considered a new breakthrough in veterinary medical literature. I hope you will read it and start the process of changing your pet companion's health and life around. And I hope you won't miss the signposts the book gives for taking the same road to optimal health for yourself and your human family.

> *God bless you.*
> *John H. Fudens, D.V.M., H.M.C.*

Introduction

How I Came to Write This Book

T*he first edition* of this book (which was called *Keep Your Pet Healthy the Natural Way* because it covered both dogs and cats) was inspired by two small poodles who recovered from diagnosed "hopeless" cases of arthritis through dietary changes only. One of the dogs, Shiki, was my own.

Shiki also inspired this new edition, in even more dramatic fashion, many years later when holistic therapy allowed her to recover completely from diagnosed terminal cancer.

Even though the first edition was continuing to sell after more than sixteen years (a very long time in the publishing world), Shiki's return from paralysis and coma to sprightly health within a few weeks made me research the advances holistic veterinary medicine had made in those years. (I hadn't looked into them previously because I write basically on alternative medicine for humans.) Once I saw how gigantic those advances are, I knew it was part of my "mission" in life to tell other people about them.

I would like to share with you right now the two case histories that inspired the first edition. I'll hold off giving details about Shiki's return from the land of terminal cancer until later in this introduction. I realize that if you are new to the field of alternative medicine, Shiki's experience sounds preposterous. I would like to lead you gradually into an understanding of just *how* and *why* holistic medicine works to achieve what seem to be wonders to those who have not investigated the field.

The first edition of this book began in the moment that my friends Brendan Robinson and Nick Cieri stood beside their totally crippled toy poodle, Little Boy, in their veterinarian's office and listened to the words: "This animal is far too advanced with arthritis to help in any way whatsoever. Put him to sleep. Please do it right now; every moment he lives is torture for him."

Luckily for Little Boy—and for all the dogs I believe will be helped by the little-known information in these pages—Bren and Nick chose to bundle up their little dog and take him home.

About a week later, I went over to visit. Little Boy was lying about six feet away from his bowl of food. He started a laborious attempt to crawl to his bowl. I say crawl, because walking—or even standing—had been impossible for the toy poodle for quite a while.

However, it was all too apparent that now crawling, too, was almost impossible. Each little leg crept out slowly, tentatively; and Little Boy squealed with pain at every movement as he tried to drag his small body along the floor.

While Bren and Nick fell over each other in a race to bring the food bowl to their pet, I found myself thinking something I never would have believed would cross my mind: "He *should* be put to sleep."

A week later, Bren phoned. "Do you think the diet for arthritis in human patients might possibly work for dogs, too?" he asked. Bren had studied such therapies for human beings extensively; I am a writer in the same field.

I thought a moment. "It might," I said. Then I added, "If it doesn't, what have you and Little Boy got to lose?"

"Right," Bren agreed. "What have we got to lose?"

Bren set to work adapting human therapy to what he could only hope were the correct differing needs of a dog. He had no book to guide him because there was none. And we did not know then that a small but growing number of veterinarians across the country were already using natural therapies for their patients.

Several weeks later, Bren called again. "Come on over," he said; "we have a surprise for you."

I was led out to the yard, where a tiny poodle of seemingly limitless energy—obviously a puppy—was playing a game by himself of leaping constantly to and fro over a low bush. When he saw me, he bounded over, tail wagging, and greeted me as if he knew me.

"Oh," I said, charmed, "you have a new little puppy!" (At the same time, I was thinking sadly that this new puppy's presence in the house meant that the nine-year-old Little Boy had been "disposed of.")

"Everybody says that!" Nick said, delighted.

"That's Little Boy," Bren said.

"That's Little Boy?" I said. "That can't *possibly* be Little Boy."

"I know it can't possibly be," Bren said, "but it is."*

Several months after Little Boy's return from the land of the hopeless, I took my own little black miniature poodle, Shiki, who was only a year old, to one of the top orthodox veterinary centers in the country; I wanted the best for my moppet. Shiki had been holding her right hind leg up in the air in a little ball and hobbling around on three feet for progressively longer periods of time. Lately, she had not been able to put her leg down at all.

"It's arthritis," the veterinarian said. "You really can't do anything for it. Just give her half a Tylenol when the pain gets too bad."

As you will see later in this book, I deplore the fact that it often takes so long for new medical ideas to supplant old, imbedded ones. Yet in Shiki's case, I myself almost fell prey to the thinking that keeps new ideas from being accepted in medicine.

Shamefully I must admit that it took me a full month to realize that there *was* something I could try for Shiki, despite the doctor's words. One night I was sitting at my typewriter unable to do much work as I sadly watched my courageous little black moppet playing happily by herself. She would throw her ball across the room, chase

---

* Little Boy died five years later, at age fourteen, of a fast-acting virus. But he was still leaping effortlessly over that bush a few hours before the virus struck.

it, retrieve it, and then growl at it for having tried to get away. Obviously this was real fun, because she was repeating the game over and over. What bothered me, however, was seeing her hobble across the room on three feet; and maybe I was imagining it, but was she starting to have trouble with one of her other legs, too?

"Oh, what's the use?" I said to myself. "I'm a medical writer; I know what is probably going to happen. She's going to get worse and worse, until she's as crippled as Little Boy used to be. She's going to have to be put to sleep, just as Little Boy was supposed to have been."

I wheeled back and ran that thought through my mind again: ". . . as crippled as Little Boy *used to be*?" ". . . be put to sleep, just as Little Boy *was supposed to have been*?"

I leaped across the room to the phone, almost tripping over Shiki, who was crossing my path in pursuit of her errant ball.

Bren answered the phone. "What is the diet you made up for Little Boy?" I asked, without taking the time to introduce myself.

"Who is this?" Bren asked.

"Never *mind* who this is," I said impatiently, and inanely. "*Just tell me what the diet is.* It might possibly help Shiki, too."

"You know," Bren said, "I was thinking that just the other day."

"The other day?" I said. "What took you so long?"

There was a pause. "I don't know," Bren said. "What took *you* so long?"

I threw Shiki's "nutritionally complete" supermarket dog foods out with the trash and started her on the more natural diet Bren had devised (which, by the way, turned out to be very close to the diet used successfully by the nutritional veterinarians whose work is detailed in this book). One day later I reported happily to my husband. "Shiki was able to put her leg down today for at least ten minutes!"

Two weeks later I was able to report, "Shiki held her leg up once today, for about two minutes."

Shiki remained free of arthritis until the day she died, of natural causes, almost two decades later.

How This Book Was Researched and Written

First, I obtained a list of veterinarians who belong to the American Holistic Veterinary Medical Association and sent them a questionnaire. This list told me their addresses and the fields of alternative medicine they are trained in (nutrition, herbology, homeopathy, acupuncture, kinesiology, chiropractic, and so on). Almost all of the doctors I chose to contact practiced a broad range of therapies, some as many as nine or ten. Occasionally, for a specific reason, I opted for a doctor who specialized in one therapy. I also had a strong preference for the veterinarians who had worked with me on the first edition. This preference came not only from loyalty but from the fact that by now these doctors have more experience in holistic veterinary medicine than anyone in history.

The responses to the questionnaire I sent told me, among other things, the disorders the veterinarians have the most hands-on experience in treating. I chose several doctors to interview for each chapter. As I had suspected, they assured me that the therapies covered in the first edition were still valid. As I also had suspected, the doctors now had numerous new therapies in their arsenals. (In the field of nutrition alone, there has been a virtual explosion of research in recent years. Many previously unknown nutrients have been discovered and studied, and new uses have been found for the ones that were known.)

I found that for disorders in which the diagnosis of terminal *sometimes* didn't mean terminal to a holistic veterinarian years ago, now it *often* doesn't. I found these doctors using newly discovered nutrients for disorders they previously had to treat with drugs or surgery. (As mentioned later, all holistic veterinarians have first received a veterinary degree in orthodox medicine.)

In short, as I listened to these veterinarians talk about their work, I kept thinking that Columbus wasn't the only one who ever discovered a whole new world.

For the most part, I have not interrupted the practical thrust of this book to cite the medical studies on which these doctors have based their work; but you should know that the doctors *are* using solid scientific bases. (Actually, it is an undisputed basic medical fact that nutrients create every biochemical reaction in our bodies. For instance, if you have a hormonal imbalance and are taking a synthetic hormone, you should realize that hormones are naturally produced every day in our bodies by certain nutrients. A holistic doctor will know how to give you the correct balance of nutrients to get your body producing the natural balance of hormones on its own— just as it always did before you got sick.) Also, you should know that when I give only one case history, it is only a representative case history chosen from many. I mention this because a number of the histories in this book will seem so astounding to you if you're new to alternative medicine that it would be easy to assume the doctors picked their one greatest success story to tell me about. And when I quote only one veterinarian, I do so only to personalize the information. It doesn't mean that there is only one doctor who uses the therapy being discussed.

What This Book Is All About

Obviously, this book is all about saving the lives of dogs. (Cats can also benefit equally from holistic therapy. I recently published a book, *Keep Your Cat Healthy the Natural Way*, devoted exclusively to our feline companions, who get different diseases than dogs do and who have different requirements for a basic preventive diet.) And as "my" veterinarians repeatedly pointed out to me, natural therapies that can cure such disorders as glaucoma, arthritis, and cancer are known to cure them in humans, too.

In this book holistic veterinarians tell you simple ways to *prevent* the disorders generally considered inevitable: cancer, heart problems, diabetes, arthritis, and so on. As I detail in chapter 2, these steps basically involve feeding your dog the diet her body evolved to thrive on—which is most probably *not* the diet you're feeding her— and can save you money, too.

Of course, there will be those of you for whom this book's prevention program comes too late, those of you with a dog stricken with a serious disease. As I have already given you every reason to expect, you will find details of successful natural therapies for many disorders.

Has orthodox veterinary medicine despaired of your pet? Have you been told to put him to sleep? PLEASE DO NOT PUT YOUR PET TO SLEEP BEFORE YOU READ THIS BOOK. You will find that holistic veterinarians often have extraordinary success with the "rejects" of traditional veterinary medicine; indeed, the majority of the case histories in this book detail recoveries of dogs who were given up on by orthodox veterinarians. As a matter of fact, time after time as I gathered material for this book, holistic veterinarians said to me sadly: "So often we get to see only the pet who has been given up on by traditional medicine. That is because many people don't think of natural medicine until everything else has been tried and has failed. While it is true that we often get good results with 'hopeless' cases, we can do even so much more when we can treat a pet in the early or intermediate stages of a disease."

The natural therapies covered in this book differ in three basic respects from drug and surgery treatments:

- The natural therapies do not tend to have the negative side effects of drugs and do not carry the dangers of surgery.
- The natural therapies do not attack just the *symptoms* of the disorder. Instead, they rebuild the total health of the body— *and the body heals itself*. In this way, as you will see, pets being treated by holistic veterinarians for one disorder tend to recover from other, seemingly unrelated disorders, too.
- Often, the natural therapies are less expensive than drugs or surgery. When the natural therapy is more expensive, it is because you are keeping your pet alive to be *on* the therapy. (A fatal dose of anesthesia—that is, euthanasia—isn't all that expensive.)

You may wonder: If nutritional medicine is so successful, why doesn't your veterinarian use it? The answer to that can be given in two parts. First, the dissemination of new medical knowledge tends to be much, much slower than most of the public realizes; and it is quite possible that your own veterinarian simply does not yet have the information put forth in this book. Another possible reason lies in the natural conservatism and skepticism of the scientific mind. This skepticism may very well have saved us from a lot of dangerous quackery, but it has also labeled as "quacks" a number of scientists later proven to be geniuses. And, as I detail later in this book, it has sometimes slowed down the use of new therapies now recognized as being responsible for saving millions of lives. For instance, antibiotics—now relied on so heavily by orthodox medicine— weren't used until a decade after they were discovered. It was obvious "quackery" for anyone to claim he had found a cure for not just one but a number of "hopeless" diseases in, of all things, the bark from a tree.

But times are definitely changing. The orthodox war against natural medicine—which at several points in recent history reached what might be called a fever pitch—has greatly died down in the last few years. It might be considered gratifying to note that the truce resulted in no small part from the will of the people. I think the tide turned when the prestigious journal for the union of orthodox M.D.s (the *Journal of the American Medical Association*) published a report that found that one in three Americans routinely visit alternative practitioners.

This surprising survey, and later results along this line that were even more surprising, led this union of orthodox doctors to urge their membership to consider learning alternative techniques.

By 1997, reportedly over one-third of this country's medical schools were offering courses in nutrition, acupuncture, homeopathy, massage, and—I might add—prayer. When I wrote the first edition, virtually no medical school offered even an elementary course in nutrition—even though it was well established by then that nutrients create every biochemical reaction in the body.

Health insurance companies have started joining the bandwagon, having realized that holistic care prevents disease and that its therapies are generally shorter term and less expensive.

Before I end this section, I would like to add one other way in which holistic veterinary medicine differs from orthodox. Holistic doctors do not tend to consider healing a dog's physical disorders to be the end-all and be-all of their responsibility. The word *holistic* used to be more often spelled *wholistic*—because in this approach to healing, the *whole* entity that comprises the animal (or human) is treated.

Holistic veterinarian John Fudens, D.V. M., expressed that idea to me this way: "The holistic view is that life is an integration of the physical with the spiritual, mental, and emotional. The physical is only an expression of the last three worlds."

Actually, I have never come upon an orthodox veterinarian who ignored an animal's psyche. But holistic veterinarians do tend to make the dog's spirit a more important part of their treatment. For instance, many holistic veterinarians now use kinesiology, a technique that allows them to diagnose not only physical problems within the dog's body, but also the emotional imprint the physical problems are causing. Holistic veterinarians explain to me that one dog with a specific disease may have a different emotional imprint than a second dog with the same disease: One dog with diabetes may be passionate and angry; another may be sad and hopeless. The differing emotional imprints play a part in the individual therapy prescribed for the individual animal.

I hope and believe that the compilation nature of this book gives you broader information—and from doctors with more expertise in the specific problem being discussed—than if I'd taken the easy way out and covered the work basically of only one doctor, as many books do. While this compilation nature has led me to track down veterinarians who specialize in one disorder—not just one part of the body, as, say, cardiologists and hematologists do—I will give a simpler example: The first holistic veterinarians I interviewed for this book told me that they hadn't seen a case of parvo in several years. The simple assumption would have been that this extremely serious disease was dying out, perhaps because generations of parvo vaccinations had led to puppies (who are particularly susceptible to parvo) being born with immunity.

But I knew that sometimes diseases are much more prevalent in some parts of the country than in others. So I talked to several other holistic veterinarians who also listed infectious diseases in dogs as an area of expertise. But this time I chose veterinarians in far different parts of the country. These doctors told me that parvo is one of the most common diseases they see. (Their successful therapy is detailed in chapter 8.)

How to Use This Book

If you have a new puppy and apply the principles detailed in the prevention chapters, you very probably will never have any use for the chapters on therapy. However, you may want to look over those chapters now, anyway: Very possibly either now or someday you may be able to help a friend's pet by alerting your friend to the information in these chapters.

If you are reading this book because you already have a sick animal, be sure you read the pertinent information carefully, especially if you do not already know a lot about nutritional medicine.

In some cases, treating your pet yourself is possible; and I have tried to indicate clearly when and exactly how you can administer treatment yourself. In treating your own pet, you *must* first have a clear-cut diagnosis from a veterinarian. Treating your pet for one disorder when he really has something quite different that just happens to have similar symptoms can be tantamount to killing him.

For the most part, however, I am against any medical treatment—either with drugs or natural therapies—that is not conducted by, or at least under the supervision of, a trained doctor.* The list at the back of the book gives phone numbers of many holistic veterinarians from around the country. If you don't live near enough to one of

---

* You will see later, for instance, that holistic veterinarians often use extremely high amounts of vitamins A and E. However, if you were to try giving the same high amounts of these two vitamins without consulting first with a veterinarian, you might cause your pet great harm. When veterinarians use large doses of vitamins A and E, they use the vitamins in a new, water-soluble form. The commonly available fat-soluble form can be highly toxic in large doses.

these doctors to take your pet in directly, I can tell you that many of them mentioned to me for this edition that over half the work they do is over-the-phone consultation.

Before sickness strikes your pet, choose a holistic veterinarian who will work with you *and* your orthodox veterinarian by phone. (Many of the nutritional, herbal, and homeopathic remedies used by holistic practitioners have in recent years become available not only in health food stores but also in drugstores. Or holistic veterinarians will mail some therapies to you. So don't be afraid that your orthodox doctor won't have the medicines needed.) In making your choice of a holistic doctor to deal *in person* with your dog, keep in mind that while the vast majority of these veterinarians use orthodox techniques when necessary for the individual case, I found a few who absolutely refused to use drugs or surgery. When these were needed, they sent the animal to an orthodox veterinarian. Do you want your dog to lose valuable time in an emergency?

Speaking of emergencies, generally these are the times when orthodox techniques are most valuable. If you're not close to a holistic doctor, take your companion to a nearby orthodox veterinarian. Get the dog stabilized, and then have the orthodox doctor consult by phone with your chosen holistic veterinarian. It would be a shame if you lost valuable time waiting to talk to a holistic veterinarian only to find out he or she would start off with the same therapies an orthodox doctor would.

Dogs are, unfortunately, quite prone to fast-acting diseases that give very little notice that the dog is ill until he is suffering an emergency. When you choose your friend's holistic veterinarian (consulting or personal), ask what homeopathics or other remedies you might keep on hand to help your dog until you can get veterinary help. A number of holistic veterinarians have told me they dispense lactated Ringer's kits to owners and teach them how to use them. These can often be the difference between life and death when the dog becomes dehydrated, which can hapen very suddenly. (See chapter 8 on infectious diseases.)

One final note about choosing a holistic veterinarian: More and more orthodox veterinarians are incorporating holistic therapies into their practices, and I have found a few who think of themselves as holistic but who still rely most heavily on their earlier training. Ask the doctor you're talking to approximately how many times he uses orthodox as opposed to holistic therapy.

A Note for Orthodox Veterinarians

First, I know that many of you have recently become interested in investigating holistic therapies for incorporation into your practice. Over the years I have received word from a number of orthodox veterinarians telling me that they were using the first edition as a basic starting point, which is certainly gratifying. But obviously the explosion of alternative medicine since 1981, when I researched that edition, has made the earlier book obsolete. Today's holistic veterinarians have assured me that nothing in the earlier book has proved invalid—but there is just so much more that can be done today, just as there have been many great advances made in orthodox medicine in those same years.

I hope this new edition will serve as an update for you if you used the first book as a starting point in your investigation of holistic veterinary medicine, or as an introduction to holistic veterinary medicine if you're just learning the ropes.

The list of veterinarians at the back of the book has been expanded since the first edition, so I have been able to give you addresses and phone numbers of more holistic doctors, should you wish to consult about something.

Now I would like to address myself to the more skeptical orthodox veterinarian.

I do not ask any orthodox veterinarian to abandon years of training, knowledge, experience, and success for an "opposite" field. I ask only that you consider adding to your success, experience, and knowledge with a successful adjunct therapy. You will see throughout this book that holistic veterinarians have not abandoned their years of training and experience in orthodox therapies. You will see surgery, antibiotics, and so on as a part of their treatment in a number of the specific case histories.

I think John S. Eden, D.V. M., expressed the above ideas very well. Dr. Eden once described his approach to veterinary medicine as "largely orthodox." He wrote me: "In my mind a combination of the two fields of knowledge seems the best of both worlds, and that is how I try to guide myself. . . . I deeply resent it when one side of this issue tries to debunk or discredit the other. It is a foolish waste of energy and only serves to prevent any exchange of information and to limit the capacity of both sides to solve problems." As Dr. Eden added, preventing this exchange of information "diminishes the ability to accomplish the common goal of seeking what is best for the animal."

The next time you have a pet in your office for which surgery or drugs offer no hope, please consult this book to see if it contains an approach relevant to that pet, consult with one of the holistic veterinarians named in the List, and try the suggested therapy before you put the pet to sleep. If the therapy doesn't work, you and your patient will have lost nothing. If it does, an animal will have been saved.

Shiki's Journey into—and out of— the Land of the Doomed

Earlier, I said I'd delay telling you about my Shiki's "miracle" recovery from diagnosed terminal cancer. I wanted to wait until I had explained alternative medicine well enough for you to understand why I'd used quotation marks around the word *miracle*. They indicate that although many people might consider her recovery a miracle, holistic veterinarians would not because they know the scientific reasons behind such recoveries.

First, I hope Shiki's grim journey will serve as a further introduction to the success of holistic medical techniques—because her "miracle" is by no means unique. (See chapter 11 for the results of a study of many years on thousands of dogs and cats diagnosed with terminal cancer: More than half went into remission and remain cancer-free today, or remained cancer-free until they died of other causes.) Second, I hope that Shiki's tale will serve as a very specific example of why I have urged in this introduction that you don't give up on your dog until you have tried holistic veterinary medicine. Third, I believe Shiki's journey will give you a more specific overview of some of the ways holistic veterinarians work differently from orthodox veterinarians.

One 3 A.M., Shiki uttered a little cry and toppled over. My husband, Joe, and I ran to find out why her legs had suddenly failed her. She was lying there helplessly, screaming and flailing her legs in the air trying desperately to right herself so she could stand again. But soon all her terrified activity ceased.

Shiki was now in deeper trouble. She was in a coma.

She was diagnosed by probably the most respected orthodox veterinary center in this country as having terminal cancer. (For skeptics who might ask why my "naturally raised" dog developed cancer, I'll repeat what I said early in this introduction—that she didn't receive a natural diet early in life, because I didn't know then what a dog's natural diet was. Also, she was sixteen when diagnosed with cancer. That's an age—equivalent to age ninety in humans*—at which most dogs have already passed on. Actually, her ancient age makes her recovery even more remarkable.)

The orthodox veterinarians told us that the cancer had invaded several internal organs and had metastasized to her brain. As if to confirm that she had cancer in her internal organs, Shiki came out of her coma just long enough to vomit up blood, then she went back to whatever netherworld she was traveling in.

As you will see, she was saved by Marty Goldstein, D.V.M., who had worked with me on the first edition of this book and whom I had called for advice on Shiki's condition.

---

* The rule of thumb that one year of a dog's life equals seven of ours seems to have been discarded—or Shiki would have been one hundred twelve in human years.

After several days at the center, Shiki was out of the coma; but she still couldn't stand, let alone walk, and she was still vomiting blood. All the center's veterinarians agreed that she would soon lapse back into a coma. They urged Joe and me to allow them to "put her out of her misery." With less optimism than Dr. Goldstein was expressing over the phone, Joe and I insisted on taking Shiki (alive) out of the center. When the attendant brought her out in his arms and put her down on the floor, Shiki fell over on her side and lay there helplessly, screaming; and the attendant glared at us for what we were doing to this poor little dog by not letting her "go."

Dr. Goldstein had, oddly (or so we thought at the time), urged us *not* to take Shiki immediately to him. "Keep her at home with you for two days," he'd said. "The first thing we need to do is to let her recover from the stress of separation and all the frightening things that are done to patients in a hospital. Give her a few days to feel all comfy and safe with you again."

But when we saw her crumpled there on the hospital floor, we felt that Dr. Goldstein was wrong. Shiki wouldn't last another two days without any medical care at all. But then again, the only medical care the center offered was to put her permanently to sleep. We carried her down to the street and propped her up on the ground while we waited for the car service to take us home. (She couldn't bend her legs to lie down face forward as animals do, you see. If we didn't hold her up, she toppled onto her side, which distressed her greatly.) Joe and I took turns kneeling beside her and holding her upright. Then I decided to test Dr. Goldstein's idea: "Once Shiki feels she's going to be safely back home with you, you'll see improvement." Gingerly, I took one of my hands off her body. If she started to topple, as I was sure she would, my other hand could still keep her basically upright.

Eventually Joe said, "Let me know when you get tired holding her up. The last thing we need right now is for her to fall over and hurt herself."

"Joe," I said, "she's been standing on her own for ten minutes."

Shiki did indeed improve further in the two days of Dr. Goldstein's prescribed "cozy time" with us at home. In those two days,

Dr. Goldstein had requested and received all the center's tests and records. As this book stresses, holistic veterinarians are all fully licensed as orthodox veterinarians, but their specialization gives them many additional tests and therapies from which to choose. So, for Dr. Goldstein, the orthodox center's tests and their results were only a starting point.

I had chosen Dr. Goldstein, of all the veterinarians who had worked with me on the first book, because I knew that he and his veterinarian brother, Robert, were conducting the research I referred to earlier and that it was showing much success. (His brother had at the time dropped out of clinical practice to devote himself fully to conducting that research.) When we walked into Dr. Goldstein's office—Shiki was slipping and sliding, but she was *walking*—the veterinarian said that, after looking at the center's information, Shiki couldn't be enrolled in the study he and his brother were running. "The center didn't prove the diagnosis of terminal cancer according to the stringent requirements of a solid scientific study."

For a brief moment, I felt that I might prefer to be dead rather than to be standing there listening to Dr. Goldstein. Shiki had fought so hard not to let this be her time to pass on, and now she wasn't eligible for a therapy that could help her because the center's veterinarians hadn't followed a particular protocol in their diagnosis. But then my mind went back to a basic tenet of alternative medicine: Bottom line, you don't treat the disease label, you treat the animal (or the human). "Well," I said hopefully to Dr. Goldstein, "even without an ironclad diagnosis . . ."

I didn't get to finish my sentence before the veterinarian said, "Absolutely. We'll treat Shiki according to what's off base in her body."

Using his training as an animal chiropractor, Dr. Goldstein found a point on Shiki's spine that was "really out of whack." He said, "Even before all this happened to her, I bet she wasn't able to stand on her hind legs the way poodles can."

True. We had thought she'd just been getting too old for athletics. (As I report later in this book, "normal" aging is not considered normal by holistic veterinarians.) Dr. Goldstein slightly twisted Shiki's neck in a way that looked as if he'd just gently nudged her to look to her left. Then he lifted her off the examining table and put her down on the floor. "Who's her favorite parent?" he asked. Joe was, as much as I hated admitting it. "Okay, Joe. Hold your hand up high in the air, and let's see if she'll try to get to it."

Shiki stood up on her hind legs, reaching toward Joe's fingers. When she realized the fingers were too high, she made a straight-up leap in the air. Shiki wasn't going toward food, because Joe had none. She wasn't even repeating a trick she had been taught. She just saw her person obviously wanting her to do something, for some strange reason, and—since she was now physically able to do it—she did it.

I'm fond of saying, from my own experience, that actually seeing the results of an alternative veterinarian's or M.D.'s work is infinitely more powerful than spending years doing research and interviews. Joe's and my first thought was that we'd witnessed a miracle. But, as I have said, holistic doctors don't consider their results astounding, simply because they know the scientific bases behind them. Dr. Goldstein said only, "Okay. That's what was crippling her hind legs. Now we have to find out what's behind all her other symptoms."

Dr. Goldstein ran a sample of Shiki's blood through a number of tests that the orthodox center hadn't conducted, including tests for levels of all nutrients. He found two vitamin and three mineral levels that were "really out of whack."

Shiki's recovery wasn't instantaneous or without cost. It was several weeks before she was back to her old spunky, bullheaded self. And the therapy was more complex than holistic therapy often is: It involved a rigidly controlled diet, several vitamin and mineral supplements, enzyme tablets, and two homeopathic remedies. But the cost of all this was about the same as it would have cost us to bury her.

Since everything in Shiki's therapy was natural and noninvasive, Shiki was spared the often gruesome side effects of surgery, radiation, and chemotherapy. Of course, she wouldn't have suffered these side effects anyway, because the major orthodox center refused to give these therapies, since she was "beyond help." She did, however, "suffer" from an intense hatred of the taste of one homeopathic.

She found it so loathsome that Joe and I had to use most of our strength to keep her small flailing body pinned down on the couch while one of us found some extra strength to pry open her mouth. But we didn't mind: We were vividly aware that this powerful, squirming dog only days before had so lost control of her brain and spinal cord that we'd been told she'd never be able to move again and would soon be dead. We found ourselves actually rooting for her to win over us.

By the way, as Shiki's body was restored to its natural balance, she recovered from cataracts, too.

PART 1

Preventing Disease and Premature Death in Your Dog: *This Is Almost Entirely Within Your Power*

Chapter 1

"Do you know what is in meat meal, the major constituent of dry dog food? . . . Urine, fecal matter, hair, pus, meat with cancer and T.B., etc."[1]
>—*Wendell O. Belfield, D.V.M.*

"When the moist foods came out, we figured they must have a very strong preservative, because they needed no refrigeration. Many of them do have a very strong preservative— formalin. Formalin is such a good preservative, in fact, that undertakers use quite a lot of it."
>—*Thomas A. Newland, D.V.M.*

"When I started out as a veterinarian, I too told everybody, 'Yes, sure, the commercial foods are all fine. Go ahead and use them. Your dog will thrive.' But I was brain-dead at the time."
>—*John Fudens, D.V.M.*

How Commercial Pet Foods May Be Killing Your Dog— and Why

If *someone suggested* you feed your dog rust every day, you would think the person was quite mad, wouldn't you? But maybe you do just that without knowing it. How about feeding her two substances that scientists use in laboratories to create brain defects in animals? How about taking a bottle marked POISON, with a skull and crossbones on its label, and sprinkling that over her food? If you feed your dog packaged or canned "nutritionally complete" pet foods—as so very many people in this country do—you may be giving him not only all of the above poisons but a number of others. This information may surprise you, because commercial food manufacturers—and even many veterinarians—tell us these foods are the "best" way to feed our pets. However, let's see what researchers and nutritional veterinarians have to say.

What Is in Commercial Pet Food That Shouldn't Be?

To begin with, let us look at what commercial pet foods are composed of in general. The Pet Food Institute has said, "Forty percent of all pet food is meat by-products and offal [wastes]." One would think that the other 60 percent would have to be better than that, but the Pet Food Institute went on to say that the other 60 percent is grain and soy meal not used for human consumption because of foreign odors, *debris*, *germs*, and so on.[2] You may remember the similar, even stronger statement by Wendell O. Belfield, D.V. M., on the first page of this chapter.

As we will discuss, today some nutritional veterinarians believe commercial foods are worse than ever.

By the way, you may have noted that Dr. Belfield wrote of tumors being put in our pets' foods. More recently I read a vivid example of that fact. A veterinarian visiting a meatpacking plant asked why the tumors being cut out from the dead animals were stored in bins, rather than thrown away. She was told there was nothing to worry about. The tumors would never reach human consumption; they would all be used in cat and dog foods.

Commercial pet foods contain a number of other "extra" substances, substances not present in natural foods and therefore foreign (toxic) to your pet's body. For instance:*

- **Sodium nitrite.** You have probably heard that sodium nitrite, which occurs in such processed foods as hot dogs and bologna, can cause cancer in human beings. But did you know that as long ago as 1972 the FDA stated that this chemical is also potentially hazardous to pet health?[3] That hasn't stopped commercial manufacturers from using it, however. You see, sodium nitrite is terribly important: it adds an artificial rosy color to some commercial pet foods. Manufacturers know that this makes a good impression on us; and we, after all, are the ones who shell out the money for these products. It is doubtful, however, that this pleasant red color makes much difference to your dog. Dogs cannot see colors.

  Sodium nitrite isn't the only unnatural ingredient used in commercial foods to add pretty colors for the enjoyment of dogs who can't see them. You may see mention on the label of red dye #2, blue dye #3, yellow dye some other number. A popular commercial cat food, which features on the box a picture of very colorful kibble, is honest enough to list several dyes as among the ingredients. But, as mentioned elsewhere

---

* Not all pet foods contain all the following harmful substances. Note also that this list does not comprise all the harmful substances that occur in various commercial pet foods.

in this chapter, if dyes aren't listed as ingredients, that is no assurance they aren't in your dog's commercial food.

- **BHA and BHT.** Scientists use these chemicals on animals in research laboratories—to produce serious brain defects. These additives also produce kidney and liver problems as well as behavior problems in laboratory animals.

- **Lead.** Researching this new book, I found indications that lead is not so prevalent in canned dog foods as it was in 1981. At that time, researchers at the Connecticut Agricultural Experiment Station had found that many canned foods contained so much lead that every time an animal ate six ounces of these foods, he took into his body four times the level of lead potentially toxic to children. So, even if this terrible state of affairs has improved, we might ask why this amount of lead was ever allowed in the first place—and what else is presently being allowed that we don't know about?

  In a recent interview, John Fudens, D.V.M., commented that "you might still find lead in some of those canned dog foods you can buy for about a dime. But I wouldn't feed those to a cockroach."

- **Artificial flavorings.** These are used to make fake food taste the way it would if it were real food. About twenty-five years ago a California physician, Benjamin Feingold, of the Kaiser Permanente Hospital, came out with a radical theory that put his reputation on the line: Many children with autism, hyperactivity, and various other personality disorders could be controlled simply by removing artificial colorings and flavorings from their diets. His theory worked so well in practice that it has since been utilized even by some of the most orthodox physicians.

  Veterinarians practicing the new field of nutritional veterinary medicine have been calling for the removal of such artificial flavorings from pet foods. R. Geoffrey Broderick, D.V.M., once said: "These same substances that are known to cause children to be unsociable, unable to learn—to choose to spend hours at a time sitting and banging their heads against a wall—these are the substances that cause your dog or cat to be nervous, hostile, and full of anxiety."

- **Salt.** This substance, while it does occur in nature, is added in unnatural proportions to many processed foods. Sometimes, Dr. Broderick said in 1981, such foods contain "one thousand times" as much salt as occurs in the natural food the processed food is imitating. You probably know the strong role excessive salt plays in causing human hypertension and heart disease. It does the same thing in dogs and is considered one of the main reasons these two diseases, virtually unknown in our pets until fifty years ago, are now top killers.

- **Euthanized cats and dogs.** Am I telling you here that the commercial foods your dog eats may contain ground-up parts of her own "people" who were put to death because they were unloved or were diagnosed as too sick to go on living? Unfortunately, yes, I am. I won't comment any further on this particular fact. I'm sure you can fill in your own thoughts.

- **Ethoxyquin.** The first questionnaire response I received for this new book came from a veterinarian who referred to himself as basically orthodox. He wrote that he had been using my first edition to start to incorporate holistic medicine into his practice but doubted he knew enough yet to contribute to this book. The one comment he did give, however, was that he felt I would find that commercial food manufacturers had "cleaned up their acts" since the first edition. Following a long tradition of veterinarians who don't specialize in nutrition, this doctor believed that commercial foods now would maintain animals' health. Hoping, for the sake of all animals, that this doctor was right in his belief that some toxic substances had been removed, I skulked in my neighborhood reading labels, as I had done in 1981 for the first book. No, everything I had mentioned before was still listed on labels. And it was only later that I found out, as I'll detail shortly, that a new law allows pet food manufacturers to put toxic substances into the foods without mentioning them on the label.

To double-check myself, I asked Dr. Fudens if he thought commercial foods had got any better in the years since the first book. "You're kidding me," he said. "In my opinion and experience, commercial pet foods have recently got much worse than they've ever been, with the road kill and the diseased carcasses, and everything else they're putting in there."

I took the same question up with Carvel G. Tiekert, D.V. M., founder and president of the American Holistic Veterinary Medical Association. He pointed out that there had been a brand-*new* poison, ethoxyquin, introduced into many pet foods since the first book, and he sent me an article by Gloria Dodd, D.V. M., from the *Journal of the American Holistic Veterinary Medical Association* (August–October, 1992). You may remember I said at the beginning of this chapter that you might very well unknowingly be feeding your dog every day from a bottle with a label featuring, in all capital letters, POISON, with an additional skull and bones as a warning for those who don't read English. I was talking about ethoxyquin.

The article was actually a letter written by Dr. Dodd to a veterinary nutritionist responsible for pet food issues within the Food and Drug Administration. Previous to her letter, Dr. Dodd had run four years of research on ethoxyquin. She began this work when a breeder contacted her after suddenly losing four champion German shepherds in a row to liver cancer. The breeder had made only one change in rearing her dogs: She'd switched them to a new commercial food that had ethoxyquin as a preservative. Soon after, another breeder told Dr. Dodd that suddenly 82 percent of her puppies were dying. Many others came into the world dead to begin with, or were malformed. The only thing she'd done differently was to switch to the same pet food.

One of the first facts Dr. Dodd unearthed was that the FDA allows a maximum of 5 ppm of ethoxyquin in human foods (which would seemingly indicate that the FDA knows it can be toxic), but allows up to 150 ppm in pet food. So it's okay for our beloved companions to eat thirty times more of this chemical than it's considered safe for us to take in. That might make sense if our dogs weighed thirty times more than we do, but obviously . . .

Maybe by now you've run off to check the commercial foods you give your dog and have noticed with relief that ethoxyquin isn't listed on the labels. Although I have recently seen this chemical mentioned on labels, Dr. Dodd states that many manufacturers who use ethoxyquin in their foods don't mention it. You may say, "I thought there was an FDA regulation that all ingredients had to be mentioned on the label." So did I. So did Dr. Dodd.

Dr. Fudens addressed this issue in an interview with me. "This is what has happened in the last few years. Lobbyists for the pet food companies got a new pet food labeling act passed in Washington," he said. "There are only about five major dog food producing companies, and they contract out to other companies for their base meal. These major producing companies add their meat and whatever else— and then what goes on their label is only what they've *added* to the base meal. They're not required legally anymore to mention on the label any junk, garbage, or poisons the original company put into the base meal."

Dr. Fudens sent me a published article indicating that the base meal may include spoiled meat cuts, ground-up flea collars, "body bags" that came in with euthanized pets, and other ingredients I'd like to shield you from knowing about.

"So if an enlightened dog owner tries to buy only commercial foods that say they're all natural, no preservatives, no artificial this or that," Dr. Fudens summarized, "the owner should realize that only God really knows what's in those foods."

In her long, impassioned letter, Dr. Dodd gave many more chilling facts. I'm mentioning only a few of them. "I further learned from the *Chemical Toxicology of Commercial*

Products," she wrote, "that ethoxyquin has a toxic rating of 3 on a scale of 1 to 6." She explained that a rating of 6 means that fewer than seven drops of a substance produces instant death. The rating of 3 given to ethoxyquin means, the veterinarian said, that it can produce slowly developing depression, skin irritation, liver damage, convulsions, coma, and eventual death.

Dr. Dodd stated that the FDA approved ethoxyquin on the basis of a study conducted by its developer, Monsanto, over thirty years ago. She gave a number of specifics of what she called the "slipshod" methods by which the study was conducted, concluding that "by today's standards of testing, [Monsanto's study] would be laughed out of the room."

But wait a minute. Let's look at one of the results Monsanto had. Of the sixty-seven puppies who were born during the study, thirty-two puppies died, a mortality rate of almost 50 percent. You may remember that it was precisely an abnormally high rate of dead puppies that prompted Dr. Dodd's four years of research into ethoxyquin in the first place.

Dr. Dodd said: "The 'scientists' claimed the deaths were due to 'underdeveloped and weak puppies'!" I'm sure you don't need me to suggest that maybe those puppies were born that way not because of karma or a fluke of nature but because of ethoxyquin in their mother's diet.

Dr. Dodd, who studied with physicians in Europe and in South America, used a state-of-the-art electronic machine developed in Germany to scientifically analyze ethoxyquin's effects in the body. She found the chemical implicated in— and I'm giving only a partial list here—poor quality of skin and hair, weight loss, obesity, nausea, diarrhea, allergies, and numerous internal stress reactions. ("There's nothing more stressing to the body than being poisoned!" Dr. Dodd noted.) She also found hypothyroidism, overall accelerated aging of the organs, tumors, and cancer of the liver with metastasis to the pancreas and spleen.

Some animals evinced strange behavior, such as incessant pacing or a "sudden development of a Dr. Jekyll–Mr. Hyde syndrome—quiet, loving pets changed to violently aggressive biting animals." Many of these were so violent that their owners euthanized them.

In those animals whose organs were not irreversibly damaged, Dr. Dodd was able to get a good recovery response in part by using a homeopathic remedy that negates the effects of ethoxyquin.

What Isn't in Commercial Foods That Should Be?

Advertising for most commercial pet foods states that the products have all the nutrients your dog needs. But do they?

If you were being paid to write ads for a dog food, would you stress that the food didn't contain any enzymes at all, even though enzymes are absolutely essential for every biochemical reaction in the body?

Yet enzymes occur, as Dr. Broderick and other holistic veterinarians tell us, in not one single commercial pet food. You see, enzymes occur in raw foods. (That fact is one of the major reasons why nutritionists urge people to eat raw fruits and raw vegetables.) Dr. Tiekert adds that a major reason nutritional veterinarians object to table scraps for dogs is that people will then be feeding their dogs basically *cooked* foods.

You probably won't find on your labels any mention of vitamin C. And yet, as we'll cover in following chapters, holistic veterinarians help prevent and cure a number of "unpreventable" and "incurable" pet problems with this vitamin. Dogs—unlike people—manufacture vitamin C in their bodies, and this fact has traditionally led veterinary medicine to the conclusion that these animals don't need to get the vitamin from outside sources.

However, this conclusion overlooks the fact that dogs always used to get additional vitamin C from outside sources: in the foods they ate before the commercial foods supplanted their natural diet. It also overlooks the fact that some pets produce much less C in their bodies than others. Further, it overlooks the fact that today's new environmental poisons (including those in commercial pet foods) actually rob the body of substantial amounts of vitamin C.

Animal behaviorists have pointed out that if your dog eats his own feces, he may not be a "bad boy"; he may simply be trying the only way he can think of to obtain some of the vitally important nutrients missing from his "nutritionally complete" commercial pet food.

Even when something that should be in commercial pet foods *is* in the foods, it may not be there in the proper biochemical form. For instance, that long list of minerals on some boxed or canned foods may look very impressive. However, those minerals are very likely to be *unchelated* minerals. These tend to pass right through the body without ever being used. Feeding your pet (or yourself) unchelated minerals can therefore be tantamount to not feeding her (or yourself) any minerals at all.

Chelated minerals, according to Richard J. Kearns, D.V. M., not only are absolutely essential in and of themselves, but also are necessary to help the body use vitamins. Therefore, unchelated minerals can sometimes seriously impair the function of the vitamins your pet gets. Moreover, unchelated minerals can sometimes store themselves in the body and help cause such modern-day problems as arthritis.

The reason for this lack of chelated minerals in pet foods is simple. As Dr. Broderick once pointed out, the unnatural forms of minerals "are a lot cheaper."

Now, what about the iron listed on your pet food's label? Well, as we have said, nutrients occur in different forms. Under the heading "iron," for instance, medical dictionaries for doctors list almost thirty different forms. One type of iron commonly used in pet foods is iron oxide. This form is more commonly known as rust. (Remember I began this chapter by saying that you might be feeding your dog rust every day without knowing it?) Then there is magnesium. This mineral is sometimes even announced on the label in the correct proportion to calcium, a subtlety not bothered with in some supplements for human consumption. (Too much calcium in relation to magnesium—and vice versa—can cause bone and joint deteriorations such as arthritis. Doctors Marty and Robert Goldstein emphasized that the wrong calcium-magnesium ratio also can be a cause of neuromuscular problems.)

However, as Dr. Broderick has pointed out, the form of magnesium most commonly used in pet foods is the inexpensive magnesium oxide. "Since very little magnesium oxide can be utilized by the body," this veterinarian said, "it is virtually impossible for the animal to *absorb* the correct magnesium-calcium ratio, even when the proportion in the box or can is correct."

In other words, even the best processed foods can be a direct cause of the new animal disease, arthritis.

What Exactly Is Meant by the Term *Natural Foods*?

Simply put, an animal's natural foods are the ones his body organs and structures are best equipped to utilize. Through evolution, the bodies of dogs have superbly adapted to maintain health on the foods that were most easily available to them in the wild. These foods are called the dog's natural foods.

It goes without saying, of course, that the foods our pets' bodies have evolved to thrive on throughout millions of years are not the processed commercial pet foods that have been manufactured for only the past fifty years. Dogs simply did not lug boxes of dry pellets around the wild with them, and they didn't take their prey home in a can. Nor was their prey stuffed with the dyes, preservatives, and other harmful additives we have shown are contained in today's pet foods.

As we have said, these commercial pet foods have been around for only about fifty years. This is not nearly enough time for a species to rebuild its body to utilize new foods for health. Three major diseases of today's pets are cancer, heart disease, and arthritis; yet in the millions of years dogs ate their natural diet, cancer, heart disease, and arthritis were virtually unknown.* These three diseases are also, of course, the main killers of human beings; again, these diseases were virtually unknown in human beings until we started tampering with our own food one hundred years ago.

---

* Scientists have ascertained this by studying well-preserved skeletons of wild dogs and cats, as well as veterinary records prior to fifty years ago.

What were dogs evolved to eat? There is no controversy here among scientists: Dogs are basically carnivores, animals who naturally eat raw flesh.*

Those of you who are interested in nutrition may point out at this juncture that human beings are supposed to have evolved to be meat eaters, too, but that in the last thirty years medical science has discovered that animal fat—and animal protein—can be detrimental to human health.

The last part of that statement is quite correct: A growing number of authorities state that animal food is at least a contributing factor to a number of our serious disorders. However, while we human animals have been eating meat for a few million years, there has not yet been enough time for our systems to have evolved to accept animal protein as a natural substance.

Let's compare a dog's carnivorous body with ours to see how the dog is adapted to be a meat eater, while we are not. Open your pet's mouth and take a look at his teeth (provided, of course, you have a sweet-tempered dog who will let you do that). You will notice that all your pet's teeth are a lot sharper than ours. You will notice also those two extremely long teeth to each side, top and bottom. (Even in my six-pound tabby cat they looked ferocious.)

Now why don't we have teeth like that? Because our teeth haven't evolved to be the teeth of natural meat eaters. They aren't sharp enough to kill another animal and tear it—raw—to pieces.

Take a look at your dog's nails. Unless you consider cutting his nails a part of his regular grooming, you see that they are very long. Women who try to grow long nails for cosmetic purposes know that human nails will usually break, no matter how well they're nurtured, long before they get as long as a dog's.

You see, the nails of your pet have evolved to this length so that he, again, can kill and tear apart his natural food: animal flesh.

But the most important anatomical difference between our natu-

---

* Don't assume that you can't possibly feed your pet his natural diet because it contains meat. As we will show in chapter 2, it can cost you *less* to feed a healthful, natural diet than you are presently paying for even the less expensive harmful commercial pet foods.

ral meat-eater pets and ourselves is the length of the intestines. Meat, in the presence of heat, tends to putrefy and send out poisons. Of course, intestines in any animal's body carry a lot of heat. Conclusion: the shorter the intestine—that is, the quicker the meat can pass through the body—the less harm it's going to do to the body.

Our intestines are very long; therefore, it takes a lot of time for animal food to make its way through them. The length of time, then, that such food is exposed to the heat of our bodies is more than ample to allow it to putrefy and send toxins through our systems. A dog, again, does not have this problem. His intestines are quite short, even considering the fact that his body is smaller than ours.

Thus, dogs—unlike us—have been carefully designed by nature to thrive healthily on meat. For this reason—and for all the other reasons we have detailed in this chapter—we are doing our pet's body a great disservice when we feed the animal the unnatural new commercial foods.

The story of the nutrient called taurine is an illustration of how natural food can maintain health, while unnatural food does not. Natural foods contain within them a number of helpful nutrients (such as taurine) that were unknown until a comparatively short time ago. Nutritional authorities believe that many others are still unknown. (Only by eating natural foods can you and your pet be certain to get the whole complement of nutrients, known and unknown, that have in the past protected our ancestors from such ailments as cancer and heart disease.)

The search that uncovered taurine began because scientists were puzzled by a new disease that was striking cats with increasing frequency: progressive retinal atrophy, a condition that leads to total blindness. Dogs are prone to this disorder, too.

Dr. Broderick once gave a dramatic medical description of this disease. "You look in a healthy cat's eyes," he said, "and you see the optic disc with blood vessels radiating out from it." (These blood vessels carry blood and all necessary nutrients to the eye, and in this way keep it alive.) "But when you look in the eyes of a cat with this disease, the optic disc looks like a saucer set apart from the rest of the eye, with no blood vessels. In other words, you see this shiny globe looking back at you unseeingly; the cat is stone blind."

When researchers recently discovered taurine, they discovered also that a lack of this substance causes at least some cases of the "new" disease, progressive retinal atrophy.

Taurine occurs naturally in meat. Cats, of course, always ate an abundance of meat when they were left to their own devices in the wild. Now that taurine has been discovered, it has been added to most commercial foods. But for many pets the addition came too late.

The question remains: How many other presently unknown nutrients necessary to pet (and human) health are not included in unnatural foods?

The next chapter will tell you how you can prevent the grim diseases considered inevitable in today's processed food–fed pet by feeding your dog his natural, healthy diet. As I have said, this diet should cost you less every week than the commercial foods you may presently be using. Be advised, however, that over the years the natural diet may end up costing you more—because your pet will probably live many more years to enjoy it.

One last word: You may at this point be vowing you will never, never, never feed raw meat to your dog because you have heard so much in recent years about the danger to us from parasites in undercooked meat. That danger is to *us*—not to natural carnivores. Again we're back to considering that our dogs' bodies evolved to be quite different from ours. Trust that holistic veterinarians will explain in more detail in the next chapter why raw meat is not harmful to our dogs. For now, just let me give a basic clue as to why a dog is not affected by parasites in the same way we are. Our bodies' basic pH balance is alkaline; our dogs' bodies are basically acidic, the exact opposite of alkaline. Imagine what happens to a parasite if it's plopped into a body full of acid.

References

1. Wendell O. Belfield, D.V. M., *Let's Live*, April 1980.
2. Cited by Frances Sheridan Goulart, *Let's Live*, October 1975, p. 44.
3. Ibid.

Chapter 2

"We just seldom see the so-called inevitable diseases in our patients when we can get the owners to raise the pets on their natural foods."

— *Robert S. Goldstein, V.M.D.; Marty Goldstein, D.V.M.; Richard J. Kearns, D.V.M.; H. H. Robertson, D.V.M.*

"Everybody laughs at me; they say I'm a specialist in geriatrics, because all my animals get to be so old. That's simply because I try to have my clients feed their pets right in the first place."

— *Richard J. Kearns, D.V.M.*

"My greatest goal is to be known not for what I've cured and controlled, but for what I've prevented."

— *R. Geoffrey Broderick, D.V.M.*

"Even the so-called 'sickly' pet can get to live a long, healthy life with the proper diet."

— *Nino Aloro, D.V.M.*

What Your Adult Dog Should Eat for a Long and Healthy Life— and Why

As *the title* for this chapter indicates, this information has been given by holistic veterinarians for an *adult* dog. Puppies, elderly dogs, pregnant or lactating dogs, and half-starved strays all have special dietary needs that are detailed in chapter 4.

This chapter is also meant to *prevent* disease in a healthy dog. If your companion is already ill, he may need important adjustments to this chapter's recommended diet to compensate for existing biochemical imbalances in his body. The chapters on disorders indicate some of these special dietary requirements.

Dogs in the wild usually did not—and still usually do not— become crippled or blind or deaf from the disorders that most veterinarians today consider inevitable. And dogs today who are raised on the diets their ancestors ate in the wild seldom become crippled or blind or deaf from the disorders that have become "normal" since the commercial pet food industry took over our pets' diets.

It is not by some unexplainable "miracle" that a pet (or a person) can be kept healthy by feeding the body the foods it has evolved to thrive on. You probably know that everything you take into your body affects your cells in one way or another: Cigarette smoke adversely affects the cells of your lungs, for instance; Valium alters body chemistry so that anxiety may be alleviated temporarily; high–blood-pressure medication sets up another biochemical reaction in your body that lowers blood pressure for a while.

Now, what one general substance do you take into your body more often, every day of your life, than any other substance? Food.

And the various nutrients in food set up more biochemical reactions in your body, every minute of your life, than any one drug can do. Therefore, when you (and your pet) take in the right foods, these foods will set up healthy biochemical reactions; when you and your pet take in the wrong foods, they will set up destructive biochemical reactions in the body. It's that simple.

Frank L. Earl, D.V.M., once expressed the idea this way: "I compare vitamins and minerals to the spark plugs in cars. These nutrients are the necessary energizers to move from one chemical reaction to another in each and every cell in the body."

So healthy, natural foods set up and maintain healthy, natural biochemical reactions in your body. These biochemical reactions set up a natural line of defense—a healthy immune system—that fights off bacteria, viruses, and parasites many times a day. Every veterinarian whose work is covered in this book has said to me in one way or another that without a healthy immune system we would all be sick every day.

For instance, let's say you're in a classroom or at a party with a person who has the flu. Ten of the twenty people in that room catch that virus; you're one of the unlucky ones. That virus didn't float mysteriously by the other ten in that room just to pick you out maliciously; it entered the body of the other ten persons, too. But the other ten had immune systems that were strong enough to say, "Get out of here; this is *my* territory," and to destroy the offending stranger.

In the same way, we all have cancer cells in our body every day. As long as our overall health is good, our immune system will keep knocking out these cancer cells.

Almost all holistic veterinarians I have interviewed over the years have asked me to please stress to readers that it is *not* bacteria or viruses that make pets sick; it is their pets' weakened immune systems that allow the disease-causing organisms to take hold.

So by restoring your pet to his natural, health-giving diet, you can restore the myriad natural biochemical reactions that give strength to his immune system. This is the "magic" that keeps pets who are fed natural diets free of today's "inevitable" diseases—diseases that were, and are, virtually unknown among animals in the wild.

Later chapters are devoted to a compilation of the work of a number of veterinarians working in the new field of holistic veterinary medicine. These chapters detail successful therapies for already existing diseases: therapies that use little or no dangerous drugs or surgery; therapies that often have amazing results with disorders currently thought basically "hopeless."

If you are lucky enough to be reading the chapter at hand on prevention because you're just starting to raise a new puppy, chances are this book will sit on your shelf for many years before you need the information in later chapters, if you ever *do* need it.

Just as every one of these veterinarians expressed to me that his or her greatest satisfaction comes in preventing diseases rather than in curing them, so I hope that the months I have spent compiling information on the successful treatment of these diseases results in some of the least-needed chapters ever written in the field of veterinary medicine.

Your Pet's Natural, Healthy Diet Will Probably Cost You Less Than the Fake Foods You're Presently Feeding Him

Before I give information on how your dog can remain disease-free and live longer, let me get one stumbling block out of the way. The dog's natural diet is high in meat, a word that raises some trepidation in people on a budget.

First of all, holistic veterinarians do not ask you to feed your dog exclusively meat. Actually, as I discuss later, feeding your dog only meat can seriously harm her. Only one-third to one-half of the dog's diet should be in the form of what is commonly called meat, and some of that can be other animal products such as eggs and yogurt.

Secondly—and very importantly—you will most probably find that your dog eats less of his natural diet than he does fake foods. As a matter of fact, R. Geoffrey Broderick, D.V. M., has reported that almost without exception pets eat one-third less of natural foods than unnatural ones. Why should a pet be so obliging? He eats less of the natural foods because these foods contain all the nutrients his body needs for good health; therefore, his body tends to retain these foods, using them to build fresh new cells, healthy blood, and so on. On the other hand, the pet's body doesn't know *what* the heck to do with the newfangled fake foods, and most of these foods pass almost immediately through the body and out again. Therefore, instant hunger. As Dr. Broderick put it: "A pound of fake food equals almost a pound of waste," or feces.

As a matter of fact, many kennel owners who deal with numerous animals in close quarters express relief that the natural diet cuts down so drastically on the amount of waste they have to discard every day. Whereas their animals were previously discarding as foreign substances (which, indeed, they are) many of the chemicals and much of the diseased matter contained in processed foods, the same bodies are now retaining the nutrient-rich natural foods for the purposes of building healthy new cells, strong immune systems, and healthy blood.

Robert Goldstein, V. M.D., and Marty Goldstein, D.V. M., have added that excessive—and costly—eating may be caused also by addiction to the chemical appetite stimulants and preservatives in fake foods. When you feed your pet natural foods, he will eat only enough to satisfy natural hunger—not to satisfy an addiction.

Another thing: Nowhere will I be asking you to feed your pet expensive steak as the basis of an optimal diet. As a matter of fact, please do *not* feed steak as the basis of your pet's diet, even if you can afford to. As we'll see a bit later when we follow your pet's ancestor through the wild, he first ate the organ meats of his prey (the heart, gizzard, liver, tripe, spleen). Steak is actually less nutritious overall than these innards. Indeed, your pet's great-great-etc. granddaddy didn't deign to eat this inferior type of meat—steak—unless his prey happened not to have been spirited away when he returned to the scene hours after dinner for a midnight snack.

Now let's compare some specific costs using present (1999) prices in my neighborhood. I'm asking you to pass up a box of embalmed kibble ($1.75 a pound) or a can of dog food ($1.80 to $2.50 a pound). I'm asking you instead to buy a pound of chicken hearts, gizzards, or livers at 99 cents to $1.19 a pound. Or a few eggs ($1.00 a dozen) or carrots (three pounds for $1.00) or a few apples (49 cents a pound). Then I'm reminding you that since your dog's body can actually *use* all the natural food it gets, your pet will probably eat only two-thirds of a pound of her natural diet for every pound of fake food.

You can probably even get your butcher to give you free some of the animal parts he normally discards that would be highly nutritious for your pet.

All this is not even considering the money you probably will not have to spend in veterinarian's bills trying to save your beloved pet's life from an illness caused by unnatural foods. As I write this, I am reminded of my friend Verna on the West Coast, who for years spent a small fortune on twice-a-day insulin shots and frequent visits to the veterinarian to control diabetes in her husky, Nijinski. Not to mention the fact that she had to greatly curtail her career in theater so as to be around two times a day to give the insulin shots. Obviously Verna loved her pet or she would have had him put to sleep, as many other owners do to "cure" diabetes. It is sad, therefore, to realize that she probably could have prevented this disease in her dog simply by feeding a natural, sugarless diet in the first place. (See the section on diabetes in chapter 9.)

In my own case, I spent a small fortune raising (and almost managing to kill) my little black poodle Shiki on the "nutritionally complete" kibble and canned foods my veterinarian—and all the ads—assured me were all she needed. She had the "inevitable" worms three times in her first year; she had gastroenteritis twice; then, at the end of that first year of her life, she developed the "hopeless" arthritis that caused her to be half crippled.

Luckily, it was just at that time that I discovered my first holistic veterinarian, Dr. Broderick, in the course of my other researches as a medical writer. Changing Shiki to the diet her body had been built for kept her free of the "hopeless" arthritis for sixteen years, until she died a natural death.

Since then I have raised three other dogs on a diet of real foods. They are all extremely healthy, extremely energetic—and extremely old.

I would say that Shiki's one year on fake foods cost me about $800 in paying for her orthodox therapies. (This was in the 1970s, so you can imagine how much more it would cost me now.) Total cost of therapy—throughout their lives—for my three ancient dogs raised on their natural diets: $000.00.

One more word about how a natural diet can save you money. As you probably know, a number of dog and cat diseases can be passed to their owners. If you have a healthy pet, you may never know how much this may have saved you in medical bills—or even in the possible loss of a loved one.*

What Your Dog's Ancestor Ate

Let's start with the average day in the life of your pet's ancestor in the wild, a day in which he had no loving owner around to provide him with things his body had not been built to deal with. I want to go through this day with your pet's great-many-times-over grandfather so you can more readily visualize the reasons for the specific suggestions we will cover later.

Ruff wakes early in the forest. There is no bowl of kibble in front of his nose for breakfast, but that doesn't surprise him. There never has been a bowl of kibble there. What does surprise him is that the half-eaten prey he had been guarding overnight has disappeared from between his front paws, spirited away in the middle of the night by some darned animal. Well, that happens. Up and at 'em. Walk, search, climb, stalk, run—in other words, exercise.

Now, when great-great-etc. granddaddy killed his prey, he ate the intestines, liver, heart, stomach and spleen first. He didn't know it, of course, but these are what we call organ meats, and they store up

---

* Wendell O. Belfield, D.V.M., for instance, reported that human beings may contract cats' upper respiratory diseases. The veterinarian also pointed to the fact that heartworms—previously thought confined to dogs—were starting to be reported in human patients. Also, Dr. Belfield pointed out that a pregnant woman can contract a serious disease—if her cat *has* the disease, of course—while cleaning feces from the litter box. The disease, called *Toxoplasma gondii*, can destroy the brain of a fetus.[1] (To be safe, if you become pregnant, you might want to prevail upon another family member to clean up after the cat until the baby is born.)

certain nutrients that are not stored in the bones and muscles. The organs of the prey also contained partially digested vegetables, fruits, and grains. These nonmeat foods provide certain other nutrients, such as unsaturated fats and carbohydrates, which are necessary for the dog, who is not totally carnivorous. Many holistic veterinarians have told me horror stories of desperately sick pets raised by well-meaning owners who were determined to raise their dogs on "natural," nonsupermarket foods. However, these owners mistakenly thought their pets were total carnivores and thus needed only meat for their natural diets.

Next Ruff went on to eat his prey's bones, fat, and muscles, to round out a full complement of vitamins, minerals, enzymes, carbohydrates, proteins, and fats.

As he later lazed in the sun, digesting his feast, he might occasionally catch himself an insect for a bit of dessert. An insect? Yes, insects contain protein and B_{12}, both of which are necessary parts of a dog's diet. (I hope this paragraph cuts down the number of distraught letters I see in veterinarians' magazine columns from owners who are sure their pets are going to die because they catch and eat flies.)

After his feast, our great-etc. granddaddy dog rested a while or otherwise amused himself before he decided he would go to the nearest watering hole for a drink. He didn't know, you see, that many years hence, many fake food labels would be saying it was best to set out a bowl of water with each feeding, or even to mix water directly with the "food" to make a nice fake gravy. Of course, neither did he have nutritionally oriented veterinarians such as Dr. Broderick around to tell him: "Drinking water at the same time as eating will make minerals pass through the body without being used and will upset the acid-alkaline balance of the system." He didn't need such specialists; it's only modern pet owners who do.

As H. H. Robertson, D.V. M., once expressed it: "All you have to do is watch a pet today who is not confined in a small apartment with his food bowl and his water bowl filled up under his nose at the same time. A free pet today will still eat first, and then later he'll go looking for a drink of water. But he'll never eat and drink at the same time."

Actually, though, your dog's ancestor didn't make many trips to watering holes. Since he was eating the diet his body had been designed to thrive on, he got most of the moisture he needed from the body of his prey. (The chapter covering disorders of internal organs discusses some of the damage dry commercial food (kibble) can do to a dog's body.)

The Optimal Preventive Diet for Your Adult Dog

The following boxed information is meant merely to sum up what we say elsewhere in this chapter. *Please read the text for important details.* Also, see the later boxed material for tips on how to feed this diet to your pet quickly and easily.

Remember always that variety is important.

The Optimal Diet

- **Animal foods:** About one-third to one-half of the daily food ration should be animal products, especially meat, preferably raw. Approximately one-sixth of the weekly meat ration should be organ meats: heart, kidney, gizzard, spleen, tripe. Provide fish perhaps twice a week and chicken and turkey often. Never give cooked bones, and be careful of bones in general.

  Other animal protein may be substituted sometimes for meat: Yogurt or raw (unpasteurized) milk can be given once or twice a week, as can one or two raw egg yolks—no whites.
- **Vegetables, fruits, grains:** Most of the rest of the daily ration should be well-cooked brown rice or cereal or whole-grain bread, cut up raw fruits and vegetables, and occasionally chopped nuts.
- **Fats:** Polyunsaturated fat (safflower oil, sesame oil, etc.) should be given daily.
- **Pure water**
- **Vitamin and mineral supplements** (some holistic veterinarians consider these optional for the healthy adult dog that is being fed the above natural diet):

  Multivitamin and mineral pill formulated for adult dogs

  Additional vitamin C

  Additional vitamin E

Quick and Easy Tips for Feeding Your Dog His New, Natural Diet

- You might want to start simply by using, for a few weeks, a high-quality non-commercial dog food in place of the supermarket pet food you and your dog have been using. This will give your dog's body a chance to become free of addiction to the impurities in the commercial dog foods. Meanwhile, you can continue your habit of simply filling your pet's bowl with prepared food a few times a day.

- Then start adding a bit of chicken, turkey, or meat from your family's own dinner—perhaps a bit of leftover that might otherwise be thrown away—to your pet's bowl. (Shift gradually from cooked animal proteins to raw.)

- Next, as you chop up raw vegetables for your family's salad, chop up a few extra pieces for your pet and put them into his bowl.

- Gradually start adding grains.

- Build a routine for your dog's diet, based closely around the one you follow for your own meals. This routine will mean you do not have to make new choices every day for your pet's menus, and it will also mean you don't have to make a separate work process out of feeding him.

  Chances are, for instance, that you tend to eat grains for breakfast. Make breakfast the meal you give your dog his grains. Chances are also that you eat salad and meat, fish or fowl at dinner; give your pet his meat and raw vegetables at dinner.

- The gradual change of your dog's diet, as recommended here, will give you a chance to reread this chapter so that the information can become "second nature" to you. After all, you don't want to have to go skimming through the chapter every day for weeks just before your dog's meal to check out something you don't remember clearly.

- When for any reason you cannot fulfill the recommendations for your pet's natural diet, it's important that you don't feel guilty. Your pet's health will not deteriorate because of an occasional deviation from the recommended diet; remember, we have termed this diet the *optimal* diet. Keep on hand a non-commercial preformulated dog food and dump that into your dog's bowl when you will be away for an extended period of time. If you oversleep and don't have even a split second to pour this food out for your dog before rushing off to work, consider his day without food a partial fast; fasts are recommended by many holistic veterinarians, as we state later in this chapter, if your pet is not chronically ill.

- The bottom line is that you should read this chapter carefully and adhere to every suggestion as closely as possible, as often as possible. If, for any valid reason, one or two recommendations are impossible for you to fulfill, then they are just that: impossible for you to fulfill. Realize that every step you take to remove your dog from a total diet of supermarket foods is bringing him that much closer to a long, disease-free life.

Meat

As we discussed earlier in this chapter and in chapter 1, the dog is basically a carnivore, or flesh eater. Through a long process of evolution, his teeth have been shaped to rip raw flesh apart. His nails can also rip flesh. His jawbones are powerful enough to chew raw flesh, and his intestines are short so that—unlike the case with our long intestines—there is little time for meat foods to become affected by body heat. Thus, they will not spoil and send toxins throughout the body.

However, as we followed our dog's ancestor through his average day in the ancient forests, we saw that he also consumed partially digested fruits, vegetables, and grains from his prey's stomach. If you see a contradiction between a dog's being a carnivore and his needing foods besides meat, a quick glance at a medical dictionary will show that members of the Carnivora family do not eat meat exclusively.

Most holistic veterinarians have traditionally recommended chicken and turkey wholeheartedly because fowl tended to be—along with veal and lamb—one of the least polluted sources of animal protein available outside of health food stores. As Nino Aloro, D.V.M., once pointed out, since chickens and turkeys tended to be killed young, they had had less time to be polluted with hormones, pesticide-contaminated feed, and so on. However, in recent years, fowl has become more contaminated, and holistic veterinarians recommend that you buy these foods in health food stores unless your supermarket carries brands that specify that the fowl has been raised naturally.

Regular supermarket veal and lamb continue to be your best bet for the least-polluted meats available outside of health food stores. But keep in mind that holistic veterinarians and M.D.s recommend all naturally raised, organic foods for an optimally healthy diet.

As we've discussed, one-sixth of your dog's meat allotment should be in the form of organ meats—thymus, spleen, kidney, heart, liver—not only because dogs ate that proportion of organ meats in the wild, but because these meats contain many nutrients that are less abundant in other parts of the animal.

Raw Meat, Cooked Meat

In the first edition, all nutritional veterinarians agreed that raw meat (accompanied by raw vegetables and fruits and cooked grains) was the optimal diet for dogs—for the simple reasons that dogs' bodies were designed by evolution, God, or Mother Nature (your choice) to thrive on these foods, and dogs fed otherwise do not thrive.

In the intervening years, the public has heard a lot more about the dangers of parasites in raw meat. But those are dangers to humans, not to dogs or cats. You see, dogs' bodies are acidic in their pH balance, while ours are alkaline—the opposite. If dogs were sickened by parasites in raw meat, the wild would never have had an adult dog.

For this new edition, Carvel G. Tiekert, D.V.M., told me: "I think the risk of giving raw meat is far outweighed by the risk of *not* giving it. The potential for parasitoxicity with raw meat is pretty small."

John Fudens, D.V.M., said that he has good success in getting his clients to give their dogs raw meat, "once I get them over their fear of salmonella and *E. coli* and all the other garbage misinformation that's out there about parasites and cats and dogs."

Veterinarians do warn, however, that you should never feed your dog raw pork or raw rabbit. These meats do carry parasites to which dogs are susceptible.

One of medical history's most dramatic scientific studies of the effect of raw versus cooked foods was begun, oddly, because an M.D. was trying to do research on something quite different. (Although this study was run on cats, it is equally relevant to dogs.) The doctor, Francis M. Pottenger Jr., was trying to standardize adrenal cortical material, and he was using cats for this research. However, he was in a quandary. So many cats were dying that he was having difficulty carrying on his study, and he did not know why the cats were dying.

It occurred to Dr. Pottenger that animals in zoos contracted the same diseases as man and died earlier than animals in the wild. It also occurred to him that animals in the wild ate raw foods, and animals in zoos often did not. And it did not escape him that he had been feeding his laboratory cats cooked meats.

Thus, Dr. Pottenger embarked on a ten-year study of three generations of cats. He fed half the cats the customary cooked meats and pasteurized (or cooked) milk; the other half he fed raw meats and unpasteurized (raw) milk. It didn't take even the first generation of cats fed cooked foods long to develop some of the new "inevitable" disorders of both animals and man: teeth loss, paralysis, irritable behavior. As time went on, heart lesions became common; so did arthritis, nephritis, hepatitis, cystitis, and so on.

Miscarriages in the first generation were about 25 percent—that is, one in four should-have-been-born kittens never made it into the world. By the second generation, 70 percent didn't make it. Of those kittens who did see the light of day, many died soon after. Many mother cats died in labor.

Lice and internal parasites were common among the "cooked-food cats"—that is, among those who lived long enough to suffer these things in the first place; so were skin lesions and allergies.

Meanwhile, the cats being "pampered" with raw foods rarely suffered miscarriages, lice, parasites, or infections. They also had calmer, more even-tempered personalities.

If you remember, Dr. Pottenger began those experiments because not enough cats were surviving the operations he was performing in his research on adrenal cortical material. Once he started giving raw foods to some of his cats, he found he could perform these operations on them with little or no problem.

By the way, my summation of these experiments is not meant to give you a sense of hopelessness if you happen to have raised a dog or cat on an unnatural diet and he now shows some of the signs of Dr. Pottenger's "cooked-food cats." You should know that in the fourth generation, Dr. Pottenger fed his "cooked-food cats" raw foods. In many cases, he was able to restore them to health.

Fish

Fish can be a good addition to your dog's diet. Fish contains polyunsaturated fats, for instance, which meat does not. We cover how crucial these fats are in a later section.

Here again, however, I must emphasize that you should not concentrate on fish for the mainstay of your dog's diet. Like any other single class of food, fish does not contain all the nutrients necessary for health. For instance, fish is low in vitamin E and in vitamin B_1. As Michael Kreisberg, D.V.M., once pointed out: "A B_1 deficiency can cause vomiting, weight loss—and brain damage."

Vegetables, Grains, Fruits

As we've mentioned, one-third to one-half of the dog's daily food should be meat. The rest should be fruits, vegetables, and grains. The latter foods give your dog a number of nutrients including carbohydrates and essential fatty acids that don't occur at all in meat but that are still necessary for your animal's health.

Partially grind up these three types of food for your dog. Remember that the bulk of these foods were obtained in the wild partially digested from the intestines of the animal prey.

An animal who has evolved to thrive mainly on raw fruits, vegetables, and grains has intestines that are long for its body. Such animals are called herbivores, not carnivores. (May I take a moment to remind you that our intestines are quite long for our bodies?) As I've mentioned, the dog's intestines are quite short. If you feed your dog uncut-up fruits, vegetables, and grains, the high amount of fiber and bulk in these foods will make it difficult for his short intestinal tract to digest them. In other words, your pet's body won't be able to utilize the necessary nutrients from these foods. In short, feed your dog his daily ration of fruits and vegetables raw because, again, cooking destroys enzymes, vitamins, and minerals. However, cut up these foods for him.

Our veterinarians stress, though, that rice and other grains must be cooked very, very well, or your pet may not be able to digest them. On the face of it, this might seem inconsistent with our previous warnings that cooking destroys many nutrients. However, rice and other grains grow naturally in very hot, sunny climates. As a result, the nutrients in these foods are unusually stable when exposed to heat.

Polyunsaturated Fats (Essential Fatty Acids)

All holistic veterinarians agree on the importance of these fats in the diet of your dog. Some veterinarians have told me that these fats are, indeed, *the* most critical nutrients.

As we'll see in later chapters, holistic veterinarians use these nutrients to help in the treatment of a number of disorders, from skin problems to cancer. As always, it's easier, cheaper, kinder, and more foolproof to prevent than to cure.

"If the animal is getting the proper proportion of fresh whole grains," Dr. Robertson has said, "he's probably getting adequate essential fatty acids. If he's not getting enough whole grains, then the owner had better supplement. The lack of unsaturated fats is the major cause of skin problems and the major reason why dogs don't absorb calcium." (The malabsorption of calcium can lead to a number of bone and joint problems.)

Research in essential fatty acid deficiency has shown that such a deficiency can also lead to stunted growth, reproductive problems, and degeneration of lungs, liver, and kidneys. Too little essential fatty acid intake is also implicated in rheumatoid arthritis and multiple sclerosis.

If you want to offer your pet an optimal preventive diet, you might add one teaspoon to one tablespoon (depending on your pet's size) of essential fatty acids a day to his diet—even if you're fairly sure he's getting enough whole grains. A bit more than necessary won't be harmful. A supplement of essential fatty acids is quite easy to obtain. Just buy a bottle of soybean oil, corn oil, sunflower seed oil, or safflower oil—the cooking and salad oils you can buy in the supermarket. The highest quality oils you can buy are cold pressed. These are available in health food stores and some supermarkets. If the oil is cold pressed, it will say so in bold letters on the label.

Dr. Robertson stated that the best source of the most potent fatty acid (gamma linolenic) is oil of evening primrose. You may have trouble getting this particular oil outside of health food stores. Dr. Kearns had a preference for cold-pressed sesame oil. "This oil does everything other unsaturated fats do," he told me, "but it also stimulates the thymus to produce T-cells, which help fight infection and cancer." Dr. Robertson and Drs. Marty and Robert Goldstein also agreed that cold-pressed sesame oil is a top choice.

As for other oils, wheat germ oil is high in vitamin E and octacosanol, and safflower oil is very high in vitamin F.

Vitamin and Mineral Supplements

For those of you whose budgets are very, very tight, I can say that a few of the veterinarians surveyed believe you'll be able to have a healthy, long-lived pet without supplements, as long as you feed him the natural diet as detailed in this chapter and give him the supplements mentioned in chapter 4 for special times in his life. For those of you who can afford a few more pennies a day (and that's all it will cost), you're on much safer ground if you give your pet supplements in the manner explained a bit later.

Readers who have been following this book closely may now be thinking they have discovered an inconsistency: "Dogs," you may say, "never had vitamin and mineral supplements in the wild." You're quite right, of course; they didn't. However, they also did not eat foods grown in nutrient-depleted earth (which both you and your pet are doing, unless you buy all your foods from well-chosen health food stores or grow all your own foods organically). And they didn't have to use much of the nutrients in their bodies for the extra job of fighting off stress from all the new poisons in the environment.

When choosing supplements, I hope you will not "build your own" vitamin and mineral supplement, for either yourself or your pet. I hope you will buy a good multivitamin/multimineral supplement, preferably from the health food store, where the nutrients are likely to be from natural sources. (Health food stores carry vitamins especially formulated for dogs.) Often, the vitamins and minerals available in drugstores are chemical copies of the real thing.

First of all, if you build your own from different sources, it will probably cost you several times more than getting all the same nutrients in one pill. But my main concern is that by prescribing your own balance of vitamins and minerals, you may very well do your pet—or yourself—more harm than good.

For instance, you may read something somewhere that convinces you that your pet needs vitamin B_6. If you give him isolated B_6 without the direction of a veterinarian, you can increase his need for the other B-vitamins. In other words, you can, by giving him B_6, make him *deficient* in the other B-vitamins. This can cause severe central nervous system damage, as well as other problems.

In another instance you may read rather simplistic statements that pregnant and lactating dogs, as well as growing puppies, need extra calcium. This is true; but what these other sources may not tell you is that you can't give a pill containing only calcium. Calcium has to be combined in a delicate balance with phosphorus, as nutritional veterinarian Dr. Kreisberg has stressed. It also has to be given in a certain ratio to magnesium or you stand the chance of causing the very health problems you're trying to prevent. In addition, vitamin D is needed or the calcium can't even be used by the body.

I have deliberately tried to make the balancing of vitamins and minerals sound complicated—because it is. I hope you will not attempt to do it on your own. For preventive purposes I hope you will follow the recommendation given here by veterinarians who have devoted their careers to the specific problem of nutrition for pets: Select an already balanced multivitamin and mineral supplement, and add vitamins C and E.

Holistic veterinarians have recommended to me that you add to the multivitamin/multimineral supplement the following additions of vitamin C for your adult dog (unless there is already part of the amount in the pill): 500 mg for a small, sedentary dog to 1,500 mg for a small, extremely active dog; 1,500 to 3,000 mg for a medium dog; 3,000 to 6,000 mg for a large dog; and 6,000 to 7,500 mg for a giant dog.

The total vitamin E you should give your pet daily is 100 IU for the small dog; 200 IU for the medium; 300 IU for the large; and 400 IU for the giant.

Saturated fat is necessary for a number of nutrients to be absorbed by the body, so feed the supplements to your guy or gal along with meat.

Ideally, you should buy a powdered supplement. If that's not possible, mash up the multivitamin/multimineral tablet in your dog's food. Why? If your dog's digestive processes are not tip-top (and if he has been on processed foods, chances are his digestive juices are *not* tip-top), the pill may pass through his system and out again without being used at all. As S. Allen Price, D.V.M., once put it: "Sometimes we give a vitamin/mineral tablet to a dog or a cat, and it comes out again later, still a whole tablet." You can see that those vitamins and minerals have not been used by the body. One more important point: There is always the possibility that a tablet might get stuck in the throat of a small animal.

How Not to Poison Your Pet with Water

Every time you fill your pet's bowl with cool, fresh water from your faucet, you may very well be bringing him that much closer to death from cadmium poisoning, copper poisoning, and/or lead poisoning. Yes, the same lead poisoning that the public is generally led to believe is caused only by eating paint peelings.

These dangerous heavy metals, of course, find it just as easy to get from your water pipes into your glass as they do to get into your pet's bowl. Many plumbing pipes are made partially from cadmium, copper, or lead; and as these metals start to erode, the water carries particles of the metal out with it.

An overload of heavy metals in your pet's body, and/or your own, can cause kidney damage, emphysema (there's a lot of the heavy metal cadmium in cigarette smoke, by the way), high blood pressure, heart disease, mental retardation, anemia, miscarriages, epilepsy, depression, and arthritis. That's only a partial list.

There is another substance that is being added *on purpose* to our drinking water. In many cities fluoride is added as a form of mass medication to help us prevent tooth decay—which might be more safely prevented by cutting out sugar, of course. Medical studies on everything from the fruit fly to mice to human beings have shown increased incidences of cancer caused by fluoride.

Dean Burk, Ph.D., once made a strong statement: "Our data in the United States indicate in my view that one-tenth of all cancer deaths in this country can be shown to be linked to fluoridation of public drinking water. That comes to about forty thousand extra cancer deaths a year. . . . [That] exceeds deaths from breast cancer." Dr. Burk was for thirty-five years a high-level researcher at the U.S. Public Health Service's National Cancer Institute in the Washington, D.C., area.[2]

That's a brief overview of the dangerous substances we drink in our tap water every day. Of course there are other contaminants, too. As I wrote the first edition, a TV reporter was announcing with some amazement that "thousands of towns" across the country had recently suffered increased incidences of various diseases and that "these diseases have been traced to human waste in the water." You have probably read similar statements quite recently.

Of course you can't cut out water, either for yourself or for your pet. Water is needed to carry wastes out of the system, not only digestive wastes but also dead body cells. However, as Dr. Robertson has pointed out, impure water does not have the "carrying power" of pure water, and many toxins and dead cells are left to float around in our circulatory system a lot longer than they should.

By now you're wishing I would stop telling you horror stories about tap water and give you a clue as to what you can do to get all those poisons out of your pet's bowl and out of your drinking glass. One simple and inexpensive thing you can do is to let your water run for five minutes before you use it. This will allow time for particles of eroded heavy metals from your pipes to be carried off harmlessly down the drain, although it won't do anything for the more than three hundred contaminants that can be found actually in the water itself.

You can help your and your pet's health even more by investing a small sum in a water filter that you can put permanently over your faucet. Investigate before you buy, however; some filters screen out more contaminants than others.

Probably you have heard of both spring water and distilled water as alternatives for the chemical-laden water that comes from our faucets. Nutritional M.D.s and D.V.M.s alike argue among themselves as to whether spring or distilled water is the better alternative. I asked a number of holistic veterinarians to tell me their preference and their reasons for it.

From their responses it seems that your safest bet may be distilled water. Even those veterinarians who prefer spring water have warned that very often such water is contaminated. If you elect to use spring water, do a bit of research to make sure it comes from pure sources. Just reading the label won't do. After all, no distributor is going to state on the label: "Bottled exclusively from contaminated springs."

Still, some nutritional writers have maintained that distilled water can be dangerous because it not only lacks desirable minerals but can also leach minerals out of the body. As for the argument that distilled water contains no desirable minerals, Dr. Robertson has stated: "The inorganic minerals that are in water are practically useless to the body." Addressing themselves to the argument that distilled water robs the body of minerals, Drs. Robert and Marty Goldstein told me that the minerals leached out by distilled water are undesirable, inorganic minerals. "Distilled water also leaches out other morbid wastes," the latter two doctors stated. Indeed, as we will see later, holistic veterinarians use distilled water as therapy for conditions such as arthritis, just because it *does* leach out undesirable minerals from the body.

Bones for Your Dog?

I know that many people have heard that bones are indispensable for their dogs. When I researched the first edition, I personally had doubts about bones because of the possibility of choking, so I asked ten veterinarians to give their recommendations about letting pets gnaw bones. Seven of the ten veterinarians voted no, two voted yes but only for a specific type of bone, and only one doctor voted wholeheartedly for bones. He cited the fact that carnivores in the wild always chewed on bones—and still do—as a way of cleaning their teeth. This doctor stated that in thirty years of practice, he has never found a pet who choked or otherwise had problems caused by a splintered bone.

Unfortunately, other veterinarians *have* seen pets who have had problems, and they voted against bones because of the possibility of choking or of splinters getting into the intestines. John C. Craige, V. M.D., for instance, said, "I remember a pitiable little Boston terrier who died with a string of lamb bones blocking his intestines. I have also seen countless dogs who couldn't pass their feces without pain from bone splinters."

I once suggested to a neighbor that she stop giving bones to her dog, Lucky. "Don't fret your head, sweetheart," she told me. "Lucky's been gnawing on bones all his life without a problem. It keeps him happy." A few months later, the dog was dead. He'd choked on a chicken bone. The neighbor was stunned. "That never happened before," she said.

It seems to me that—while problems with bones may be rare—bones can kill. In this regard, I remember one of my earliest interviews with an M.D. when I was starting out as a medical journalist. "My editor wants you to comment on the fact that this form of cancer affects only 10 percent of men," I said.

The researcher answered: "The comment I have is that when a disease affects 10 percent, or 5 percent, or even 1 percent of the population, if it happens to *you*, the statistic is 100 percent."

Dr. Aloro was most strongly against giving bones to pets. He stated that bones, far from keeping the teeth healthy, can harm them quite drastically. "When my clients don't listen to me and give their pets bones, I find the teeth get chipped; they break; they get otherwise ruined because the roots get weakened." As if that weren't enough, sometimes the teeth even get "filed down to the gum line." Dr. Aloro did, however, recommend soup bones—which don't tend to splinter—*for teething pets,* whose baby teeth are meant by nature to come out soon, anyway. These bones help loosen the baby teeth.

Dr. Tiekert, who entered "the bone question" for this new edition, said: "I'll throw this in for whatever it's worth. I like to give animals ox tails if the owners can get them. Animals are not likely to break teeth on these bones. I do a lot of veterinary dentistry, so I see many animals who break their teeth off chewing on *hard* bones. But with the ox tails, animals get quite a bit of gristle, so they get a lot of precursors for ligaments and cartilage." (That means that gristle sets in motion in the body the biochemical reactions that produce two substances vital for healthy joints and bones. Thus, gristle can help prevent disorders that cripple.)

Does Dr. Tiekert know of any animals who have choked on ox tail bones? "I've never seen that happen," he said. "But of course there's always a potential for choking whenever an animal chews on anything."

Drs. Robert and Marty Goldstein told me for the first edition that most of today's dogs that are raised on processed dog food "do not have strong enough teeth or digestive juices to handle bones as safely as their ancestors did"—and still do—in the wild. In contrast, dogs who have been on natural diets for long periods of time tend to have strong digestive juices that can dissolve bits of bone, preventing these bone fragments from getting imbedded in the intestines.

Important: If you have always heard that dogs absolutely must have bones, maybe this discussion has not convinced you otherwise.

Please at least don't let your dog have bones small enough to swallow or fragile enough to splinter as he gnaws on them. And take the advice of many holistic veterinarians *not* to cook any bones you give your pet. Dr. Craige explained that cooking denatures the collagen (a protein) of the bone, making it harder to digest. While dogs do chew on bones in the wild, they obviously aren't cooked bones.

I have been talking until now about real animal, fish, or bird bones. What about plastic bones, rawhide bones, and milk bones? When you buy these you are using the fake products holistic veterinarians spoke against so strongly in chapter 1. One veterinarian warned: "These artificial products must be excluded from the diet of *all* pets." And this was the veterinarian most strongly in favor of *real* bones for pets.

Additional Tips

A Chocolate Treat for Your Dog? No!

Chocolate is dangerous for both dogs and cats. It contains a chemical called theobromine, which can cause urinary incontinence, seizures— and death.

Food Combining

How you combine food groups can be crucial to your dog's health. Why? The digestive organs secrete enzymes to break down food so it can be properly used by the body. When carbohydrates and proteins are eaten at the same time, the protein enzymes go to work first, and the digestion of carbohydrates must wait. While the carbohydrates are waiting around to be digested, they ferment and release toxins in the body.

Proper food combining might more aptly be called *not* combining foods: Give only meat (or other heavy proteins such as eggs or milk) at one meal; give carbohydrates (fruit and grains) for the other meal. Vegetables, though, may be given with either grains or heavy proteins.

This easy step can not only be helpful in preventing the release of toxins in your dog's body, it can also help prevent pancreatitis (inflammation of the pancreas). Holistic veterinarians discuss just how serious this disease is—and how many other conditions it can lead to—in chapter 9, which discusses problems of internal organs. You see, the pancreas spends much of its work time producing enzymes to aid in digestion. Asking it to try to produce two sets of enzymes at one time—to help digest both proteins and carbohydrates—can cause this hard worker much distress.

Is all this true for people, too? Yes. Rather than eating cereal and toast with ham and eggs for breakfast, you might consider eating cereal, fruit, and toast—all carbohydrates. If you are troubled by puzzling bouts of gas, you might see if proper food combining puts an end to them.

Don't Spring This New Diet on Your Dog All at Once

For one thing, any sudden major change in a diet can prove upsetting to the body and cause digestive disturbances. For another, a dog addicted to sugar or other unnatural additives in commercial foods is not unlike a person addicted to alcohol. If you take away all his additives abruptly, he may suffer intensely from withdrawal symptoms.

Start slowly. Add just a bit of his new diet at a time for about a week, then gradually add a bit more. In this way, not only his digestive system but also his taste buds can get a chance to become adjusted to the new (though ancient) diet.

You might want to see chapter 4, my personal story of my dog Rambo, who suffered because of a quick change in diet.

How Much to Feed Your Pet and How Often

First I am going to repeat the information on calories from the first edition. I'm doing this because I think calories are still the general approach to the idea of how much food you should feed your dog. But dealing with calories can become complicated for someone who isn't a nutritionist. After the information on calories, I will tell you about a newer, easier approach given me by two holistic veterinarians I talked to for this new book.

Most nutritional veterinarians are loath to recommend how many calories you should feed a dog, and rightly so. As Dr. Aloro said: "Of course I have in my office all those nice charts about calories and fat, et cetera, per pound of the animal's weight. But for practical purposes, they are fairly useless. The charts deal with the average animal. In reality, most animals are not average; each pet is an individual."

What Dr. Aloro said is true. Feeding the same number of calories to a 20-pound dog who spends his days running around the yard and to a 20-pounder who spends his days snoozing at your feet could result in one half-starved dog and one bloated butterball.

Even feeding an equal number of calories to two dogs of the same weight, age, and exercise habits won't work for certain to maintain perfect weight. These two animals might have quite dissimilar metabolic rates: One dog might burn up only half as many calories a day as the other. As Thomas A. Newland, D.V.M., once pointed out, the same disparity is true of people. "We all know people who eat everything and stay thin, and we all know people who eat little and get fat."

Holistic veterinarians recommend this sublimely commonsense rule of thumb: If your dog starts gaining weight, cut down a bit on his food and encourage him to exercise more. If he starts losing weight, indulge him in a bit more food. Another easy-to-follow rule of thumb about your dog's weight: You should be able to *feel* her ribs—that means she doesn't have a lot of extra fat around them. But you should not be able to *see* her ribs—that means she doesn't have enough fat around them.

However, I'll give you a base to start from, because I know your dog's new natural diet won't be coming out of a box or can that provides you with simplistic instructions for your "average" dog. Try starting him with about 50 calories a day for each pound he weighs. But no matter how many calories you include in your dog's new diet, watch his weight carefully for a while.

The following is an example of why Dr. Aloro and other holistic veterinarians are reluctant to deal with *average* calories for *individual* animals: The average recommendation for dogs worked out to 500 calories a day for my 10-pound poodle and 600 calories for my 12-pounder. Yet both Shiki and her daughter, Little Lady, maintained their weight to the dot for some fifteen years on 800 calories a day.

You can easily get inexpensive books and pamphlets that give calorie counts of most foods. Maybe over breakfast one day, circle those foods you'll be feeding your dog. Then you'll be able to find the calorie counts quickly. You'll probably be surprised how fast you memorize them and don't need to look them up anymore.

Now that was, as I said, the traditional advice about doling out your pet's food. But for this new book, several veterinarians told me that they go by *volume*, not calories. In other words, if you have a small dog that maintains her weight on a cup of food a day, one-third to one-half of that cup should be meat. At her other meal, give her the remaining half to two-thirds in grains and vegetables.

How often should you feed your dog? Traditionally, we have been told on boxes of kibble to leave dry food out for the dog to eat at will all day.

This advice is a far cry from that of veterinarians who specialize in nutrition. First, of course, these doctors don't recommend foods in cans or boxes. Second, "We don't like to feed them what we call free choice, leaving any food down all the time," John B. Limehouse, D.V. M., told me in a recent interview. "We like to feed them twice a day, and what they haven't chosen to eat after maybe thirty minutes, we advise you just go ahead and pick it up." Dr. Limehouse explained that the reason for this seeming cruelty is, as always, the goal of keeping your dog's carnivorous body as close to nature as possible. "In the wild, dogs stalk their food, they chase it, they struggle with it, and after the kill, they play with it. So by the time they get ready to eat it, their bodies have worked up to producing what you might call a crescendo of enzymes. I feel that when we let dogs nibble throughout the day, they're not developing a sufficient amount of enzymes to always do a good job of digesting their food and actually *using* the nutrients." The veterinarian added that often with dogs who have been allowed to nibble at will, "we wind up having to supplement them with extra enzymes" to get them back to full health.

To express this from a somewhat different angle, remember that dogs' bodies weren't formed to be those of grazers (such as cows, who *can* stay healthy by nibbling all day). Dogs need "fasting" time between meals so their bodies can become acidic—their normal, healthy state. Smelling food and nibbling all day keeps dogs' systems alkaline, the *opposite* of acidic.

Norman C. Ralston, D.V.M., summed up these facts in another way while talking to me about heart problems for a later chapter. Expressing himself passionately, as he usually does because he cares so deeply about animals, he interrupted himself to say: "You can talk about heart problems, you can talk about urinary problems, you can talk about other problems. But the biggest mistake people make with dogs is to overlook their basic nature. Dogs were designed by God—or nature if you don't want to talk about God—to go from feast to famine." After discussing some of the above facts about necessary changes in a dog's body, Dr. Ralston said, "Dogs need to get hungry so that they can stay healthy."

He added that he once had the same problem in his house: "My wife was wanting to leave food out all the time for our cat. 'Well,' she said, 'I'm afraid he might get hungry.'" Dr. Ralston managed to convince her that the cat was *supposed* to get hungry. Before going back to the subject we had been talking about, the veterinarian commented: "Now our cat is seventeen years old, and he's a healthy son of a goon."

Fasting

Here, we're talking about longer-term fasting than we were in the previous paragraphs. If you already believe in occasional fasting for yourself because you feel that the digestive system should have a rest now and then to let the body rid itself of toxins, you'll be glad to know that there's a rationale for fasting your dog occasionally, too. Do you remember Ruff, our composite great-great-etc. grand-daddy of today's dogs, whose evolving body shaped your dog's car-nivorous body and its needs? Well, Ruff didn't get lucky enough to snare a catch every day. So Ruff and all his billions of descendants have bodies designed to be healthy if they have to fast occasionally for a day.

All the recommendations I know of suggest you fast your adult dog over two years of age for twenty-four hours once a week—if you want to "get into" fasting at all. *Of course, you must give him water during the fast.* If your dog is between four months and two years of age, fast him for only half a day every week, and a full day once a month.

Warning: Do not fast your chronically sick pet without the *personal* guidance of a veterinarian who thoroughly understands fasting. (Close guidance by phone is okay, if you feel assured the veterinarian will be quickly available by phone in case of an emergency.) The poisons that concentrate in the body before they are expelled can kill a degenerated pet. I know you may have read elsewhere that fasting can help many sick dogs recover—and it can. But don't use this technique on your own, even if the book or article seems to have given you precise instructions. (Sometimes writers give detailed instructions for something they know should be done only under close professional guidance because they fear readers won't consult doctors for one reason or another. The writers feel they should at least give some structure to what readers might otherwise "make up on their own.")

If you opt for occasional fasting, give your companion some extra-special attention while depriving him of food, and don't fast him while you're not home.

Here I feel I should address myself to readers who may think that dogs don't have the same "feelings" as humans. (I doubt that many of you reading this book believe that, but I try to cover all bases; and I've known compassionate "animal people" who have told me in no uncertain terms that dogs aren't affected by the death of loved ones. Also, I have read articles written by experts saying that if you lock a dog away all alone in a strange room while someone renovates your house, the dog cries piteously only to get your attention—not because she is suffering emotionally.) It's true that Ruff, your dog's great-great ancestor, didn't have a human around to console him whenever he had to go without food for a while. But Ruff *never* had a human. Your dog *always* has, and so he has learned to depend on you for many things that Ruff never dreamed of asking a two-legged animal for. Faced with no food for a day, Ruff would probably have said to himself: "Heck, no food today. Okay, I've survived this before. Let me take a nap and I'll go hunting again tomorrow." Your domesticated dog may think, "Oh, no. No food in my bowl! This has never happened to me before. I can't get out of this place to hunt, because I'm all locked in. I'm doomed, that's what I am!"

Some holistic veterinarians suggest that you take a more "hands-off" approach toward regular fasting. Dr. Robertson has said, "Your pet is the one who knows when he should fast. Whenever a dog or cat doesn't feel in top form, the first thing he'll do is stop eating. Leave it to him. He has a better idea of when he should fast than we do." (In this regard, you should have some concern if your pet goes off his food. But if he does, perhaps the worst thing you can do without professional guidance is to force-feed him. Think back, for instance, to the times you've felt nauseous: Would you have thanked *your* loved one for forcing you to take food into your stomach?)

Milk Products

I know that many people consider milk an excellent food for dogs. This *is* true of puppies: After all, all mammals start life living exclusively off the milk their mothers so graciously provide. However, let's investigate this for a moment. If you're feeding your grown dog milk, you're feeding him cow's milk, aren't you? (That's pretty much the only kind you can buy in most stores.) As a puppy your companion got milk, naturally, from his mama—but it was *dog's* milk. Just as kittens naturally get cat's milk from their mamas, and human babies naturally get human milk from their mamas.

Richard J. Kearns, D.V. M., once stated the above ideas this way: "I feel that milk is an unnatural food unless it goes from nipple to host by suction." The doctors Goldstein added that cow's milk contains growth hormones that serve to take a 40-pound calf and build him to a 700- to 1,000-pound cow. "This is great for the cow," the doctors said, "but not for the dog."

Having said all these negatives against milk, let me add that holistic veterinarians believe that raw, unpasteurized milk (especially raw goat's milk available in some health food stores) can be a good addition to your dog's weekly diet—*if your dog shows no signs of being allergic to milk.* On the plus side, milk contains calcium. In the wild, dogs and cats got calcium from chomping on the bones of their prey; this book asks you to consider very carefully before giving bones to your pet. Therefore, you must find other means to give him the calcium his body evolved to thrive on. Raw goat's milk is a good way.

Yogurt may be an even better way to provide your pet with calcium. Yogurt tends to cause fewer animals (and fewer persons) allergy problems. It also contains a type of "friendly" bacteria that is extremely important to the digestive health—and therefore the total health—of your pet (and yourself).

The common belief is that allergies cause basically only stomach and skin problems. However, Alfred Jay Plechner, D.V.M., who has studied allergies extensively, has stated that nearly any disease in the body may be primarily or secondarily related to a food allergy. Nutritional M.D.s make similar statements about human diseases.

If your dog has bouts of diarrhea, simply cutting out milk might "miraculously" cure the diarrhea. However, as we've said, allergies can cause almost any symptom. So if your pet has *any* problem that your veterinarian has not been able to explain or treat successfully, I hope you'll ask the doctor to consider the possibility of allergies to milk and other foods.

Your Dog's Food and Water Bowls

Joseph Stuart, D.V.M., once pointed out to me that your pet's bowls should not be the common plastic ones that so many owners use. Dr. Kearns agreed, adding that there is a chemical reaction that can cause many pets to lose pigment from their noses. Dr. Kearns also advised that aluminum dishes can cause aluminum toxicity and ceramic dishes can cause lead toxicity. He recommended stainless steel or glass dishes as the safest. Nutritional M.D.s make the same recommendations for us.

If your dog's water bowl starts to show discoloration, look to your tap water. In my recent book on psychiatrists who treat mental problems using natural therapies *(Healing the Mind the Natural Way)*, I included the case history of a woman who for years had been diagnosed as having a serious psychosomatic disorder that refused to yield to psychological therapies. It was "psychosomatic," you see, because no physical reason for her array of symptoms could be found on the usual orthodox diagnostic tests. When her puppy also developed some of her "imagined" symptoms, the woman found it hard to believe that a pet could catch "mental" disorders from his owner. A discoloration in his water bowl led to her having her water pipes tested. They had many times the level of copper considered safe. She and her puppy had copper poisoning, and both were easily cured of their symptoms by nutritional doctors.

How to Supplement Your Dog's Diet with Inexpensive Packaged Foods

Your pet's healthy diet might include occasional servings of prepared dog foods bought at a store. Right now you're getting ready to throw back at me all the grisly facts we covered in chapter 1 about packaged pet foods from supermarket shelves. What I am recommending here are packaged pet foods available primarily at health food stores and some enlightened pet shops and grooming shops. The prepared foods I'm referring to here are more closely tailored to your pet's needs, tend to come from more natural sources, and may not contain the poisons that plump out the commercial pet foods.

These purer prepared foods can serve as a nice source of balanced nutrition now and then: for instance, when you're not going to be home in time to serve a meal. And they can be just about invaluable when you have to leave your dog in the care of someone else. You can more easily expect a friend or kennel owner to shake out some kibble from a bag than to deal with raw meat balanced with grains and raw fruits and vegetables.

Surprisingly, these more natural prepared foods are often no more expensive than the lethal packaged foods in supermarkets. Are these distributors, then, philanthropists? No. But for one thing, as we covered previously, the more nutritious a food is, the less a pet will eat of it, because he will need less to fulfill his body requirements. For another thing, you don't have to pay these distributors for nationwide TV ads. As Dr. Newland pointed out to me in 1981: "A few seconds' TV commercial costs $60,000 to $150,000." (We can easily imagine the cost nowadays!) "I ask you, is there any nutritional value in this hot air? If you buy the product, you are paying for this advertising, right through the nose," the veterinarian said.

Now, if there are fairly good prepared foods available, why have I bothered you with everything I've told you in the earlier part of this chapter? Because your dog cannot thrive on these foods as a *mainstay* of her diet. They should be used only as an occasional supplement. And if they are used often, they themselves should be supplemented with the nutrients they're lacking. These more nutritious canned or packaged foods are still not raw, and they're missing the enzymes that can be found only in raw foods—more accurately, your pet is missing out on them. I think you'll find that adding the enzymes already makes the packaged food more expensive than a completely natural diet. And some of these less poisoned foods consist basically of lamb and rice, or another combination of basically two ingredients. If you use these as a basis of your dog's diet, in addition to enzymes, you'll have to supplement with omega-3 and omega-6 fatty acids to make up for the fact that she doesn't have any fish in her diet. These "two-ingredient" prepared foods also leave your dog vulnerable to developing allergies because of eating the same foods every day.

Another argument against serving even the purest packaged foods as a mainstay of your dog's diet is that the longer foods sit around in packages or cans, the more nutrients they lose. And once you open the package or can, exposing the food to air, the nutrients start disappearing even faster, through the oxidation process.

Here you might have every reason to expect me to make things easy for you by simply giving you the brand names that holistic veterinarians recommend for occasional supplementation of a natural raw-food diet. I did do that in the first edition, although some veterinarians warned me not to, saying that many producers of the purer prepared foods become greedy over time and start substituting artificial ingredients for the more natural ones in order to make a bigger profit. When I tried again to make a list of brand names for this new book, I found that holistic veterinarians were telling me that until very recently they were recommending, say, three specific brands, but that number was now down to one because the other two distributors had started seriously tampering with the quality of their products.

But do you know what? I *can* simplify the choice for you. Call the offices of a few holistic veterinarians (see the list at the back of the book) and ask what they're recommending at the precise time you're reading this. I suggest calling more than one holistic veterinarian because you might find brand X, say, to be one of four choices of the first doctor, but brand Y is a choice of that doctor as well as two other veterinarians. I'd assume, then, that brand Y would be the more educated choice. Since busy veterinarians can sometimes be hard to get on the phone for a simple question like this, try just asking the secretary what the doctor recommends.

If, for some reason, you'd rather "go it alone" on choosing a prepackaged food for an occasional supplement—or if you want to double-check the veterinarian's recommendation—here's a very quick rundown on what you should look for on labels, once you think you have found a noncontaminated food in a health food store, pet shop, or grooming shop. First of all, the label should state that there are no artificial preservatives, colors, or flavorings. Recently, even some supermarket foods state "no artificial preservatives or colors." If you read the label carefully, you'll probably see that there are artificial *flavorings*. That's not good enough for your dog. Some labels state "no added" preservatives or whatnot. The word "added" is a clue that the sources of the product might have *started off* with preservatives or whatnot. In addition, the label should not contain the words *meal* or *by-products* after any of its ingredients, for the reasons given in chapter 1. And the label shouldn't list any of the other "no-no's" covered in that chapter.

Somewhere along the line, the label should read that the product has one or more preservatives. But haven't I said that preservatives are practically going to make your pet keel over on the spot? I've warned against *artificial* preservatives. If you don't have any preservatives at all in prepackaged food, there's nothing to prevent it from spoiling while it sits on the shelf—before you even buy it. The label you're investigating should specify *natural* preservatives, such as vitamins C and E.

Avoid using too often a product that lists fish early on the label, which indicates it's a major ingredient. Too much fish robs the body of vitamin E. And if you come across a product that claims you can use it for both dogs and cats—as I have—ask yourself: How can a product fulfill at the same time the needs of dogs, who thrive on a diet of 33 to 50 percent meat, and the needs of cats, who thrive on a diet of 60 to 75 percent meat?

Let me add a final word to discourage you from using prepared foods often: As covered in chapter 1, a new labeling act allows labels to claim products are "all natural" even if they contain many poisons.

A Vegetarian Diet for Your Dog?

In the first edition, I reluctantly gave specifics of a vegetarian diet that came as close as an unnatural diet *could* to having the potential to keep a pet healthy. I pointed out that people who were vegetarians themselves because they believed meat wasn't healthy for humans were on the right track because our bodies aren't those of carnivores. But they were definitely on the wrong track if they tried to make their carnivorous pet into a vegetarian. However, I felt I couldn't offer an argument for readers who refused to feed meat to their pets because they couldn't bear to contribute to the slaughter of other animals. (I was afraid that these readers might feel they should switch to poisonous fake supermarket foods, and I hoped to help them do less harm by suggesting the best possible vegetarian diet.)

Now I offer the argument against a vegetarian diet that one reason animals are killed is to provide animal parts to manufacturers of your dog's supermarket foods. So, by paying for these foods, you are still helping to contribute to the death of these animals. But instead of giving your companion the parts of the animals that can bless her with a long and healthy life, you're giving her tumors and the like. Perhaps the fact I discovered for this new book—that the commercial foods contain parts of bodies of euthanized dogs and cats—will solidify your decision not to switch your dog to these foods.

For this book, I questioned a new batch of holistic veterinarians about whether it is ever okay for owners to feed a vegetarian diet to their dogs. The responses I got were even more vehement than they were in 1981. For instance, John Fudens, D.V.M., answered me—and I quote him directly—"Never, never, never, never. Absolutely no. Never."

The veterinarian continued: "I don't care what our own religious or philosophical viewpoint is. You don't love your animals if you try to make them vegetarians." Referring to the vegetarian dogs and cats who have been brought to him in ill health in his thirty-four years as a veterinarian, Dr. Fudens said that the pets had become vegetarians because of their owners' perspectives, "not from the animals' points of view." He added that "once you balance out these sick animals' diet with some meat, you should see how happy and healthy they become: like fleas on a sick dog.

"Dogs and cats are not herbivores," Dr. Fudens summarized. "God made them as carnivores—whether we like it or not—and they need animal protein."

Dr. Tiekert said: "These are dogs and cats we're talking about; they're not little people. And I think we should use diets that are appropriate for their digestive systems—not ours. If we force on dogs and cats our philosophical desires about vegetarianism, I don't believe we're thinking about what we *have*. If you've chosen an animal who's by nature a carnivore, and now you want to make him into a vegetarian, why did you get that animal in the first place?"

Dr. Tiekert suggested that people considering buying or adopting a dog and feeding him a vegetarian diet should first look at a lot of pictures showing wild dogs carrying the bodies of dead animals in their mouths.

I still have a nagging fear that some of you will continue your dog on a vegetarian diet. If you absolutely must, at least have a diet drawn up by an animal nutritionist who knows how to balance amino acids.

But you can see why I'm not including a vegetarian diet in this edition. It would go against my conscience. Also, I'm afraid the veterinarians who worked with me on this book would shoot me.

Summary

The holistic veterinarians who worked with me on this chapter have given you detailed information on nutrition, which is the source of every biochemical reaction in our dogs' (and in our) bodies. You now are armed with the most important information presently known to give your adult dog a supremely healthy and long life. Specific nutritional information for puppyhood and other special stages in your dog's life will follow in chapter 4.

But first, in the next chapter, let me give you information on the misuse of vaccinations—yes, orthodox veterinary medicine's major way of attempting to prevent disease. As I will detail there, holistic veterinarians consider standard vaccinations to be almost as important— some consider them of equal importance—in destroying our pets' health as a steady diet of unnatural and poisonous food. These veterinarians will tell you how you can vaccinate your dog safely—and with less expense than the regimen presently recommended by most orthodox veterinarians. We'll also see that perhaps the present regimen is fast falling out of favor even with conventional doctors.

As usual, this information will also be relevant to the health of you and your human family.

References

1. Wendell O. Belfield, D.V. M., *Let's Live,* July 1980, p. 139.
2. Cited by Jim Sibbison, *Bestways,* April 1982, p.42.

Chapter 3

Vaccinations Can Be Your Dog's Worst Enemy or His Best Friend: How You Can Make the Right Choice

"Standard vaccines are the single biggest cause of immune system damage in animals and humans. All chronic disease in animals is traced to genetics and standard vaccinations before anything else."
—*John Fudens, D.V.M.*

"Overvaccination is the *main* problem (along with malnutrition) that affects our pets today."
—*Michele Yasson, D.V.M., C.V.A.*

"A practice that . . . lacks scientific validity or verification is annual revaccinations. Almost without exception there is no immunologic requirement for annual revaccination. Immunity to viruses persists for years or for the life of the animal. Successful vaccination to most bacterial pathogens produces an immunologic memory that remains for years . . ."
—*Tom R. Phillips, D.V.M., and Ronald D. Shultz, D.V.M., in* Current Veterinary Therapy XI, *p. 205*

"Since I have been using homeopathic vaccinations [nosodes]—for the last fifteen years—I have never had, to my knowledge, a single animal come down with any disease that was vaccinatable."
—*John Fudens, D.V.M.*

When I worked in 1981 with numerous holistic veterinarians for the first edition of this book, I didn't find any who really liked the idea of giving vaccinations, because of the potential dangers to the animal. But there were basically only two choices in that era: either give standard, orthodox vaccinations or give none. So I included in the book the details holistic veterinarians provided for making standard vaccinations as nontoxic and as effective as possible. (I repeat these details at the end of this chapter for those of you who might still feel, after reading the following new information, that your dog's health can benefit most from a specific standard vaccination. You can also use these details if you still feel you want to give your dog the full regimen of standard vaccinations throughout his life. But I'm betting that you won't want to do that by the time you get to the end of this chapter.)

One major reason I wanted to update the first edition was that I knew that many holistic veterinarians, in the last decade and a half, had been trained in homeopathy, a natural field of medicine that only a few were beginning to use in 1981. (Homeopathy is not, however, a new, untried field; it was developed in the late 1700s.) Just before starting to work with doctors for this present edition, I found that holistic veterinarians were now using homeopathic nosodes to protect against disease. I wondered where that would lead.

The first veterinarian to answer my questionnaire, John Fudens, D.V.M., wrote me a heavily underlined note stating that genetics and vaccinations were the major causes of disease in our dogs.

My first thought was that this veterinarian was probably on the extreme edge of the vaccination issue. But within days, I'd received several more completed questionnaires from holistic veterinarians, all of them saying that standard vaccinations were one of the two major causes of disease in animals, and all heavily underlined for emphasis. I should stress that in the questionnaire I never asked for any doctor's thoughts on vaccinations. These were all veterinarians who—in part because they now have homeopathic nosodes as a safer, surer way to prevent diseases than the standard vaccinations—at last feel free to warn strongly against the conventional vaccinations that they had never believed in seventeen years ago.

After talking to other veterinarians and doing some reading in technical publications, it was clear that I couldn't just easily update the first edition's several paragraphs on vaccinations, as I'd planned. This subject was of the utmost importance and warranted its own full chapter. I knew that most of you have been taught to believe—and I believed this, too, until I researched the first book—that standard vaccinations are the most important step we can take to prevent disease in our animals. I know my readers to be intelligent, seeking people; and I wasn't going to convince many of you to give up the usual vaccinations by saying, in a few paragraphs: "They're bad because I've looked into the matter and have deemed them to be bad."

As I said, my goal in the early 1980s was to tell you what holistic veterinarians advised you to do to avail your dog of the *best* that standard vaccinations offered while advising you how to save your dog from the *worst* they offered. My goal now is to give you guidelines as to when you can safely do away with harmful standard vaccinations altogether; when you can safely use only homeopathic nosodes; when your best bet might be to mix and match; and when your dog may be better off without either vaccinations or nosodes.

The bottom line as always, though, is that you should consult, at least by phone, with a holistic veterinarian for advice about your own, unique dog. You may wonder why these doctors can't just draw up a simple regimen, as orthodox doctors do: vaccination X for all dogs at such and so an age, vaccination Y every so many years throughout the dog's life. Orthodox veterinarians sometimes think in terms of "a dog is a dog is a dog," while holistic veterinarians tend to think in terms of: "Okay, this animal is a dog. Now what are his or her specific needs?" A lot of what a holistic veterinarian recommends will depend on your pet's age, general health, lifestyle, and—as we will see later—even the part of the country in which he shares his home with you.

If you don't live anywhere near a holistic veterinarian, don't worry that you won't be able to avail your dog of homeopathic nosodes. As I detail later, this is as easy as waiting a few days after talking on the phone and then picking up the prescribed nosodes from your mailbox. (These nosodes are given by mouth; you don't have to know how to inject your dog using a needle.)

What Are the Dangers of Standard Vaccinations?

On the covering page of this chapter, I gave a few of the passionate comments against orthodox vaccinations sent to me, unsolicited, by holistic veterinarians. Cat breeder Celeste Yarnall in her book *Cat Care, Naturally*[1] found many other holistic doctors damning these vaccinations. She cites, for instance, Richard Pitcairn, D.V. M., whom I know as one of the earliest holistic veterinarians in this country and one of the earliest to specialize in homeopathy—and who also, Yarnall points out, has a Ph.D. in immunology. (Immunology is the medical specialty that includes vaccinations.) Yarnall cites the doctor as saying that the majority of problems facing veterinarians today stem from vaccinations. (There's that same idea again!)

Checking to see if I could find a major holistic veterinarian to balance all these strong statements against standard vaccinations, I talked to Carvel G. Tiekert, D.V. M., founder and still executive director of the American Holistic Veterinary Medical Association, whom I consider a conservative holistic veterinarian. By that I mean he doesn't express his knowledge in terms of black and white, and he takes pains to back up empiric evidence with controlled scientific research. I asked if he agreed with the strong statement that traditional vaccinations are one of the two major causes of modern-day illness and death in pets. "I think that's still to be proven per se," he said, indicating that the mass of scientific studies generally needed before a new medical fact is accepted had not yet been completed. So I had my more conservative viewpoint, I thought for a split second. Then he added, surprisingly, "But I *do* agree with that statement."

Dr. Tiekert went even further to talk about another fact I'd heard several times recently: that even orthodox veterinarians are showing increasing signs of turning against overvaccination. (Yarnall states that many veterinarians have told her that they no longer believe in vaccinating *at all* but are afraid to buck the system.) "I think," Dr. Tiekert said, "there's certainly enough evidence coming up within the conventional world saying that we've been way overvaccinating animals, that academia is going to be radically changing the suggestions of how often animals should be revaccinated. There is no longer a huge amount of controversy that we've probably been advised not only to overdo the frequency of vaccinations but also the amount of diseases we vaccinate for—particularly at the same time."

Indeed, holistic doctors consider the harm that standard vaccinations can do to a body as a separate disease in and of itself: They call this medical disorder vaccinosis. Many seriously ill animals who don't respond to other treatments get better when given a homeopathic remedy that's known to combat the damaging effects of vaccines. You might consider this possibility if your dog is sick and veterinarians haven't been able to help him.

Even a very shortened list of the possible symptoms of vaccinosis explains how a dog can be assumed to have some other disease: symptoms of cystitis, inflammatory bowel disease, nephritis, aggression, chronic upper respiratory infections, destructive behavior, seizures.

When we allow a dog to be vaccinated with the standard vaccines, we are putting into his system a small amount of a modified or killed virus that causes the disease we want to protect him against. The idea is that this will produce antibodies against the virus, and the antibodies will protect the dog if he's exposed in the future.

One problem with this hope is that if the dog doesn't already have a strong immune system, the injected virus may produce the very disease we were trying to protect him from.*

Some holistic veterinarians go just about ballistic when you mention *multiple* vaccinations: that is, when a number of viruses are put into one needle and shot into the dog all at once—as is often done with standard vaccinations. "This confuses the immune system," is how one veterinarian expressed his objection. *Confuses* it? As if the immune system had a mind? Elsewhere in this book I give an explanation of how the immune system works, based partly on a video of a magnified immune system actually at work. It's composed of cells that act for all the world like well-disciplined army battalions, each with its own job to do and each capable of sending out signals when the "soldiers" need help. (Those signals were actually visible on the magnified video.) To explain simply the *confusion* that multiple vaccinations can cause: Let's say your dog's immune system is healthy, and all the battalions are resting. Suddenly a red alert goes out: "Incoming invaders!" The battalions come to attention: "Is it *my* enemy, or another battalion's enemy?" Under normal circumstances, only one type of virus enters the body at a given time, so the battalion that is best equipped to fight the virus quickly rushes to battle. But with a multiple vaccination, the immune system realizes that "It's many different enemies all at once!"

You can see how the various battalions can now become *confused*, to use the veterinarian's word—getting in each other's way as they race to defend their entity's body, and losing their normal elegant organization. The problem is now more complex than the immune system is used to: Which enemy should we attack *first*?

The above scenario, remember, was for a *healthy* immune system taking care of its dog. But if we send many invaders at once into the body of a dog whose immune system is already weak, we may virtually destroy that immune system—and the dog.

All the above possible havoc becomes compounded because we are told to repeat some multiple vaccinations often throughout an

---

* Dr. Tiekert disagrees with this statement.

animal's lifetime. The quote from *Current Veterinary Therapy* on the covering page of this chapter gives an indication of how unnecessary many of these revaccinations may be.

Holistic veterinarians also object strongly to the additives in vaccines, which can include—among other objectionable items—pus, blood, urine, feces, aluminum, antibiotics, acetone, and formaldehyde.[2] How are substances like pus, urine, feces, and formaldehyde supposed to help our dogs resist disease? Don't ask *me*.

As if all this weren't bad enough, the more we vaccinate, the more we may be opening the way to have viruses mutate and change into new viruses. Did you know that there is now a brand-new form of AIDS? This disease is now attacking cats. Yarnall cites Jeff Levy, D.V.M., as believing that feline leukemia evolved because of vaccinating for panleukopenia. (The two viruses look a lot alike under a microscope.) "And then with the vaccination for feline leukemia, the cat just came up with a different disease . . . feline AIDS."[3]

I know full well that if your family includes a cat as well as a dog, I've just given you a whole new, and awful, disease to worry about in your cat. Not only that, but—as I write this, anyway—orthodox veterinary medicine has not yet developed a vaccine for it. (Although perhaps we should be thankful for that.) Let me remind you that your cat will most probably never get AIDS if he's on the diet his body evolved to thrive on. Also let me assure you that in the chapter on infectious diseases, in this book's new edition for cats *(Keep Your Cat Healthy the Natural Way)*, I detail a very successful therapy for feline AIDS from a holistic veterinarian, Jack Long, V.M.D., who also has noted the similarity between feline leukemia virus and feline AIDS. He'd already had years of experience successfully treating feline leukemia.

By the way, I have been informed that, at least as I write this, AIDS is not known to strike dogs.

Yarnall details a number of frightening facts about how specific standard vaccines can do more harm than good (pp. 26–29). I'll mention only one vaccine. In 1903 the United States military went to the Philippines and started vaccinating for smallpox—although the disease had always been virtually unheard of there. Two years later, the Philippines had a major epidemic of smallpox. Australia banned the vaccine when two children died after being inoculated, and in the next decade and a half after the smallpox vaccine was unavailable, the continent had only three reported cases of smallpox. Here in the United States, we continued to vaccinate for smallpox until 1966, when Dr. Henry Kempe convinced Congress that, according to Yarnall, "fewer people were dying from the disease than from the vaccination."

Are Homeopathic Nosodes Effective? Are They Safe?

"I've got to be honest with you," Dr. Fudens told me. "Since I've been using the nosodes, for some fifteen years, I have never to my knowledge had one animal break in any way, shape, or form." As well as dogs and cats, Dr. Fudens treats horses holistically and protects them with nosodes. "I've never had one animal I know of come down with a sickness, disease, or germ that was vaccinatable. It may have happened, and I didn't hear about it," he admitted. But he added that he feels owners wouldn't hesitate to complain if a pet had come down with a disease they'd had the pet vaccinated against.

Michael Lemmon, D.V.M., writing in 1996 in *Animal Guardian* (Vol. 9, No. 3), noted that "nosodes have a long history of effectiveness in South America, England, and Europe." One fact he cites is that in 1974 a meningitis epidemic in Brazil left many thousands of victims. The nosode against this disease was "highly successful" in preventing thousands of other persons from being affected by the epidemic.

Citing technical publications, Dr. Lemmon stated that recent research from England during an outbreak of kennel cough showed "far greater protection with kennel cough nosodes than injectable and intranasal vaccines." And in Buenos Aires, doctors routinely use nosodes to prevent people from succumbing to a number of diseases, including influenza, measles, and diphtheria. "After many years of this practice," Dr. Lemmon reported, "they have observed a very high immunization level."

Dr. Tiekert (our "conservative" holistic veterinarian for this chapter) expressed what I've found to be the overall view of holistic veterinarians on the safety of nosodes: "Yes, I think they're completely safe." In the next section, we'll see that Dr. Tiekert does, however, question how well nosodes work to prevent a few of the diseases some veterinarians use them for. Of course, standard vaccinations by no means always work either—and no doctor I know of considers them anywhere near completely safe.

How Can You Choose What to Do about Vaccinating Your Dog?

Dr. Fudens expressed to me the optimal goal I believe most holistic veterinarians share: "You make the animals' immune systems so darned healthy that they blow off any virus or bacteria that's audacious enough to try to attack them. That's the ideal: that you don't vaccinate an animal even with the homeopathic nosodes, and they never get sick." (You may find Dr. Fudens' statement surprising, in view of the fact that in this chapter he has been such a champion of homeopathic nosodes. However, he is now talking about his *optimal* goal. And, like other full-fledged holistic veterinarians, he likes to tamper as little as possible with an animal's body—and he doesn't want to charge owners for unnecessary services.)

Although I strongly recommend you don't follow the above route of no vaccinations at all without talking to a holistic veterinarian about your individual dog, I do know that the above goal is not just utopian. Years ago I took in a stray dog who, it turned out, had been infected with the very serious parvo virus while trying to keep herself alive on the streets. (The disease is spread through feces, and she was probably eating these because she had little or nothing else to nourish her.) While this country's most esteemed orthodox veterinary medical center rushed Doggie off to intensive care (the isolation section because parvo is so contagious), the veterinarian told me that my two cherished miniature poodles were almost sure to come down with the disease, too. She chastised me for not having vaccinated them against parvo "before it was too late."

The truth was I hadn't vaccinated them against *anything* since they'd got the obligatory initial vaccines when puppies. (Parvo hadn't been a problem in those years, so they'd never been vaccinated against it even as puppies.) I'd been following what I'd learned in working on the first edition of this book about the dangers of standard vaccinations and had been banking on safety from the fact that my poodles never mingled with other dogs who might be carrying viruses. (I would have given my poodles, Shiki and her daughter Little Lady, several homeopathic nosodes, but they were virtually not in use then.)

Now I had brought into their home a dog carrying a lethal virus. *How could I have been so dumb?*

I called Richard J. Kearns, D.V. M., one of the major veterinarians from the first book. Could I give massive amounts of vitamin C (a major fighter of infections)? Could I . . .

Dr. Kearns told me I didn't need to do anything because my poodles had strong immune systems from years of my feeding them their natural diet.

"But they were never vaccinated *against parvo!"* I as much as shouted into his ear over the phone.

"Doesn't matter," Dr. Kearns said.

The holistic veterinarian was right. While the highly contagious parvo virus was almost surely waging a war with my poodles' immune systems, neither Shiki nor Little Lady was disturbed enough by the battle going on within their bodies to have even a momentary loss of appetite. Their immune systems must have won the war swiftly and easily.

Dr. Tiekert not only strongly advised that you consult, if only by phone, with a holistic veterinarian about your individual dog—but also that the veterinarian be one who practices in *your area of the country.* "For instance," he said, "Lyme disease is a significant problem in my area" (Bel Air, Maryland). "We've had quite good luck with nosode protection for this disease." So if Lyme disease is a problem where you live, you might use nosodes to protect your dog against it.

But if you have a dog who can be exposed to parvo, you might do best to use the standard parvo vaccination along with the nutritional help at the end of this chapter to ward off negative effects. Why? Dr. Tiekert said: "If you talk to a number of holistic practitioners, and look at the scientific data, you'll see that we don't do so well with preventing parvo. I've known of a number of litters that have died from this virus after receiving nosodes."

Another thing you should discuss with a holistic veterinarian when setting up your dog's individual protection program is your companion's personal lifestyle. For instance, does she roam around free part of the day, so that she may come into contact with other animals? Or is her outdoor time limited to her yard, or to walks with you holding her by a firm leash? Giving one illustration of how important this single facet of lifestyle can be, Dr. Tiekert said that "even many, many, many conventional veterinarians don't vaccinate 'inside' cats for feline leukemia. They can't justify the risk. Although we don't know the full extent of that risk, a lot of orthodox practitioners simply say 'There's no real reason for me to assault this cat's immune system with a vaccination when the cat never goes outside.' " He stressed, though, that in his area, "you see a fair amount of cats who develop feline leukemia if they go outside without having been vaccinated."

Dr. Tiekert indicated that if your dog never comes in contact with other animals, there may be a number of vaccinations she doesn't need.

Dr. Fudens, like Dr. Tiekert and every holistic veterinarian I questioned, believes that often "less is better," as I mentioned earlier. And he agrees that treating your dog as *an individual*, rather than as *a dog*, will lead to a healthier, longer life for him. "When I have virgin [never previously vaccinated] puppies or kittens come in," he said, "I start them off with nosodes for the first one, two, or three years, depending on their lifestyle."* Dr. Fudens continued, "I'm absolutely against giving the standard initial vaccinations. After that we evaluate the dog's health and how well the client is taking care of him and

* Dr. Fudens asked me to stress here that he also puts all animals on a natural diet and keeps them on it for life.

the exposure the dog may have to any disease or contamination. And then—depending also on the owner's perspective—we may continue some of the nosodes, or we may stop them completely."

Perhaps oddly, Dr. Fudens indicated that sometimes his clients "cannot make the break with vaccinations for whatever reason," and he has to coax them not to continue using nosodes when he finds them unnecessary. "I just try to convince them: Don't even use the nosodes anymore—you'll just be wasting your money. Susan or Sam or Max will never get sick from a virus or bacteria."

Giving another example of not overusing even the homeopathic nosodes, Dr. Fudens said: "A lot of technicians who work with conventional veterinarians use me as the veterinarian for their own pets. And they worry a lot about bringing diseases into their animal's home from all the sick animals where they work. When they first bring their pets to me, this is of course a very legitimate concern. But," Dr. Fudens went on, "I detoxify the animal and put him on a constitutional homeopathic. Then, if I find his health is as high as possible, I tell the owner, 'Hey, he doesn't really need these nosodes because he'll never get sick on you.'" The veterinarian added: "And this has worked out very well."

In summary, the bottom-line recommendation from holistic veterinarians is that if you use standard vaccinations at all, use a very limited program. Don't use them for diseases for which effective nosodes exist. Never vaccinate for more than one disorder at a time, and don't keep repeating the vaccinations. Also, if you must use a standard vaccine, protect your dog nutritionally against its dangers, as detailed at the end of this chapter.

How to Give Your Dog Homeopathic Nosodes When You Don't Live Near a Holistic Veterinarian

Before I discuss how easy it is to surmount this seemingly insurmountable problem, let me say that I've seen detailed published instructions on how to make your own nosodes. The instructions I happened to read weren't written by veterinarians, and the authors didn't indicate that they'd been working closely with doctors. I sincerely hope you won't try to help your dog that way. Even assuming the instructions are 100 percent accurate, they seem to me to require you to learn critical aspects of a medical field without an instructor to guide you or to check you for accuracy. I wouldn't trust myself to be able to do that—especially since in homeopathy minuscule differences in ingredients are crucial.

So what *can* you do? First of all, maybe you live a lot closer to a holistic veterinarian than you think you do. Check the list at the back of the book.

If you do live uncomfortably far away, remember that an overall recommendation of this chapter was to call and discuss your dog's individual protection needs with a holistic veterinarian. After a holistic veterinarian helps you work out your dog's specific needs for homeopathic nosodes, the doctor will simply *mail* you the specifically chosen nosodes to administer to your dog yourself.

If you're still thinking of homeopathic nosodes as being much like standard vaccinations, you're now saying: "But I don't know how to inject vaccines." When I was also in a primitive state of knowledge about nosodes, I put myself in your place and took this "problem" to Dr. Fudens. "No, no, no," he "explained" to me. "The nosodes aren't injected into the body by needles. You just put them into your dog's mouth.

"We don't just send the nosodes through the mail and leave clients to their own devices," Dr. Fudens continued. "We send three little bottles and give them specific instructions on how much to put in their pet's mouth. And," he added, "if owners have questions about the simple instructions, I stick with them. I'm available to them on the phone."

How to Minimize the Negative Effects of Standard Vaccinations

In case, for any reason, you must opt now and then for a standard vaccination, I'm repeating in this section the advice holistic veterinarians gave in the first edition. The veterinarians working with me on the new book tell me this advice is still up-to-date.

You can take some easy steps to prevent the two major short-comings of standard vaccinations: the fact that they sometimes cause the disease they're meant to prevent, and the fact that they sometimes just don't work to prevent it.

First, don't vaccinate your dog when he is showing any signs of illness. If your pet is already ill, his immune system may not be able to produce the antibodies the vaccination is supposed to stimulate, and he stands a chance of being overwhelmed by the small amount of virus in the vaccine and succumbing to the illness he's being vaccinated against.

Second, make sure your pet receives the following supplements for two to three weeks before and after vaccination:

- **Vitamin A.** 10,000 IU a day for a fifty-pound dog; 2,500 IU a day for a ten-pound dog.
- **Vitamin E.** 400 IU a day for the larger dog; 200 IU a day for the smaller.
- **Vitamin C.** 5,000 mg (5 grams) a day for the larger dog; 2,000 mg (2 grams) a day for the smaller. Start the C at 500 mg a day and increase every second day until the recommended dosage is reached. Give the dosage in stages, two to four times a day. (Introducing large amounts of C suddenly can sometimes cause diarrhea.)

Third, realize that *vaccinations do not take effect overnight*. Don't take your dog to a groomer, kennel, or other animal gathering place for two weeks after the vaccination shot.

And don't let yourself be talked into any of those multiple-vaccination injections—or into the idea that vaccinations require lifetime repetitions.

Summary

Get the advice, at least by phone, of a holistic veterinarian who practices in your area and who knows the infectious diseases your dog stands a chance of being exposed to. Also discuss your dog's personal lifestyle (indoor or outdoor), his medical history, and his diet.

Now let's move on to investigate ways to keep your dog in prime health during special times in her life, such as puppyhood, pregnancy, and old age. Although if you are reading this while your dog is a puppy, she probably will live many, many years without ever becoming old.

References

1. Celeste Yarnall, *Cat Care, Naturally* (Boston: Charles E. Tuttle, Co., Inc., 1995), p. 22.
2. *Ibid.*, p. 35.
3. *Ibid.*, p. 24.

Chapter 4

"Dead mothers and dead babies: We seldom see them anymore if the mother is fed a natural diet with supplements."
—*John E. Craige, V.M.D., Richard J. Kearns, D.V.M., and many other holistic veterinarians (from 1981 to 1998)*

"Many people come to us with old, degenerated pets for whom other veterinarians have told them there is no hope. When the owners see how their pets become young again—and recover from the 'hopeless' disorders—they start taking themselves and their families to nutritionally oriented physicians. They realize, 'If nutritional medicine can work wonders for my pet, it can work wonders for us, too.' "
—*Robert Goldstein, V.M.D., and Marty Goldstein, D.V.M. (in 1981)*

"Quite often, acupuncture used alone really brings dogs and cats diagnosed as dying back to life.

"What we're all looking for, when we try to have our patients given good nutrition and when we treat with alternative medicine, is for the animals to enjoy a very high quality of life and to live this life as long as possible. Everybody knows there are two different ways to grow old. Many animals (and people) grow weak and debilitated long before they should, living out the later years of their lives as mere shadows of what they were in their younger years. Our goal is to keep pets vital, healthy, active, and loving until that inevitable day when death comes—and when it does, it comes swiftly and without pain."
—*Phillip Racyln, D.V.M. (in 1999)*

Special Diets for Special Times in Your Dog's Life: Pregnancy, Lactation, Puppyhood, Senior Citizenship

How to Prevent Problems of Pregnancy and Birth

Holistic veterinarians have found that many of the "nonpreventable" pregnancy problems and deaths just suddenly stop occurring when simple nutritional steps are taken for the expectant mother. Forward-thinking M.D.s have for decades been reporting the same sudden disappearance of pregnancy problems and deaths in human mothers, not only in clinical results, but in scientifically conducted studies.

I have read statements by orthodox veterinarians that one in four puppies will be born dead or will die shortly after birth—and that this is "normal." But as you can see from the statement by holistic veterinarians on the previous page, this high toll definitely need *not* be normal, if only the expectant mother is fed right.

Here are two specific case histories from my own life to illustrate what holistic veterinarians state. My miniature poodle, Shiki, who bore her babies before I knew what a dog's natural diet was, did lose one of her four puppies within hours, fulfilling the mathematical prophecy I've since read by orthodox veterinarians. I fed Doggie, the stray I brought in years later, a natural diet throughout her pregnancy. Although orthodox veterinarians estimated that she was "too old" to bear healthy puppies and to remain healthy herself, she and all *six* of her babies lived and are still alive many years later, fulfilling the prophecy of holistic veterinarians. Although five of her progeny were raised by other people on the "nutritionally complete" commercial foods and have had various health problems, Mr. Sandman was raised by us on natural foods and has never been sick a day in his life.

(By the way, I'm not advocating that you breed your dog if she's in her later years. The elderly Doggie and our elderly Labrador mix, Rambo, did their family planning without consulting me.)

Even if you're quite positive you have had your dog on the optimal preventive diet, as detailed in chapter 2, for quite a while, all the nutritional veterinarians I've talked to over the last decade and a half agree that her pregnancy is a time you *must* add supplements. This is a time of extreme stress to the mother's body—something no reader who has borne a child needs to be told. And it's not such an easy time for the unborn babies, either.

It doesn't take much imagination to realize that one body that is now suddenly trying to provide for several more bodies within her own needs some help. Nutrients that have been sufficient to keep one body running smoothly aren't going to become, magically, enough to keep a number of "newcomer" bodies going nicely. Unless more nutrients are given, someone's body is going to have to be robbed—probably both the mother's body and the tiny developing bodies—and everybody is going to suffer.

Orthodox veterinarians, of course, recognize this fact. As a result, they may recommend that the prospective or nursing mother increase her food, sometimes to three or more times her normal amount. However, nutritional veterinarians believe it is not a greater *quantity* the mother is desperately seeking when she wolfs down triple the amount of food, but more *nutrients*. Indeed, most of the holistic veterinarians I asked told me they find that the mothers-to-be in their practices that are given additional nutrients in the form of a supplement generally choose to eat only a little more than they normally do.

With nutritional supplementation, holistic veterinarians and nutritionally minded breeders report the virtual disappearance not only of dead mothers and babies but also of many birth defects: cleft palates, "swimmers" (newborns who are huge and, as one veterinarian put it, just "lie around, feet sprawled out and helpless"), and animals born with only a thin covering of skin over the brain. (Usually these babies die when the tiniest pressure touches this part of the brain.) Richard J. Kearns, D.V. M., once told me that when the mother dog has been fed properly and given the right supplements, there is a virtual disappearance of puppies born with malformed legs and tails, spinal curvatures, and other birth defects.

For those of you who like to know about scientific studies behind medical statements, let me point out just a few of the very many studies proving that vitamin deficiencies can cause birth problems—and that supplementation can help prevent them. One experimenter deliberately fed too little vitamin A to a number of pigs. One sow thereupon presented to the world eleven baby pigs—all without eyeballs. Other pigs in the experiment produced piglets with too many ears. When experimenters put enough vitamin A back into their diets, the same pigs produced healthy offspring.[1] This study was published, by the way, in an orthodox medical journal—in 1933.

A number of studies have been run concerning birth problems and wheat germ oil, which has a high vitamin E content and contains another natural substance, octacosanol. I have read scientific studies going back to 1926 on cattle, branching off to studies with humans in 1937, and continuing on to more modern studies. Some of the results of the studies on humans show premature births reduced to *half* their previous level when wheat germ oil was given, babies' deaths in emergency resuscitation *entirely eliminated*, miscarriages *almost halved*, and only *20 percent* of the "usual" number of babies born dead.[2] I saw those studies reported in 1971.

One reason I've mentioned how long ago all those studies were conducted is to indicate how many years it can often take for nutritional research to get disseminated into the offices of most doctors who don't focus on nutrition. Remember that a little earlier I mentioned that holistic veterinarians for many years now have seen the virtual disappearance of puppies born with only a thin covering of skin to shield their brains? Those puppies had what is technically called a neural tube defect. In a book I recently published on nutritional help for mental problems *(Healing the Mind the Natural*

Way), I noted that established medicine had finally listened to years of studies showing that if expectant mothers took a small amount of the nutrient folic acid, there was a dramatic drop in the number of babies with neural tube defects. These defects include brains outside the skulls and spinal cords outside the spines—if there is any brain or spinal cord at all. Finally it is officially recommended that women take in a certain amount of this vitamin—which nutritional M.D.s had been recommending to their patients for years. Who knows how many babies suffered these tragic defects—needlessly—in the years established medicine ignored the scientific studies? (The natural diet you feed your dog contains folic acid, and the multivitamin/multimineral supplement holistic veterinarians recommend contains it, too. But just in case a specific brand doesn't, check the label before you choose a supplement for your pregnant dog.)

Your dog may be happily nursing her little ones and suddenly develop muscle spasms, a high temperature, and convulsions—symptoms of eclampsia. She may die. The *least* that can happen is that the new mother's milk production stops and she rejects her babies. I have found some orthodox veterinarians estimating that every time a dog has puppies, she has one chance out of twenty of developing this condition. Yet innumerable holistic veterinarians for both editions of this book report that they have yet to see *one case* of eclampsia in a dog or cat on a proper nutritional program. A major reason these animals don't suffer this disorder may be the fact that their natural diet contains magnesium, and so do the multivitamin/multimineral pills we've recommended.

Why am I mentioning magnesium here? For over sixty years, obstetricians have considered injections of large doses of the mineral to be the preferred way to stop convulsions in a woman with eclampsia. Yet it was only a few years ago that it occurred to researchers that maybe magnesium in small doses could help *prevent* eclampsia. Donald R. Davis, Ph.D., reported in my *Healing the Mind* book in 1995 that finally such studies had been run. And they had found that supplements of small amounts of magnesium during pregnancy help to prevent not only eclampsia but the full syndrome of preeclampsia, of which convulsions are only a part. (The list of symptoms of preeclampsia takes up formidable space in medical dictionaries. A shortened list includes extremely high blood pressure, kidney disorders, blood cell destruction, eye damage, fluid in the lungs, and bleeding in the brain. So you can see how lucky we are that research on nutrition has found that all this havoc to our dogs can be easily prevented.)

Also, nutritional veterinarians such as Dr. Kearns rarely find litter runts. Whelping time is cut in half; pets who could never breed suddenly breed, even with the same mate; and uterine atony has virtually disappeared. (Atony is a weakening of the uterus during the birth process that traps the tiny puppy in the uterus without oxygen while it is trying to help itself be born. Obviously the puppy dies, or at best survives with severe brain damage. Isn't it painful to think of all the puppies over all the years who have died needlessly in this way only because their mamas weren't offered a natural diet and a daily supplement?)

Cesarean operations are often done in a last-ditch attempt to save the mother's life and/or the lives of her little ones when birth complications result, just as such operations are performed on human mothers. As long ago as the early 1980s, Wendell O. Belfield, D.V.M., reported that he offered his clients with newly pregnant animals a choice: "You can pay a few dollars for some vitamins now or pay $250 or more for a cesarean operation later on." With the simple nutritional supplementation, Dr. Belfield reported he had cut the number of cesarean operations he had to perform by at least 95 percent.[3] Other holistic veterinarians have reported similar results to me.

While you may have started this chapter thinking you'd have to be God to have the power to prevent any disaster resulting from your dog's pregnancy, I believe you've seen by now that you don't have to be anything but a human being with up-to-date knowledge about nutrition. We're not talking about miracles; we're talking, as we always do in this book, of the scientific fact that nutrients control every biochemical reaction in the body.

Before I give more information on how you can prevent all the previously mentioned strong possibilities of death, deformity, and pain—for your dog, her babies, and yourself—I think I should say a few words to those who fear you can't take the time, or don't have the money, to feed your pregnant dog a natural diet. First, I beg you to carefully read chapter 2 regarding how quick and easy it can be to feed the optimal diet, and how it can actually save you substantial money. If you're still convinced you can't feed a natural diet, I'll give you the suggestion of Phillip Racyln, D.V.M., who worries about people who won't, for whatever reason, feed their dog a raw-food diet. Since the first edition, Dr. Racyln told me in an interview, a number of good prepared diets have come out that are especially made for the pregnant or lactating dog or cat. "The real key," he said, "is to use only an all-natural prepared food."

But then Dr. Racyln presented some of the same quandaries other holistic veterinarians gave in chapter 2. (Please, for your dog's sake, particularly note in that chapter that even the best prepared foods don't contain enzymes, which are absolutely crucial for good health.) For instance, Dr. Racyln said, "You can't believe a label just because it states that the products are all natural. They still might use by-products that contain chemicals that don't have to be listed on the label." Chapter 1 details that by-products also include such "natural ingredients" as tumors discarded from slaughtered animals and the remains of cats and dogs who have been euthanized. Dr. Racyln added a few problems not even covered in chapter 2: For instance: "The quality of the grains of some products that are labeled 'all natural' may be really poor." He pointed out that when people read that a product contains brewer's rice, they tend to assume that the product contains rice. But, he said, brewer's rice has very little nutrition in it compared to the brown rice recommended by nutritional M.D.s and holistic veterinarians.

So Dr. Racyln's comments lead us back to the recommendation given in chapter 2: If you feel you *must* (and we all hope you *don't* feel you must) feed a prepared food as the mainstay of your dog's diet, make phone calls and consult with several holistic veterinarians for recommendations of the most *closely* "all-natural" prepared foods for your pregnant or lactating dog available at the time you read this. If you use these prepared foods, it becomes even more imperative that you use the highest-quality multivitamin/multimineral supplement, adding the extra vitamins C and E in the dosages recommended a little later in this section. Dr. Racyln added that, if the most closely "all-natural" food recommended to you has the real truth printed on its label, you'll see that you should supplement the food with enzymes and essential fatty acids. (Trust me that at this point you will be spending substantially more money than if you fed your canine companion the truly natural diet her body evolved to thrive on. Again, that diet is detailed in chapter 2.)

For those of you who already know how easy and inexpensive it can be to feed a truly natural diet to your dog, here are a few simple modifications to make in accordance with the changes going on in her body during and immediately after her pregnancy: First, give her more fat and protein than usual. Dr. Racyln pointed out that a large dog who is likely to have eleven puppies will need a greater increase in fat and protein than a small dog who will have only one or two babies. Second, it would be of optimal benefit to your dog if you divide her food into four or five smaller meals a day, rather than feeding her two larger meals, as was recommended in chapter 2 for the average healthy adult dog. Large meals can overload an expectant mother's stomach, already being crowded by her growing babies, and can cause serious digestive problems. Also, be sure to offer the mother-to-be more water than she normally drinks. It will help to flush wastes out of her kidneys, which are at this time not only flushing out her own wastes, but also those of her fast-forming babies.

As mentioned earlier, offer her more food than before. But don't fret if she doesn't choose to "eat for two" (or four or eleven), because you'll be giving her extra nutrients in the form of supplementation.

For that supplementation, buy a bottle of dog multivitamin/multimineral supplement from a health food store, your own veterinarian, or a pet store.* As already mentioned, make sure the supplement contains magnesium and folic acid. Buy the supplement already in powdered form, or mash pills up in her food.

Give the supplement as directed. Do not double or triple the

---

* Dr. Racyln believes these supplements should be obtained only from a veterinarian.

recommended amounts at your own discretion. As discussed in chapter 2, it is possible to overdose your pet—and yourself—with vitamins and minerals. It is even more possible to throw out of whack a delicate *balance* between two or more nutrients if you decide to add a little more of "this" or a little more of "that."

However, as also discussed in chapter 2, the dog multivitamin/multimineral pill you buy will most probably contain no vitamin C at all, and it will probably contain too little E for your pregnant pet and her soon-to-be offspring. As I touched on briefly, vitamin E has been shown to be especially helpful for preventing problems connected with pregnancy and birth. The nutritional veterinarians I surveyed for this edition gave the same recommendation as did the doctors I surveyed for the first edition: For a small pregnant dog, add 1,500 mg of vitamin C to the supplement; for the medium dog, 3,000 mg; for the large, 6,000 mg; and for the giant, 7,500 mg. The doctors recommend adding the following amounts of vitamin E: for the small dog, 100 IU; for the medium, 200 IU; for the large, 400 IU; and for the giant, 600 IU. Usually holistic doctors recommend a small amount of the nutrient selenium whenever vitamin E is given, because they both work better together than when either is used alone.

John B. Limehouse, D.V.M., noted that if a dog (or a cat or human) has not been taking vitamin C, she can get diarrhea if you suddenly give her large amounts all at once.

Foods and Supplements for Lactating Dogs

Holistic veterinarians give the same recommendations for basic diet, vitamins and minerals, and number of feedings for a lactating dog that they gave in the previous section for the pregnant dog. This short section covers only the variations you should make once your dog has given life to her puppies and is now involved in feeding them.

Oats should be a high proportion of the "working mother's" whole-grain allotment, because this food helps produce breast milk. So do goat's milk and grated raw carrots, so they may play a larger role than usual in her weekly allotment of protein and vegetables.

For those of you interested in herbs: The marshmallow plant and fennel will also help mothers produce milk. A bit of garlic in mama's food may pass itself along in her milk to help prevent in her babies the all-too-common problem of worms.

"During her first week of lactation, your dog needs about one and a half times the calories she normally requires," Priscilla A. Taylor, D.V. M., told me in an interview. "One way to do that is to bump up the volume." That is, if you normally feed her one cup of meat and two cups of grains and vegetables, feed one-and-a-half cups of meat and three cups of grains and vegetables. "Another way is to add a tablespoon of flaxseed oil for every cup of food you normally give her."

When the new mother enters her second week of lactation, "she requires basically twice the amount of her maintenance calories," Dr. Taylor said. "Then, during the third week, through the end of lactation, she needs roughly three times the amount of her maintenance level."

The veterinarian stressed that "you must be really sure that your dog is getting adequate calcium and phosphorus." As we say often in this book, the *balance* of synergistic nutrients is crucially important: "The intake ratio should be about one and a half times the amount of calcium to phosphorus," Dr. Taylor stated. "Otherwise, she will draw calcium from her own body stores for the puppies."

Special Information for Feeding Orphaned, Unweaned Puppies

I certainly don't expect your dog to die during or after childbirth if she's been on a natural diet with the recommended supplements, but just in case you come upon an orphaned puppy in some other manner, I want to ensure that you know how to give him the best of care if he hasn't been weaned.

Cow's milk, the milk you get at all supermarkets, is not an acceptable substitute for the milk of a mother dog, who does not produce cow's milk any more than a mother cat (or a human mother) does.

Dog's milk is richer in protein and fat and has less of the offending milk sugar lactose in it. Goat's milk, preferably raw, is the top recommendation of many of our veterinarians, since it is much closer in nutritional composition to the milk of dog mothers than is cow's milk. Goat's milk is most easily available in health food stores. Don't dilute it.

For optimal health of your orphaned puppy, fortify the milk with the following, which has been recommended by veterinarians Marty and Robert Goldstein: To 2 ounces of goat's milk, add ¼ teaspoon cold-pressed sesame oil, ¼ teaspoon unfiltered raw honey, and 1 raw egg yolk (*no* egg white). Dr. Kearns recommended adding thymus extract to the formula, 10–15 mg daily for each pound of body weight. *Give everything in drop (liquid) form for preweaned puppies.* Dr. Racyln recommended strongly that you add one of the new products called probiotics.

Why are you being asked to add anything to the goat's milk? Certainly, mother dogs don't add anything to *their* milk. No, but Mother Nature does: Most notably, the mother's protective antibodies are passed along in the milk to the puppies. (This is why orthodox and holistic M.D.s alike recommend that human mothers breast-feed their babies.) Thymus extract and sesame oil are natural ways to build a strong immune system. The egg yolk adds fat and protein, and the honey adds simple sugars to bring the goat's milk closer to dog's milk.

If you can't get goat's milk, you can get special formulas approximating dog's milk from veterinarians. Call a holistic veterinarian (see the list at the back of the book) to make sure the formula your orthodox doctor recommends actually has all the nutrients your foundling puppy needs.

Nino Aloro, D.V.M., has recommended that you prepare the following formula, which has more of the desirable protein and fat than cow's milk: Blend 4 ounces evaporated milk, 4 ounces water, 1 egg yolk (no egg white), and 1 tablespoon raw honey. Keep refrigerated, and don't heat before using.

A puppy under a week old should be fed every two hours night and day. After the first week of his life, start cutting down very gradually on the number of feedings until you are feeding your four-month-old puppy three times a day. After six months, you should shift to two feedings a day.

The doctors Goldstein stress the following point: "Feed the puppy until the abdomen is slightly larger than the chest. *Don't overfeed.*" Actually, the veterinarians not only underlined those last two words, but used three exclamation points to emphasize how important they feel this point is.

Michael Kreisberg, D.V. M., added several helpful tips on feeding the orphan. "Wake the puppy before mealtime and let him eliminate." To this, Dr. Aloro added that "sometimes, to help elimination, it is necessary to massage lightly the area around the anus with a soft cloth wet with warm water." Dr. Kreisberg advised that you place the baby "on his stomach when you feed him. Don't let him nurse too rapidly from the bottle, because puppies can get colic just as easily as babies can."

Weaning of the puppy can start *gradually* at three or four weeks.

Now that the orphan is weaned, and you have a firsthand appreciation of what new mother dogs have to go through every day, let's move on to discussing how to keep the little fellow healthy until he's an adult. (At that time, you'll need the information in chapter 2 until he enters his "golden years.")

The Optimal Preventive Diet for Puppies

Until you begin weaning your dog's babies, relax and leave all feeding worries to her. After all, she'll be feeding her little ones with the same natural food she would be feeding them in the wild. In other words, the new puppies in your home are now getting off to the same natural start as their ancient ancestor, Ruff, did. Of course, I'm assuming you're feeding mama her natural diet so that the milk she produces will have a minimum of poisons and a maximum of nutrients and antibodies.

But, as you know, your mama dog will stop feeding her babies at a certain point. In the wild, she would by now have given her chil dren some training on how to obtain their own food. She hasn't had that opportunity in your household, so now she as much as says to you, "Okay, I've done all I can. It's your turn."

Once the puppies are weaned, you should be giving them five small meals a day, including two meat or fish meals. (Remember as always to vary all foods, and especially don't give fish more than twice a week.)

Your newly weaned puppy still has his baby teeth; it's not until he's an ancient seven months old that he'll get all his strong adult teeth. So don't ask your baby dog to struggle with a whole slab of meat; mince it up into tiny pieces for him so he won't be in danger of choking to death.

As for the amount of food given at each of the five meals, two teaspoonsful should be about right if your puppy's breed indicates that when he is all grown up he will weigh about 10 pounds. (Adjust the number of teaspoonsful upward according to how much his breed weighs as adults.) Increase the amount gradually as your puppy gets bigger. Keep in mind to feed the puppy only until his abdomen is slightly larger than his chest. If the puppy still seems greedy for more food, picture the size of his stomach before you're tempted to throw a few more teaspoonsful of food on his plate: At ten weeks, if the little guy is going to grow up to be 10 pounds, his stomach is only the size of a walnut! So you can see that even an additional "treat" of one extra teaspoonful could extend that walnut-size tummy almost to the point of bursting.

By the end of the three months, you should feed your puppy only four times a day. By now the intensive demand of his body for protein will be reduced somewhat. Now is the time to start adding a small portion of *mashed* vegetables and *well-cooked* grains to the diet, inching the little guy toward the diet (chapter 2) that holistic veterinarians recommend for healthy grown dogs. Also, by now you don't have to mince the meat into tiny pieces; just chop it into small chunks.

When your puppy gets to be four to six months old, reduce the number of meals to three, cutting down on the amount of milk rather than on the quantity of meat and grains.

Of course, our recommendation in chapter 2 to cut down on calories for the healthy adult dog if he starts to gain weight won't hold true for your puppy. After all, if he *doesn't* gain weight, something is pretty drastically wrong.

You might ask your veterinarian to give you a healthy weight range for your particular puppy's breed at each stage of growth. Then step up or cut down on the amount of food if he slips out of that range.

By the time your puppy is six months old, you might try two meals a day, and you might begin letting him eat as much as he wants at each meal. Remember our rule of thumb to check whether the dog is too fat or too thin: You should be able to *feel* his ribs (he's not too fat), but you shouldn't be able to *see* them (he's too thin).

Dr. Limehouse suggested that you keep puppies "a little bit on the thin side, especially the larger breeds." He said that this practice results in fewer bone and joint problems, such as arthritis and hip dysplasia.

You will see throughout this section that veterinarians give specific recommendations for preventing the crippling disorders that traditionally have so plagued larger-breed dogs. Robert J. Silver, D.V.M., spoke to me extensively on this subject, and he focused not only on faulty nutrition but also on giving these animals too much exercise, particularly as puppies. "When the animal's joints are not yet fully formed, and the bones are still soft, then if someone runs the animal a lot, that puts a lot of stress on the joint. This stress remodels, or changes the actual shape of, the joint. The stress can also contribute to laxity in the ligament." (You might want to look at chapter 5 on crippling disorders at this point.)

Dr. Silver added that some "eager-beaver" breeders over the years have fed their puppies too much protein, "maybe to make them grow bigger or have more energy, perhaps because the breeders feel they can get better prices when they sell the animals." Dr. Silver called this a form of "overnutrition" that can also contribute to developmental bone diseases such as hip dysplasia.

The veterinarian further noted that holistic veterinarians nowadays are not routinely feeding "puppy-chow" prepared foods to large-breed puppies. "The accepted practice recently is to recommend adult-maintenance foods that have adequate protein, but not enough so that you speed up the natural development of the bones in a large-breed puppy," Dr. Silver said.

Even those few holistic veterinarians who believe supplements aren't really necessary for a healthy adult pet who is receiving his natural diet recommend a multivitamin/multimineral supplement during the first year of a dog's life. When your puppy is full-grown, the nutrients he eats will be used to keep his cells, bones, and organs as they are, but in this first year he needs a lot of extra help so that those bones and organs can grow fast enough.

Holistic veterinarians recommend a multivitamin/multimineral supplement formulated especially for dogs to help the puppy through all the physical stresses of growing. These doctors suggest you add to that supplement vitamin C in the following amounts: for small breeds, one to six months—250 mg; six months to one year—250 mg, eventually to 500 mg. For medium breeds, one to six months—500 mg, eventually to 1,500 mg. For large breeds, one to four months—500 mg, eventually to 1,000 mg; four to eighteen months—1,000 mg, eventually to 3,000 mg. For giant breeds, one to four months—750 mg, eventually to 2,000 mg; four to eighteen months—2,000 mg, eventually to 6,000 mg. (Lately, a few holistic veterinarians have suggested even more vitamin C for large-breed puppies. You might consult one of these doctors for the thinking that's current when you read this.) Add 100 to 200 IU of vitamin E, depending on the age and size of your puppy.

Do not give tablets whole to a puppy. Buy the supplements in powdered form or crush the tablets and spread them over his food. There is a danger of choking on a whole tablet.

Dr. Kearns stressed that it is vitally important to check with your veterinarian regarding the proper temperature climate for your puppies.

When it comes time to get good homes for some or all of your naturally raised pups, I'm assuming you'll have no trouble doing that because the little ones will have such beautiful coats, bright eyes, and sweet dispositions that people will fall in love with them on the spot. At this point, you have the chance not to let all your good work go for naught, and not to let your puppies down at the last minute. Impress upon the new parents the importance of a natural diet, and give them a copy of this book so they can have the same details you used.

When I compiled the first edition, the average person thought that people who believed in holistic medicine were "weirdos." But these years you don't have to worry about that: Things have so changed since the early 1980s that now anyone who doesn't have at least an open mind to the importance of a natural diet must have been "living in a barn" for many years. For instance, in the early years of the first book, I gave copies to everybody I knew who had a dog or cat. They all said, in one way or another: "Thanks, but no thanks. I'm going to do what everybody recommends." ("Everybody" was usually the ad writers for commercial foods and, sometimes, an orthodox veterinarian.) In recent years, I can't count how many of these same people have called me asking what the natural diet is for their new dog or cat, or asking for the name of a holistic veterinarian.

If you sense you're talking to someone who, for whatever reason, isn't sincerely going to try to keep your puppy healthy with a natural diet, you might opt to find a better home for him. Or get the person to promise that, in return for your gift of this beautiful, healthy entity, he or she will at least read the early chapters of this book.

The barest bottom line I suggest you tell such a new parent is to realize that *any* sudden change in a pet's diet can make him sick; and that if the puppy is suddenly changed to commercial foods after being on a natural diet, the person should expect such symptoms as vomiting and diarrhea. To prevent this, the new parent should keep the puppy on his natural diet and only gradually add in the fake commercial foods.

I'd like to make this point—that *any* sudden drastic change in diet can make a pet sick—very solidly, because it may apply to your pets in many different situations. Suddenly changing a dog from commercial foods to a natural diet can do just as much harm as suddenly changing him from a natural diet to a commercial one. To drive this point home, I'm going to share with you how stupid I was many years ago in introducing my new charge, Rambo, to a natural diet. I was eager to start Rambo on real foods when I brought him home from the animal "shelter" where he had been dumped. I knew the "shelter" had not given him natural foods, so I wanted to set him on the road to a long, healthy life instantly.

My new puppy loved the foods I gave him, but he couldn't keep them down. He'd eat, then vomit; eat, then vomit. This type of reaction to a sudden change in diet had been mentioned only in one or two sentences in my first edition, and as a result I'd frankly forgotten about it—a major reason I'm drumming it in this book.

Rambo seemed to be in particular distress one 3:00 A.M., and I ran frantically to my books written by orthodox veterinarians, who stated that my puppy probably had a bowel obstruction and needed immediate surgery. So I dragged Rambo off in the middle of the night to the nearest veterinary center open twenty-four hours. This is the center I mention often throughout this book as having probably the best reputation in the country for orthodox veterinary medicine. The veterinarians there confirmed my fear that Rambo had a serious condition.

They kept Rambo in the hospital for a week, giving him every test standard veterinary medicine knew of. He was still vomiting up almost everything he ate. If for no other reason than I've already told you what I did wrong, you're following Rambo's problem more smartly than I was, and you realize that not only had I suddenly switched this poor puppy to a natural diet, but the orthodox doctors had switched him suddenly back to a fake-food diet. Nobody had given his digestive system a chance to get used to either diet.

After they'd had Rambo in the hospital for a week, the veterinarians told me that "every known diagnostic test" showed that Rambo had no physical problems. (When orthodox tests can't find any physical reason for symptoms in people, doctors often send the patients to psychotherapists because they believe the symptoms are "all in the patients' heads," but dogs don't tend to get diagnosed this way.) The veterinarian in charge of Rambo's case said that, at a loss, she'd contacted "a major specialist in the country on puppies who vomit everything up." She told me this doctor had said that "sometimes puppies just get into the *habit* of vomiting."

So, after subjecting Rambo (and myself) to a week's separation, I paid the veterinary center a lot of money and took my new puppy home with me, still vomiting up almost everything he ate because, as I'd learned, he had developed that "habit."

Faced now with a puppy that the best orthodox veterinarians couldn't help, it finally dawned on me to wonder if the answer might be in the book I myself had compiled years before. I started reading the book word for word until I found the short mention: If you make any sudden change in diet, your dog or cat may suffer digestive disturbances, including heavy vomiting.

Since the latest diet that Rambo had had suddenly thrust upon him was fake commercial food, I figured his digestive system was now closer to becoming adjusted to that. Gritting my teeth, I went out and bought a bag and a can of fake food and fed him that for a few days. Sure enough, this poor puppy who had vomited every day of his life with me *finally* stopped. Then I gradually gave him less commercial foods and more natural ones. In this manner, Rambo gave up his diagnosed "habit" of vomiting. He has been on a natural diet for many, many years now, and has never again vomited once.

You may wonder why I didn't call a holistic veterinarian rather than taking Rambo to an orthodox center. It's true that a holistic veterinarian, hearing that I had just gotten the puppy, would have suspected a sudden change in diet as a possible cause of his digestive distress. (Not being specialists in nutrition, none of the orthodox veterinarians thought of that.) But remember that it was the middle of the night when the orthodox books gave me reason to believe that Rambo was suffering an emergency. As I urge in the introduction, in an emergency get your pet to the nearest veterinarian quickly; and I state that in emergencies virtually all holistic veterinarians will rely mainly on the same techniques as orthodox doctors.

Caring for the Older Dog

As I said in the introduction, it is my greatest hope that you will not destroy your dog ("put her to sleep")—no matter *what* is wrong with her—until you have given holistic veterinary medicine a chance to work its natural wonders. This holds true not only for dogs diagnosed as "surely" dying of the disorders we'll cover in later chapters, but also for pets falling apart in general from the problems of old age considered "normal" in dogs fed poisonous commercial pet food.

For the first edition of this book, back in 1981, I had no trouble gathering case histories of dogs diagnosed as "dying from old age" who recovered from their infirmities and lived many more years with the health and joy of life they'd had as puppies.

For this new book, in 1998, I asked Dr. Taylor to contribute one or two case histories of an aged, dying dog restored to good health through holistic therapy—a dog whose recovery might be considered a "miracle" by people not yet knowledgeable in holistic medicine. When Dr. Taylor heard my question, she laughed. "You want only one or two?"

She chose to tell me about Boomer, who came into her mind first. "Boomer, a poodle, was about seventeen years old when we started seeing him," the veterinarian said. "He had no hearing and very little vision. The poor little guy's body was so degenerated that he didn't have a single tooth left in his head." But the loss of ability to hear, see, and chew food was, according to Dr. Taylor, not Boomer's biggest problem. "His greatest challenge," she told me, "was very severe chronic arthritis of the spine that would cause his back to just seize up."

I think you can imagine how many dogs of Boomer's age with his severe physical problems are put to sleep every year because owners think that the dogs can't be helped. It's kinder to put them gently "to sleep" than to let them suffer. But, as many case histories and statistics throughout this book show, "hopeless" dogs often don't appear hopeless to holistic veterinarians.

Dr. Taylor addressed herself early on to Boomer's diet, as holistic veterinarians generally do. "He was on a conventional commercial dog food, and we had his dad put him on a home-*cooked* diet." Dr. Taylor indicated that feeding a raw-food diet to an elderly dog who has been eating commercial foods all his life is "probably not the most appropriate choice, because he may not have the digestive strength to really metabolize raw foods." (Other holistic veterinarians have not expressed that idea to me in discussing elderly dogs, although this book recommends often that a dog's natural diet be introduced gradually—in part to build up the digestive strength Dr. Taylor worries about. However, one major reason I made this book a compilation of the experience of many doctors was to give you various viewpoints. You might consult a holistic veterinarian on this point, discussing your elderly dog's specific dietary history, age, health, etc.)

The protein part of Boomer's diet included various meats such as beef, chicken, and turkey, "which are tonifying meats," the veterinarian said. She added that "lamb is sometimes too hot, too warming for an older animal." However, the choice of meats for a specific elderly dog depends on the problems the animal comes in with.

For grains, "usually in an older animal, I recommend millet or barley," Dr. Taylor said, "especially in a dog who has arthritis, as Boomer did. Barley helps clear some of the dampness and pain in the joints. Oats are sometimes a good choice, because they help strengthen the sinews." Dr. Taylor stressed, as have all other holistic veterinarians I've worked with over the years, that grains should be thoroughly cooked.

As for vegetables, "with this particular dog, we leaned toward the more tonifying vegetables, such as beets and some of the dark-green leafy vegetables like spinach," the veterinarian told me.

Boomer also got a fatty-acid supplement that included omega-3 fatty acids. "Sometimes in an elderly dog that's quite deficient nutritionally, we will give small amounts of the herbs spirulina or chorella," Dr. Taylor said. But she warns against several remedies sometimes used for younger dogs: "Blue-green algae is too intense for these older guys; they don't tolerate it well because it's too strong energetically for them. The same is true for barley grass and wheat grass; they detoxify the body too fast for an elderly dog." As veterinarians mention often in this book, too many toxins leaving the body at one time can overwhelm the body's liver if it's not strong enough to filter those toxins.

For Boomer's specific case, Dr. Taylor also used a few Chinese herbs "that are very gentle, easily assimilated and metabolized, and that are known to be tonics for the blood and for the chi." (You'll note that one of Dr. Taylor's goals with elderly animals is to use natural therapies that heal *gently*.)

Boomer also got a homeopathic constitutional remedy and a few acupuncture treatments.

Dr. Taylor said that Boomer "made a remarkable improvement" in all his health problems and came back from the brink of death "quite nicely." The poodle—who seemed sure to die at the already ancient age of seventeen—lived happily until he was twenty-three years old.

Dr. Racyln said in an interview that "often, acupuncture used alone really brings dogs diagnosed as dying back to life." But he chose to give me a specific case history of a "doomed" dog who needed more help than he often must offer.

The veterinarian told me of an elderly dog named Tess, an airedale who was brought to him when she was thirteen years old. Tess had severe arthritis, chronic skin and dental diseases, and long-standing ear infections. Her people had taken her to several other veterinarians who basically couldn't do anything to help the dog. "When her owners brought Tess to me, they had pretty much decided to euthanize her," Dr. Racyln told me. When he first saw Tess, it was easy to understand why she seemed so hopeless to other doctors: "Her skin looked absolutely terrible, and she was so riddled with arthritis that she could hardly even move." (For a similar case history of a dog with "hopeless" arthritis, from a couple of decades ago, see the Introduction.)

Nevertheless, Dr. Racyln said that he talked the owners out of putting Tess to sleep. "The first thing we did," he said, "was to switch the diet to an all-natural dog food. We put Tess on essential fatty acids as a supplement for her skin problems. We treated her acutely, to get rid of the infections, with orthodox antibiotics and antiinflammatories. And we started treating with Glycoflex, a product containing glycosamines, which are well-known among holistic M.D.s and veterinarians to help arthritis."

The veterinarian added: "We cleaned her teeth, because dental health is a very integral part of the body's overall health, since bacteria in the mouth get into the bloodstream and cause problems. So we got Tess under anesthesia and cleaned her teeth. While we had her under anesthesia we also cleared her ears out really well. Then we worked with her people on keeping the environment in the ear really clean and dry—because holistic medicine is just as much environmental medicine, and you can look at the ear as a mini environment. A key to keeping infections of the ear under control is to keep the ear's environment nice and dry. So we put natural supplements directly in the ears to keep them dry."

Dr. Racyln also put Tess on a nutritional supplement and on enzymes.

Only three weeks after Dr. Racyln talked the dog's people out of putting her permanently "to sleep," they called to say that Tess was now "a different dog" than the one they had brought to him. Her crippling arthritis was already so improved that she could not only move around okay, "but she's running around again, for the first time in years." Dr. Racyln added that the skin and ear problems also cleared up and never returned.

The veterinarian said that Tess went on to live another two and a half years beyond the time she was supposed to die—"and she was active, healthy, and happy until the day she died."

Even in 1981, when holistic veterinary medicine was in its infancy, Dr. Belfield told of Clyde, a ten-year-old collie mix. Clyde could no longer control his bladder. He couldn't control his bowels. He had no energy, and he couldn't eat. As if to add a final indignity to the dying Clyde, flies, attracted by his sickness, swarmed constantly around the poor animal's head and body.

Clyde's owner loved him and couldn't stand to see him suffer so. Not knowing that nutrients have the biochemical potential to rebuild the body, Clyde's owner brought him in to Dr. Belfield and tearfully requested that his beloved pet be put to sleep.

Dr. Belfield asked if the owner would like to try vitamin and mineral supplementation.

It was only a few weeks later that the owner returned to Dr. Belfield's office and reported that Clyde could now control his urine. He could control his bowels. He was running and leaping about.

Clyde's owner had one question, though. Could vitamins and minerals do something like this for humans, too?

As Dr. Belfield summarized this case history, it had been over a year since Clyde's owner had wanted him put to sleep. Clyde was still doing fine.

And Clyde's owner and the rest of his human family were taking vitamin and mineral supplements.[4]

What Not *to Do for Your Senior Citizen That You Are Normally Told to Do*

It's often considered just about axiomatic that you should cut down on your dog's calories when he gets into his later years. One basic reason is that today's fake-food-fed pet starts to slow down at that time; he hasn't the energy or strength to exercise the way he did when he was a youngster. The reduced exercise, of course, leads to reduced caloric expenditure; and lower caloric expenditure without lower caloric intake equals more weight. Overweight can lead to heart disease and other life-threatening disorders, the same as it can in people.

However, if you have been raising your dog for several years on the natural diet proposed in this book, I would urge you *not* to cut down arbitrarily his caloric intake as he grows older. Chances are he will still have the physical energy and the psychological outlook of a puppy, and curtailing his calories might result in an emaciated dog who wonders why he is suddenly being punished by not being given enough food.

Here's a case in point: I myself own (perhaps more accurately, am owned by) a nineteen-year-old puppy, a eighteen-year-old puppy, and a thirteen-year-old puppy. All have been on natural diets for years. When I open the door to the yard for them, several times a day, they shoot out like three rockets. They run to the back of the 85-foot yard, then zoom back toward me, again like rockets. (The rocket called Rambo is a bit slower than the others because his legs are much shorter.) They repeat this game tirelessly (up to an hour or more at a time), stopping only now and then to bark at the "cat with the attitude" in the next yard, until I call them in to get their food. If there's anything they enjoy more than their exercise, it's their food.

As mentioned, one reason we're often told to reduce calories in the older pet is that animals fed unnaturally tend to slow down and exercise less as they get older. This is not considered depriving the pet, because these animals also tend to start to lose their *appetites* as they enter their senior years. As I just indicated, my three elderly puppies are even more enamored of their food than they are of their intense exercise.

A few holistic veterinarians I interviewed for this new book worried if I'd recommended, in the first book, less protein for the older dog, because it was a common thought in those days that you should give an older dog less protein. No, I hadn't recommended less protein, because even back then that idea was discounted by veterinarians who specialized in nutrition. However, when I heard that this idea might still be floating around, I looked at the labels of some present-day pet foods for "seniors" and found them declaring that one reason their food will help your pet is that it has lower protein.

Dr. Racyln talked to me in detail about this issue. "A lot of people, including those who put out some of the so-called highly nutritious prepared foods, are still saying that you have to cut down protein for older dogs. This is based on two theories," he said. "One is that all older dogs have some sort of low-grade kidney disease. And the other is that when you have low-grade kidney disease, low protein helps."

How scientifically solid are those two theories? "The original studies that were done on the association between kidney disease and normal-protein diets were done on something like six laboratory rats," Dr. Racyln said. "And when they were fed a normal-protein diet, they already had kidney *failure*—not minor kidney disease. But the experimenters concluded, on the basis of that handful of rats, that you shouldn't use a normal-protein diet in animals with low-grade kidney disease." And remember that the other false assumption is that all older dogs have low-grade kidney disease.

"I think," the veterinarian went on, "it's stretching it quite a bit to conclude that normal, healthy older animals need low-protein diets. I don't think that's true at all."

Dr. Racyln added that, although the few high-quality prepared foods he occasionally recommends put out special formulas for the geriatric pet, he keeps his patients on the adult formulas.

The veterinarian stressed that he is talking here about—just as he said—the normal, healthy older animal. "You should know what your animal's kidney function is before making a decision about what type of diet the animal needs." This may be a good time to remind you that this entire chapter is written for *preventing* future disease in *healthy* animals at special times in their lives. If your dog is ill, please read the chapters on disorders for information to help her recover.

Dr. Limehouse expressed the same ideas as Dr. Racyln a bit differently: "It's no longer considered true that you should give an older dog less protein just because he's an older dog. If his blood tests show he doesn't have kidney problems, you should not reduce the protein levels." The veterinarian explained that animals (and people) need protein to build muscles. "And the older any of us gets, the harder it is for us to make muscle mass. So if we cut down on protein, our muscles can get quite thin and scrawny." So maybe the myth that we should cut down on all older dogs' protein can be contributing to the fact that it is normal for older dogs fed fake diets to become progressively weaker.

What You Should *Do to Keep Your Older Dog Healthy*

As mentioned in chapter 2, some holistic veterinarians consider a multivitamin/multimineral supplement optional for the healthy adult dog, while others think this supplement should be given as a matter of course. If you took the option not to use a supplement, you should start your dog on one as she enters her later years. Chances are that as she grows older, her body will be able to utilize a smaller proportion of the nutrients she takes in. As is true for dogs of all ages, a multivitamin/multimineral pill formulated especially for dogs should be used, preferably one obtained from a health food store.

Holistic veterinarians recommend that for older dogs you add to the supplement 200 IU of vitamin E daily for the small dog, 400 IU for the medium and large, and 800 IU for the giant. If you followed the recommendation in chapter 2 for the amount of vitamin C to add for the healthy adult dog, increase that amount now as your companion enters her "golden" years. Your older pet's ability to produce vitamin C in her own body may be diminishing. Both C and E are antioxidants, which means they slow down oxidation— the process that's mainly responsible for aging. Even that yellowed (aging) picture in your photo album got that way through oxidation.

There are several different forms of vitamin E, and Dr. Limehouse stated: "We like the natural form, d-alpha-tocopherol."* The form of E should be listed on the label of any supplement you're considering.

While the holistic veterinarians I have consulted since 1981 have often suggested a very light role in supplementing for the healthy adult dog being fed a natural diet, every doctor stressed supplementing your older dog with antioxidants. If you keep up with nutritional news for humans, you've been hearing a lot about antioxidants in recent years, particularly for people of advanced age. Since 1981, the number of known antioxidants has grown extensively, and these years holistic veterinarians suggest giving the older dog a few of the newer antioxidants, as well as vitamins C and E.

* Note that this is not a misprint for dl-alpha-tocopherol, the form of E you can most easily find in drugstores.

Dr. Limehouse said that he particularly likes the recently discovered coenzyme Q10. Dr. Taylor recommends that a healthy elderly large dog, such as a Doberman, be given 90 to 100 mg a day in divided doses. Dr. Racyln tells me that he uses this coenzyme and other antioxidants in all his older patients.

Another newly discovered and studied antioxidant is Pycnogenol. I asked Dr. Limehouse about this antioxidant. "We like that," he answered. He pointed out that some of the Pycnogenols are made from pine extract, and some are made from red grape seeds. He cautions that if your animal lives in an area with pine trees, he may have developed an allergy to pine. "Then you have to be careful to use the grape seed extract."

Grape seed extract also tends to be cheaper than the pine extract.

You might also ask a holistic veterinarian about adding the natural substance lecithin to your dog's diet. Lecithin helps prevent heart attacks and can help dissolve blood clots.

Dr. Taylor frequently recommends digestive enzymes for older dogs, "and I recommend they be given with every feeding," she told me.

Dr. Limehouse, who recommends digestive enzymes for dogs of all ages, told me: "The older a dog is, the more I think he needs these enzymes." Digestive enzymes help the body to *use* the nutrients it gets; this is one of the many abilities that often decrease with age.

Dr. Limehouse also supplements older dogs (as well as younger dogs) with omega-3 fish oils (essential fatty acids)—at least if they're not getting natural sources of fish every week, as recommended in chapter 2.

Dr. Racyln, speaking of herbs he commonly uses for older dogs, "many of which weren't available ten years ago," said he particularly recommends ashwaganda, an Indian herb. How does this presently little-known herb help an older dog? "It's considered an adaptogen," Dr. Racyln told me, "meaning that it helps the body go back to its normal state of being. It's a good balancer. It gives energy, makes older dogs more alert, and helps their vital functions."

By the way, Dr. Racyln does not use ashwaganda for cats. Holistic veterinarians have told me of other herbs they use with good results for dogs that can be toxic for cats. Please don't try to use information in this book for a cat who also shares your home unless you consult a holistic veterinarian, at least by phone. (See the list of holistic veterinarians at the back of the book and my book *Keep Your Cat Healthy the Natural Way*.)

"We also use fatty-acid supplements in older pets," Dr. Racyln continued. "Holistic veterinarians have known for a long time that fatty acids are essential for a good skin and coat. But more recently we've learned that fatty acids are good for cardiac output, so we use them in all older pets, especially those with cardiac disease. These nutrients are also wonderful for joint pain, so we use them in conjuction with other supplements for arthritis and general old-age stiffness." Dr. Racyln adds that fatty acids can also help improve renal and liver function.

"So," Dr. Racyln summed up, "if I get an old, stiff dog walking in to my clinic—who has, say, the early stages of heart failure and his liver isn't functioning well—the first thing I do is to put him on the Indian herb ashwaganda, coenzyme Q10, antioxidants, and fatty acids." Dr. Racyln added that he would also immediately start to change the dog over to an all-natural diet. In several decades of reporting on nutritional medicine, I haven't found one M.D. or veterinarian who didn't stress that a healthy basic diet was of prime importance for recovery, as well as for prevention.

If your dog has spent much of her life on commercial foods, she may have lost many of her teeth. You can—and should—help her by mincing up her meat for her, as you did when she was a puppy. Half-chewed food will be half-digested food, which means her body won't be utilizing many of the nutrients she takes in. And there is always a possibility of choking to death on half-chewed food.

Feeding a Half-Starved Stray Dog

The dog you find wandering about the street may appear to be half animal, half skeleton. If you absolutely cannot take the starving entity home with you, at least until you can restore him to health and try to find him a home, *any* food you may be carrying with you—or can get your hands on quickly—may help keep the animal alive long enough so that he can find an adoptive parent.

If you can take the unfortunate being home, don't succumb to what might easily seem like the "commonsense" idea of letting your half-starved foundling eat unrestrainedly. Give small feedings, four to eight times a day at first. And gradually add just a little bit more food at a time. Dr. Aloro said, "It may take as long as ten days before a half-starved dog or cat can be trusted not to harm himself by overeating."

If you do let him eat, right off, all he seems to want, you could be leading him, as Dr. Kearns pointed out in the first edition, to protein poisoning, inhalation pneumonia, convulsions, and other problems.

Dr. Kearns recommended that raw honey and fluids are of prime importance when you first get the dog home. "Solid foods can always wait." You might at first also give a little yogurt.

The fluids that Dr. Kearns recommended are vitally important because the animal may be dehydrated or in danger of becoming so. For this new book, Dr. Racyln explained that "the idea with raw honey is to get some high-quality simple sugars into the dog." While Dr. Racyln doesn't recommend commercial foods as a mainstay of a healthy pet's diet, he did say there are a few commercial products that are "a bit better than just raw honey" for a half-starved stray. As this new book was written, this veterinarian recommended Nutrical because it gives "not only the simple sugars and carbohydrates but also many vitamins and minerals." He also recommended Hills A/D and Purina CV. "The CV stands for cardiovascular," said Dr. Racyln, "but it's also good for cases like this."

Agreeing with Dr. Kearns that "you should certainly keep the animal off solid foods to begin with," Dr. Racyln added that you shouldn't do this for too long. When you introduce solid foods, "start him off with something light. And you certainly want to give some probiotics at this time, because the animal's intestinal flora are sure to be unbalanced. Give the probiotics *between* his small meals, not with them." Dr. Racyln further stated: "If you are knowledgable in Chinese herbs, you can certainly add some tonifying herbs."

Probably the easiest, least expensive, and healthiest solid diet you can start your stray on when he's ready for regular foods is a diet of cooked chicken or turkey and brown rice. (As mentioned in chapter 2, don't feed heavy proteins like the first two foods at the same time as carbohydrates, such as brown rice.) Fowl and brown rice are particularly high in nutrients and are easily digestible. We can assume the unlucky fellow is likely to have problems digesting things for a while to come. (Well, he *was* unlucky; but now he has you.)

We're suddenly recommending *cooked* chicken or turkey since raw foods are not recommended for your stray pet, partly because they would probably be a sudden drastic change of diet for him. Chances are his previous owners didn't feed him the delicacies of a natural diet; and who knows what he has been managing to dig out of garbage cans to keep himself alive? As discussed earlier in this chapter, any sudden change of diet—even a change for the better—can cause digestive upset even in a healthy dog; and now we're trying to help a dog whose digestive system is probably already in much distress.

Do give a *powdered* multivitamin/multimineral supplement daily to your new pet. I call him your new pet, even though you may be quite sure you are just keeping the abandoned animal a few days until you can find somebody else to take him off your hands. If you're like many of us, you'll end up looking back years from now and realizing that he became your new pet the moment you saw him looking at you, with sad eyes, for help on the street.

In that regard, in *Keep Your Cat Healthy the Natural Way* I tell of how my husband, Joe, and I took in a stray cat "overnight," who ended up sharing her life with us for some twenty years. The same kind of thing happened when I first saw Doggie. (I mention Doggie several times in this book in relationship to her continuing inspiration to me of how natural diet and therapies can prevent and cure.) I named her Doggie when I picked her up off the street, starving to death—my idea being that I would give her only a "generic" name, not a real name of her own. In this manner, you see, I would not become bonded to her while I tried to find her original owner. I wasn't aware that dogs can become bonded to humans—and can *lead* the bonding process. (Several holistic veterinarians have pointed out to me that dogs often "xerox" their person's emotional state. I, for one, am living proof that people can xerox their dog's emotional state—even when the dog in question *isn't* their dog.)

With food, I lured Doggie off her street corner. She had tenaciously planted herself there for many days. Was she waiting patiently for her people to have a change of heart about having ditched her and come back and pick her up? Had she been abused by her people, run off, and chosen this street corner because it offered her the company of a couple of "junkyard" dogs, similarly deprived of love, whom she could relate to through the barricades that separated them? I'm never going to know the actual answers to those questions, but I do know that for months Doggie cringed whenever Joe or I raised our hands in a simple gesture. (Now she assumes these gestures mean "play time.")

With much misgiving, Doggie followed my promise of food out into my yard, where I was certain she would be very happy, my yard reminding her of her ancestral forest and all that. For days, I spent much of my time on the phone, trying to find her real owners or at least someone who would take her off my hands and promise her a good home. But Doggie didn't enjoy my yard, her "new forest," at all. She spent her days sitting by the sliding glass door between my office and the yard, looking in on me longingly and crying softly. (I have often read that dogs' eyes can't convey different expressions. But maybe, like me, you know darned well that they can.)

Finally, one day Doggie was sitting out in the rain, ignoring it completely, while she continued to stare in at me and whimper softly. I hadn't taken this dog into our house because I didn't know what diseases she might be carrying, and I didn't want her to infect my two precious miniature poodles. (The chapter on infectious diseases shows how my poodles did end up exposed to the very serious disease parvo, which Doggie was carrying. But it had no effect on them, thanks to the fact that they had been on natural diets for years.) One reason I had put her into the yard was that it had a sort of a barn, and I assumed this dog would have, as the saying goes, "enough sense to come in out of the rain." Now I wondered how dumb this stray dog could be, not to realize she had easy shelter.

Finally, exasperated, I went out myself in the rain and led Doggie into the barn. She easily understood that I had led her into a nice shelter, but she understood also that I was right there *with* her. (Meanwhile, I was starting to realize that I had spent the better part of a week's work trying to help a dog I didn't care about.) Doggie at last fell asleep in the barn. I went back to my office and resumed my phone calls to try to get her off my hands. It was maybe ten minutes before Doggie woke up, realized I was no longer with her in the barn, and was back sitting outside my sliding glass door, looking at me mournfully and whimpering softly, in the rain.

Needless to say, Doggie's instinctive knowledge that she had found a good entity to bond with proved to be stronger than my intellectual knowledge that I had *not*, and Doggie and I have been together for some fifteen years now.

References

1. Fred Hale, "Pigs Born without Eyeballs," *J. of Heredity*, March 1933, p. 105.
2. Carlton Wade, *The Rejuvenation Vitamin* (New York: Award Books), 1970, p. 122.
3. Wendell O. Belfield, D.V.M., and Martin Zucker, *How to Have a Healthier Dog* (Garden City, New York: Doubleday and Co., Inc.), 1981, p. 107.
4. *Ibid.,* p. 141.

PART 2

**Natural Ways of
Healing the Mildly
Ill, the Very Ill,
and Even the
"Terminally" Ill**

Chapter 5

New Help for Crippling Disorders

"Acupuncture has a very high success rate with crippled animals whom conventional therapies have not helped."
—*Sheldon Altman, D.V.M. (specialist in veterinary acupuncture)*

"I think the nutrients glycosaminoglycans must be included in any treatment of arthritis, hip dysplasia, or other crippling disorders, because of their invaluable influence in healing those problems. These substances help produce healthy tendons, ligaments, joints, bones, and cartilage. They are safe for dogs, cats, and humans.

"The omega-3 fatty acids are also invaluable: For one thing, they are natural antiinflammatories that are a lot safer than the antiinflammatory drugs commonly used."
—*Robert J. Silver, D.V.M.*

"My current approach to hip dysplasia and ligamentous disease has been quite effective in most cases."
—*Jack Long, V.M.D.*

"In the more serious cases of ruptured discs, my routine approach is to inject the downed dog with sodium ascorbate [vitamin C] for three to five days. Normally this is all the time it takes to bring the animal back to its feet."[1]
—*Wendell O. Belfield, D.V.M.*

"I have successfully treated more cases of dogs with arthritis than I could possibly remember. I chiropractically adjust them, put them on a more natural diet, and choose nutritional supplements according to what the individual dog tests out to need. Typically, these dogs get well and end up running around and playing in a month."
—*Neal K. Weiner, D.V.M.*

Writing in 1981 in *Veterinary Medicine/Small Animal Clinician* (p. 1307), Sheldon Altman, D.V.M., a specialist in veterinary acupuncture, pointed out that "until recently, chronic pain and chronic degenerative diseases in animals were seldom treated. Because of economics, inconvenience, and concern for suffering, the usual solution to these problems was euthanasia." Euthanasia is, of course, a "nice" word for killing the animal before he may have chosen his own time to die.

Unfortunately, we can't ask the dog or cat if he himself has given up on living.

Since orthodox veterinarians started treating more animals for crippling problems, they have been using, in part, the following drugs: painkillers, muscle relaxants, tranquilizers, antiinflammatories, and corticosteroids. Nerve blocks and neurectomies are also used for large dogs. "In many cases," Dr. Altman said in 1981, "these therapies are unsuccessful or are contraindicated because of the presence of some other disease." The veterinarian said that when these treatments don't work or are contraindicated, practitioners must then either use an unconventional therapy or destroy the animal.

In the same year Dr. Altman wrote those statements, holistic veterinarians were detailing to me for my first book their alternative therapies for crippling disorders and were reporting good to excellent results in the majority of cases, even those that didn't respond to orthodox techniques. In this new book, holistic veterinarians tell you of the new therapies developed since the early 1980s that offer even more help.

The following is general information on what holistic veterinarians suggest you do—*and don't do*—to help your dog with a painful problem that's started to, or already has, crippled him.

First, *don't* give him "human" painkillers unless you call a holistic veterinarian (see the list at the back of the book) and get an okay for a specific painkiller for your individual dog. Many of the usual analgesics—as well as other types of drugs you can buy easily without a prescription—can be very toxic, even lethal, for animals.

With that warning, you may be tempted to take your dog immediately off a drug she has been *prescribed*. It is true that virtually any drug has potentially serious side effects. Cortisone, for instance, as Ihor John Basko, D.V.M., once pointed out to me, may produce in some patients "weakening of muscles, including the heart; stress on the kidneys; suppression of the immune system—and decreased healing." Also, while cortisone can cover up the pain of a crippling disorder, it does nothing to heal the disorder itself. So your dog may take to using the still-diseased joint (which he wouldn't do if the pain were not being artificially covered up)—thus causing further degeneration to the joint.

Yet I talked to some fifteen holistic veterinarians about taking your dog off a prescribed drug, and they all agreed that you should phase these drugs out gradually and then only under the supervision of a veterinarian. So make that a point you take up when you phone or visit a holistic doctor.

As with most drugs, there are safer, and usually less expensive, natural alternatives. For instance, vitamin C has been known for many years to be an effective deadener of pain. As Phillip Racyln, D.V.M., pointed out to me in a recent interview, omega-3 fatty acids are now known to help joint pain, "so they're part of what I always use for arthritis and general old-age stiffness," he said.

S. Allen Price, D.V.M., is also careful to keep the salt content of the diet extremely low, since salt can increase pain. This veterinarian also told me for the first edition: "I have very good success in pain alleviation with castor oil packs over the joints. This is quite simple

to do. Just soak cotton in castor oil, wrap the cotton around the affected limb, and secure it with bandages. Leave the dog's toes outside the bandage; the pet will continue to walk as long as he can feel
his toes touching the ground." The castor oil decreases the inflammation that causes pain. It also increases circulation, and increased
circulation promotes healing. Thus, the oil is working not just to
mask the symptom of pain, but to alleviate its causes.

Norman C. Ralston, D.V. M.—saying that his goal is not just to decrease the severity of a crippling disorder, but to get the dog "to feel
well and run everywhere"—told me of a twelve-year-old mixed
breed who was brought to him "paralyzed, down completely." When
veterinarians speak of a "downed" dog, they refer to one who is so
crippled he can't stand. "We used acupuncture to get her up," Dr.
Ralston told me, "and two natural substances to reduce the pain.
And of course we worked on her nutrition." The veterinarian added
that the dog's person was so impressed with the results of this
therapy that she made up a before-and-after picture study, which
she titled "My Story." The "after" pictures show the dog running and
jumping.

Dr. Ralston concluded, "The dog did very well for four years. But
then, at sixteen, she 'went' mentally. The owners believed she
wanted to leave, and they had her put to sleep."

Basic Suggestions for Treating Arthritis and Other Crippling Disorders

As is the case with most disorders, any printed therapy—orthodox
or alternative—can be used only as a suggestion for your particular
pet. Every individual body chemistry is unique—a concern that is
one of the major tenets of holistic medicine. For instance, my miniature poodle, Shiki, remained symptom-free for sixteen years of what
a veterinarian at one of the country's most esteemed orthodox
medical centers had diagnosed as a case of arthritis for which "nothing could be done." (She died peacefully, with no suffering, a natu-

ral death of old age about fourteen years later than the veterinarians predicted we would have to put her—unnaturally—to sleep. In other words, following an idea I put forth early in this chapter, Shiki chose her *own* time to die. My husband and I didn't choose it for her.)

The therapy we found for Shiki was simple: a natural diet, the addition of a multivitamin/multimineral pill, and a bit of apple cider vinegar spread over her food every day. (This form of vinegar adds acidity to the body's basic acid/alkaline balance.) However, I would not dream of guaranteeing that these three steps alone would achieve a similar control for your particular pet. For one thing, Shiki was only a year old, so she had youth on her side; for another, she had been on the harmful commercial foods for only that year, and they hadn't had much time to wreak a general degeneration of her body. She also happened to have had an indomitably spunky, devil-may-care spirit that left her particularly unsusceptible to psychological stress.

It always worries me when I read short articles that seem to promise that they contain all the information readers need to treat their dog or cat, or themselves, on their own. As mentioned in earlier chapters, many holistic veterinarians are available these days for phone consultation if you don't live near them (see the list at the end of this book). Hopefully, you'll use the information in this chapter as inspiration to help your dog holistically, and as groundwork for drawing up your own specific questions for a holistic veterinarian and for understanding what this doctor prescribes for your companion.

The box below gives some "classical" holistic suggestions for treating arthritis and other degenerative problems such as hip dysplasia. But, as you might expect, advances have been made in recent years that *add* to the chance that your dog can have a complete recovery without surgery or drugs. I give these advances immediately following the box.

As always, holistic doctors will modify treatment for each pet after scientific testing of individual body chemistry.

Some Classical Holistic Treatments for Arthritis and Other Cripplers

- **Phase out drugs**. Gradually withdraw drugs, *under the supervision of a veterinarian*, as the natural therapy begins to take hold.
- **Phase out old diet.** Gradually eliminate chemical-filled processed foods and replace with a natural diet over a period of one or two months.
- **Begin a natural diet.** This diet differs somewhat from the preventive diet in chapters 2 and 4. That diet is to maintain health in an already healthy animal. Now we are dealing with a dog who has different requirements to rid him of a disease. The new diet should contain: 25 percent finely chopped fruits or vegetables; 50 percent flaked grains (brown rice, millet, or oatmeal, soaked in hot water until soft); 25 percent ocean fish (lightly steamed), raw milk or cheese, fertile raw egg yolks, yogurt or cottage cheese. Red meat and chicken should totally be eliminated and perhaps gradually added back to the diet as the animal recovers. However, some arthritic animals cannot tolerate the return of red meat to their diet.
- **Offer only pure water.** Give pure steam-distilled water only. Distilled water helps remove undesirable mineral salts from the joints. Do not allow your pet access to water during the meal or for one hour before or after.
- **Fasting your pet.** This gives the digestive processes a rest and allows the body to eliminate stored toxins. Some doctors recommend a thirty-six-hour fast weekly and a two- to three-day fast every three months. The fast consists of removal of solid foods and the offering of steam-distilled water, fresh carrot and celery juice, or a broth made by adding the skin of four potatoes to one quart of distilled water and simmering for fifteen minutes. *A fast should be administered only under the supervision of a veterinarian experienced in monitoring animals during fasts.*
- **Supplement your dog.** For a 30-pound dog, based on two meals a day: brewer's yeast, 2 teaspoonsful per meal; kelp, 1 teaspoonful or three tablets per meal; whey (preferably goat's), 2 teaspoonsful per meal; vitamin C, 1,500 mg per day; vitamin E, 200 IU per day; pantothenic acid, 200 mg per day; bone meal or eggshell, one tablet per meal; cod-liver oil (cold-pressed), 1 teaspoon per meal; wheat germ oil (cold-pressed), 1 teaspoon per meal; lecithin (granules or liquid), 1 teaspoon per meal; vitamins A/D, 5,000/400

IU, one capsule per meal. As the dog improves, these dosages can be adjusted downward to minimum daily maintenance dosages.
- **Massage your pet.** Massaging affected joints with your fingers will increase circulation and therefore help promote healing.
- **Exercise your pet.** Moderate outdoor exercise—such as a fifteen-minute walk twice a day—can be helpful.

The boxed material recommends several antioxidants that were available when I wrote the first book. Recently, a number of new antioxidants have been discovered that can result in what at one time would have been considered "wonders." As Robert J. Silver, D.V. M., said in a recent interview: "I've got a list of new antioxidants an arm long."

Dr. Silver continued: "All these new antioxidants are fine to use, from the viewpoint of the animal's health. But I think it's best to keep things simple and try to keep everything as inexpensive as possible for people. We shouldn't get carried away with telling people they have to buy expensive, fancy, hard-to-get, hard-to-administer antioxidants."

Using those criteria, this veterinarian's major recommendation from among the new antioxidants is grape seed extract, which other holistic veterinarians recommend strongly elsewhere in this book. Dr. Silver said that "grape seed extract is probably the antioxidant of the '90s."

Pointing out that the simplest antioxidants to use are vitamins C and E—already recommended in the boxed information—Dr. Silver added that another antioxidant, selenium, should always be used when you give vitamin E. "We're finding that E and selenium work together in harmony even better than each of them works alone," the veterinarian said. Other holistic veterinarians—and related new studies sent me by research institutes—back up Dr. Silver's use of selenium with vitamin E.

Dr. Silver added that vitamin C is "only one small part of the big picture in terms of collagen production and repair." Important coworkers with that vitamin are the minerals manganese, calcium, and magnesium. "And lately," the veterinarian said, "we have found that other very important coworkers are the minerals boron and copper." He noted that the more we learn of the interrelationships between various nutrients and the workings of the body, "the more we understand how complex these interrelationships are." He also noted that "there is a simple solution" to the complexity of taking in all the right nutrients needed to keep all body processes healthy: "Eat real, unprocessed foods." If you have read only part of one chapter elsewhere in this book, you have already read of holistic veterinarians' passion for a diet of the dog's natural foods. (I detail these natural foods in chapters 2 and 4.)

Glucosamine Sulfate

Continuing to give new information in use since the first edition of this book, Dr. Silver offered details about the glycosaminoglycans, especially glucosamine sulfate.

First, however, Dr. Silver pointed out that he usually will pre-scribe glucosamine along with several nutrients that work well with this substance for crippling problems: vitamins C and B complex, and the omega-3 fatty acids. The veterinarian stated: "All my clients get my lecture about these fatty acids because they're so very valu-able globally for keeping the body healthy. Just two of the properties they have that specifically help crippling disorders is that they're antiinflammatories and antioxidants. I have found that these ex-tremely important nutrients are across the board either not present in the diet, or—because they are easily destroyed by light and heat [as in commercial processed foods]—are destroyed before the ani-mal gets to eat the food that naturally contains these nutrients." Dr. Silver specified that the omega-3 fatty acids are found only in cold-water fish, such as salmon, halibut, and cod. (The preventive diet given in chapter 2 recommends that you give your dog all her foods except grains raw—and that you feed her fish a few times a week.)

"The glycosaminoglycans are compounds that I think must be included in any treatment of arthritis, hip dysplasia, or any other crippling disorder because of their invaluable influence in healing these disorders," Dr. Silver said. He added that glycosamine sulfate is "safe for dogs, safe for cats, safe for humans" and that it is no problem to give to a pet because it can easily be added to their food, and it's tasteless.

Dr. Silver explained how glycosaminoglycans work: "They are molecules that are combinations of sugars and amino groups. And they're used by the fibrocytes, which are cells that produce fibrous tissue and collagen. Fibrocytes also produce what is called the ground substance, which is what all the cells sit in that holds the cells together."

As Dr. Silver explained, one of the substances that fibrocytes produce from glycosaminoglycans is collagen, a protein substance. How important is collagen? It acts as the body's cement; it is connective tissue that literally holds the parts of your body together. Frank L. Earl, D.V.M., once gave me a vivid description of animals with severe collagen problems: "They look like they've become unglued. They look like they're falling apart before your eyes." Actually, without collagen we would all—people and animals alike— *literally* fall apart. Our bodies would collapse into hundreds of uncoordinated, unconnected pieces.

Collagen helps form tendons, ligaments, bones, and cartilage— all very important parts of our bodies that must be strong and healthy if we're not to become victims of a painful crippling disorder, or if we are to recover from one of these disorders.

Many of us—and many of our pets—are walking around (or trying to) with various stages of collagen disorders. These disorders in humans include rheumatoid arthritis, rheumatic fever, and a condition characterized by anemia, hemorrhages into the skin, and bizarre central nervous system symptoms (thrombotic purpura).

The body normally creates its own glucosamine sulfate from glucose and the amino acid glutamine. But if a metabolic defect prevents utilization of these raw materials, the body won't be able to produce enough glucosamines; in turn the fibrocytes won't be able to produce healthy cartilage, tendons, ligaments, and bones.

Dr. Silver explained that by adding glucosamine sulfate directly in the diet, "you can be certain that you are giving the cells of the joint the material they need so they can create healthy cartilage," even when the body cannot make its own glucosamine sulfate.

How Can Acupuncture Help Your Dog?

I'd like to start this section with a case history of Thor, who had a crippling disorder that wasn't responding to orthodox therapy and who was healed by acupuncture used alone.

Thor was a male miniature poodle who had been diagnosed by a very prestigious animal medical center as "a classic example of spondylosis" (chronic degenerative disc disease). Before this, Thor had been a very active dog and had exhibited the poodle breed's penchant for walking around on his hind legs. But Thor had begun finding it difficult to put any pressure on his hind legs, even for "regular" walking. He also started to fall down frequently.

For three months Thor was treated with the drugs prednisolone, Valium, and aspirin. They seemed to alleviate his pain but did little to improve his walking. Also, when the drugs were withdrawn for twenty-four hours on several occasions, the poodle had difficulty controlling his bowels and urine and suffered from vomiting and loss of appetite.

Then Thor was taken to Marty Goldstein, D.V.M., who gave him only two acupuncture treatments. Thor's owner also gave him several acupressure treatments at home after having been taught the technique by Dr. Goldstein. Less than two months after being taken to Dr. Goldstein, Thor had returned to nearly normal, except he showed "a slight hesitancy" before jumping up on chairs, according to his owners. The last I heard about Thor, he had been free of problems for five years.

Acupuncture is a nondrug, noninvasive technique of healing that has virtually no side effects. It is sometimes assumed to be a "new" therapy (and therefore, to skeptics, an *unproven* therapy) by those in this country who have not taken the time to learn much about it. Actually, this "new" therapy has been practiced for five thousand years in the East and since the 1700s in Europe. But surely, you may think, using acupuncture to treat *animals* must be a brand-new idea. Not true. For instance, recently a treatise was discovered that gave specifics for how to use acupuncture to treat elephants. It is estimated that the veterinary acupuncturist—or whatever he may have been called in those days—wrote that advice three thousand years ago. It wasn't until the 1950s that acupuncture slowly began to be accepted into medical practice in America. By 1984 there were some four hundred veterinarians in this country who regularly used acupuncture as part of their practices.

Acupuncture is often erroneously thought to be of value only in alleviating pain. Even if that were *really* all that acupuncture could do, you can see that it might be of great value to your dog with a crippling disorder, since pain is such a debilitating symptom. But acupuncture also helps other problems associated with crippling disorders. Actually, Dr. Altman stated that the majority of animals referred to acupuncturists suffer from arthritis and various forms of paralysis or neuropathies (inflammation and wasting of the nerves).

Also, controlled investigations on animals have shown that acupuncture can have beneficial effects in treating shock, ulcers, and abnormal heart rhythms. Case studies have shown that acupuncture can be of value in a wide variety of nervous, reproductive, urinary, digestive, respiratory, and circulatory problems.[2] The National Association for Veterinary Acupuncture noted as long ago as 1977 that "acupuncture has been used to treat a number of other conditions, including certain eye problems, dermatitis, deafness, general debilitation of old age, and epilepsy.* In fact," they stated, "about the only thing that acupuncture is not recommended for is acute infections."[3] Dr. Altman adds that acupuncture can sometimes even bring animals out of comas and respiratory arrest.

How Does Acupuncture Work? Traditional Chinese medicine explains acupuncture in terms that often sound weird to the Western ear: *yin* and *yang*, the negative and positive; and *chi*, the life force. Dr. Altman, quoted in the *Journal of the American Veterinary Medical*

---

* A number of case histories in this book attest to the fact that accupuncture can help many problems.

Association in November 1992, said: "The Chinese terms scare us. We understand the sympathetic and parasympathetic nervous systems, but if we call them *yin* and *yang*, we're going to raise eyebrows." He said, though, that our physiology is simply traditional Chinese medicine "being looked at from a different point of view."

I, too, find concepts like *yin* and *yang* rather mystical, so I'm giving this brief explanation of how acupuncture works in terms of the more scientific (if you will) research done since acupuncture has been incorporated into Western medicine. We have documented quite well that one way acupuncture controls pain is because the needles release endorphins and other hormones that are known to lessen the brain's perception of pain. We have come up with *theories* about additional ways that acupuncture alleviates pain—through various neural mechanisms. But I think details of these are better left to a textbook.

Effects of acupuncture other than pain alleviation are believed to be mediated via the autonomic nervous system. As the journal article explained, nerves from certain acupuncture points overlap with nerves from various organs in the spinal cord. Stimulating these acupuncture points causes a reflex arc, which results in autonomic nerve responses. This explains why an acupuncture point for a specific organ may not be directly over that organ.

For treating crippling problems, an acupuncturist will stimulate specific acupuncture points that lie over nerves, muscle/tendon junctions, or motor points.

DOES ACUPUNCTURE RELIEVE ONLY THE SYMPTOMS, AS DRUGS OFTEN DO? No. The idea behind acupuncture is that symptoms and diseases result from disturbances in the normal strength and pattern of energy through the body. As Ihor John Basko, D.M.V., once explained to me: "We run tests to determine the underlying *causes* of the symptoms. The chosen acupuncture treatment is designed to correct this underlying cause. Acupuncture actually returns the body to a healthy, balanced state—*where it will heal itself*. Since the healing comes from within, it is self-perpetuating."

Dr. Marty Goldstein and his brother, Robert Goldstein, V.M.D., noted here the pervasive importance of a natural diet: If the condition being treated is due to a degenerative metabolism caused by poor nutrition, acupuncture will give only temporary relief *if the diet is not improved*.

Is ACUPUNCTURE EXPENSIVE? The rule of thumb I've been given is that the price of an acupuncture treatment is approximately equal to the cost of a regular office visit plus one vaccination. Yes, but how many treatments might your dog need? Is acupuncture one of those therapies (like insulin for diabetes) that has to be maintained for life? Of course I can't specifically answer the first question, but I can say that your dog definitely won't require lifetime acupuncture treatment. Remember Dr. Basko's statement above: Since acupuncture helps the body to heal itself, the healing is self-perpetuating. Consider also Dr. Altman's study, detailed a bit later, in which he had a high rate of success with, usually, a *maximum* of eleven treatments—on animals most of which had been found incurable with orthodox treatments and were also well up there in years.

However, as I've just hinted, acupuncture is often successful in dogs (and cats) who are considered "hopeless" and are set for euthanasia. (Actually, Dr. Altman reported that the majority of animals referred to him for acupuncture treatment had failed to respond to conventional therapy.) A course of acupuncture treatments will cost more than putting your dog down. (Since putting your dog permanently "to sleep" is a simple, one-step procedure, it's relatively inexpensive.) Acupuncture will cost more in dollars, that is. It will, of course, cost substantially less in guilt and sorrow.

You may be able to cut down the number of acupuncture treatments needed by applying acupressure. Ask your dog's doctor to show you this technique. Acupressure uses the same principles as acupuncture but is done with the fingers rather than with needles, so the only training it requires is learning which parts of your dog's body you should touch to help the specific disorder. It is less effective than acupuncture, but often can be used as a helpful adjunct.

WILL ACUPUNCTURE HURT OR FRIGHTEN YOUR DOG? Since one of the major uses of acupuncture in animals, and people, is to deaden pain—it is even often used as the only anesthesia during surgery—it would hardly make sense that acupuncture is painful. As for the needles frightening your pet, dogs and cats do not tend to have the apprehension of needles that we do. Both Dr. Basko and Dr. Altman reported that often while the acupuncture needles are inserted in place, the animal will snatch the opportunity to take a nap. (Imagine you or me snatching a nap after getting a needle at the dentist's.) Dr. Altman told me: "About the only time my patients get emotional is when I have accustomed them to a treat after therapy and then don't give them this treat after one particular session. *Then* they put up a fuss and a racket."

WHAT ARE THE CHANCES THAT ACUPUNCTURE MIGHT HELP YOUR PET? As we have said previously, acupuncture has an impressive success rate with a number of disorders. Dr. Altman has done a rather large study of acupuncture as treatment for a number of dogs and cats with crippling disorders. Most of the animals in Dr. Altman's study had been treated by conventional methods for a long time—unsuccessfully. Further weighting the study toward potentially poor results, the veterinarian didn't reject any patients, even if improvement seemed unlikely. And the average age of the animals was eight and a half years, so they were hardly youngsters. Dr. Altman treated most animals with acupuncture eleven, or fewer, times. Some of the veterinarian's results follow. (For simplicity, I have focused on the statistics for the extreme categories of response.)

- **Hip dysplasia:** Of eighteen animals treated, seven had 75 to 100 percent improvement, five had 50 to 75 percent improvement, and only one showed little or no improvement.
- **Paresis (including partial paralysis, tremors, and seizures) in the small dog and cat:** Eighteen of twenty-seven animals had 75 to 100 percent improvement, while only four showed 0 to 10 percent improvement.
- **Paralysis in the small dog and cat:** Eleven of twenty-seven animals had 75 to 100 percent improvement, while ten had 0 to 10 percent improvement.

- **Pain (cervical disc) in the small dog and cat:** Of eight patients treated, five had 75 to 100 percent improvement; only one had 0 to 10 percent improvement.
- **Central nervous system disorders, such as ataxia (muscle incoordination) and chorea (uncontrollable and ceaseless jerky movements):** Of twelve animals treated, one had 75 to 100 percent improvement, four had 50 to 75 percent improvement, and only four showed little or no improvement.
- **Chronic arthritis:** Of nineteen animals treated, five had 75 to 100 percent improvement; two had little or no improvement.
- **Miscellaneous pain syndromes:** Eleven of twenty-five animals showed 75 to 100 percent improvement, while three had little or none.
- **Traumatic peripheral nerve injury:** Six of ten animals treated had 75 to 100 percent improvement; two had 0 to 10 percent improvement.[4]

Please remember how this study was more weighted toward failure than toward success. Another important point was made by the National Association for Veterinary Acupuncture, of which Dr. Altman is a member of the board of directors: The technique and other treatments are not mutually exclusive. Thus, your pet may benefit *even more* by acupuncture used with another therapy. For instance, Dr. Basko commented that the association's reported results for arthritis and intervertebral disc syndrome can be improved by 20 to 40 percent when Chinese herbal therapy is added to the acupuncture. Since the association reported a 60 percent success rate in animals with chronic cases of intervertebral disc syndrome *that had not responded to either surgery or conservative treatment,*[5] Dr. Basko's estimate would bring the success rate for these "hopeless" animals to 80 to 100 percent, just by adding one more natural therapy.

Dr. Basko was commenting in 1981 on the association's 1977 statistic. Remember that holistic veterinary medicine has added many new techniques since then.

If you want to try acupuncture for your dog, you are much luckier than readers of the first book because so many more holistic veterinarians have discovered the effectiveness of acupuncture and have been trained in this therapy. Check the list of holistic veterinarians at the back of the book to find the nearest one who uses this therapy.

With acupuncture, there are a few problems that you don't have with most other natural therapies: Obviously, holistic veterinarians cannot send you this therapy through the mail, as they might send, say, homeopathics or nutritional supplements. And you can't ask your orthodox veterinarian to work over the phone to learn to use acupuncture from a holistic doctor, because acupuncture is a hands-on therapy that can't be learned by just listening to words.

If you don't live near a veterinarian who uses acupuncture, ask yourself: Am I *sure* I can't spend the time or money to travel to the nearest veterinarian who is trained in acupuncture? If your answer is yes, try calling holistic veterinarians near you. Discuss your dog's medical problem. You may find that these veterinarians have other therapies that can help your dog, and because so many holistic veterinarians keep adding acupuncture to their areas of expertise, you may find that a nearby veterinarian has been trained in acupuncture since I wrote this book. And be sure to ask the doctor if acupuncture's cousin therapy, acupressure, wouldn't be almost as helpful as acupuncture. (Remember that you can use acupressure yourself.)

Additional Ways to Help Crippling Disorders

In a recent interview with me, Dr. Ralston gave further details of his basic approach for arthritis and other crippling problems: "The first thing we do," he said, "is to find out what's *causing* the problem. Then we go back and correct the cause," rather than attacking the symptoms. To find the cause, Dr. Ralston uses contact reflex analysis, or kinesiology.

"We often find that the cause is a malfunctioning thyroid gland or adrenal gland due to nutritional deficiencies," the veterinarian said. "So then we know we have to add the nutrients that naturally keep that gland healthy. We also try to *remove* anything from the body that would interfere with healing. For that, we use a lot of homeopathy."

Dr. Ralston added that he finds that cleaning the dog's teeth can also be very helpful in healing crippling problems. Why? Dr. Ralston believes that tartar from teeth can break off, enter the dog's body, and be deposited around the joints.

The veterinarian explained a basic way he judges how to modify initial therapy as the dog starts to get better (which usually happens in about two weeks). "One key we use is when the animal just refuses to take the medicine he's been taking until now without complaining about it. We feel that the dog knows best—after all, it's *his* body and *his* spirit—and so we ask the owner to let us test the dog again at this point. What we usually find is that the dog was right: The dosage he needs has gone way down, and he shouldn't be taking the original dosage anymore."

I asked Dr. Ralston to comment on the use of intravenous vitamin C, which was the treatment of choice for serious cases of some crippling disorders in the early 1980s when I wrote the first book. "While that's no longer the usual preferred treatment these days," he said, "it *becomes* the preferred treatment if the animal's body *says* it is."

Hip Dysplasia

Jack Long, V.M.D., stated that "hip dysplasia strikes fear and sadness into the hearts of many dog owners and breeders. It causes degeneration, pain, and lameness in the hips of many dogs." In a recent interview with me, he explained that the term *dysplasia* means malformation. A normal hip is a true ball-and-socket joint. Dysplasia produces joints in which the ball doesn't fit correctly in the socket. Severely affected dogs cannot move their hips at all.

Let me tell you about Leigh, a golden retriever who suffered hip dysplasia many years ago. Leigh belonged to Dr. Robert Goldstein, and it was this dog's affliction that led the veterinarian and his brother, Dr. Marty Goldstein, to shift the emphasis of their practices from orthodox to holistic.

Leigh had developed symptoms of hip dysplasia when he was little more than a puppy. It was rated grade 3, radiographically. (The disorder is rated on a scale from 0 to 5; a grade-3 case is a pretty bad one.) Leigh had been fed exclusively one of the "better"—and more expensive—commercial dog foods. By the time he was six years old, he had "much difficulty in getting up," Dr. Robert Goldstein told me, "and was in almost constant pain. He also had chronic skin and ear problems. Leigh was getting long-acting cortisone injections every two to three weeks and topical medications for his dermatitis." Surgery seemed to be the next step.

Luckily for Leigh—and luckily for all the dogs and cats whose lives have been saved by the veterinarians Goldstein (see, for instance, their exciting new work with cancer detailed in chapter 11)—the brothers were then studying human nutrition and were "in the process of transforming our own health," Dr. Marty Goldstein told me. "After seeing the tremendous improvement in our own general well-being, we decided to adapt the same basic rules for our own pets."

The results for Leigh, both veterinarians said, "were astounding."

The common belief is that dysplasia is hereditary, or genetic. This belief, of course, makes the disorder appear to be virtually impossible to prevent. As long ago as 1981, however, holistic veterinarians were telling me that hip dysplasia was due to nutritional deficiencies before and after conception and during puppyhood, when the bones and joints are developing rapidly. This view, of course, makes the disorder quite preventable, and several holistic veterinarians reported that hip dysplasia had completely disappeared in their practices in dogs treated preventively merely with vitamin C. Nutritionally enlightened breeders from around the world were reporting the same experience.

For this new book, Dr. Ralston maintained firmly that hip dysplasia is not a genetic problem at all but a disorder caused solely by a lack of proper preventive nutrition. This might explain the observation sent me by Dr. Long, that while many breeders in recent years have been using "genetic selection" (x-raying the breeding stock before use) to try to prevent the puppies from having dysplasia, "many pups still develop hip dysplasia. And most breeds have had their breed standards for hip conformation decline over the past twenty years." (Dr. Long believes that genetics can influence whether a dog is susceptible to certain health conditions.)

Citing in part the research of Robert Nolan, D.V.M., a past president of the American Veterinary Medical Association, Dr. Ralston said that "it's the early nutrition that's the cause of the hip dysplasia problem, and not this genetic misperception, which needs to be straightened out."

Dr. Long stressed that another important factor in damage to ligaments and connective tissue is too little—or too much—exercise. Excessive exercise may be an especially strong factor in work, sport, and high-energy breeds.

Nino Aloro, D.V.M., pointed out to me that, while hip dysplasia has traditionally been thought confined to large-breed dogs, it is now appearing in shih tzus, Pekingese, and Pomeranians. Perhaps that lends more credence to the idea that heredity is not the only cause.

The orthodox therapy for hip dysplasia is drugs and surgery. Dr. Ralston commented: "I don't find this business of surgery works. You take a heavy dog [most dogs with hip dysplasia are large]; that dog needs all the strength he can have to maintain that joint. And if you go into that joint and start cutting, you do nothing but make it weaker." The veterinarian added that an owner had recently come to him who had been told "he should spend $5,000 to have a hip operation on his dog." Dr. Ralston told the owner that he didn't have to spend that much money for a holistic approach that "really can work."

Drs. Long and Ralston use, instead of surgery, a technique called proliferative therapy. "I was trained in this by an M.D. in Germany," Dr. Ralston said, "and the technique has been like a godsend for me."

In proliferative therapy, long, fine needles are placed around the joint and ligaments in such a way as to stimulate *connective* tissue growth and strength. (Remember that the problem with hip dysplasia is that the ball is unstable within the hip socket.)

Dr. Long said that "very severe cases can be treated with implants of very small gold-plated beads injected into selected acupuncture points to provide continuous stimulation."

Dr. Ralston, explaining that the gold beads "set up a little battery in there to relieve the pain," commented: "The problem I had with gold beads was that the body would recognize them as a foreign substance and would sometimes move them around. So a lot of times I'd have to repeat the procedure.

"However," the veterinarian added, "with proliferative therapy, you create a permanent cure because it causes the body to lay down the tissue that's needed to tighten the joints." He noted that animal studies have proved that. In rabbits, for instance, it may take only seven days for the body to create the needed tissue, "although sometimes you may have to repeat the procedure at that time."

Dr. Ralston will also choose one homeopathic from among several that help tighten joints, and he uses natural remedies to reduce pain. Once the dog is recovered, he no longer needs any of these therapies.

Dr. Long told me that the therapy he uses for hip dysplasia and ligament degeneration diseases also includes some or all of the following treatments: vitamins C and E and the trace mineral selenium; selected herbal and homeopathic remedies, enzymes; collagen supplements; acupuncture; and chiropractic. Of course, the treatment he lists as number one is a high-quality diet, "preferably home prepared." (See chapters 1 and 2.)

The veterinarian stated that his current approach "has been quite successful in most cases."

"Wobbler" (Cervical Syndrome) Disorder

This disorder involves destruction of the collagen of the neck (cervical) area of the spine. Since collagen is the body's "glue," some of the symptoms lead to the term "wobbler" disorder.

Dr. Ralston told me that cervical syndrome is "a more intense problem" than other crippling disorders. (Heather's story in this section will illustrate vividly why the veterinarian made that statement.) "I have fair to good success in restoring these dogs," Dr. Ralston told me. I asked his estimate of the degree of success *orthodox* therapy has. "I don't know of any orthodox therapy that will help in wobbler syndrome," he said.* Then, because doctors are well aware that there might be a therapy somewhere that they don't know about, Dr. Ralston added, "Maybe there's somebody out there who knows of an orthodox technique that can help. If so, I'd appreciate hearing about it."

For this very serious disorder, Dr. Ralston depends heavily on proliferative therapy, mentioned earlier in this chapter. "But you have to treat the dog all the way up to the cervical discs." As mentioned previously, these discs are high up on the spine, in the neck area. "Then you get your best results by combining this therapy with good nutrition." The veterinarian added: "Once again, this is an unnecessary disorder caused by poor nutrition."

The following case history of a severely advanced case of wobbler syndrome was reported in my first book—when holistic veterinary medicine was still in its infancy. I ask you to imagine at which point during the two years of unsuccessful orthodox therapy you might have opted to put your pet mercifully "to sleep," if she were going through all this.

Heather was a nine-year-old Doberman pinscher whose descent into hell, as it were, started with difficulty walking up and down steps. Then she developed a urinary infection and started falling down when she went outside to urinate. Next, Heather began to howl and tremble in pain as she tried to walk. She became unable to see in front of her. If you tossed something at her to catch, she would just stand and let it hit her nose, because she didn't know it was coming.

---

* In reviewing the manuscript for this chapter, Dr. Altman commented that there are surgical techniques that can relieve pressure on the spinal cord and stabilize the cervical vertebrae.

Heather's personality changed, as will ours when we are constantly debilitated, in pain, and scared. Children, whom Heather had always considered her "pets," now terrified her. If someone raised a voice in her presence, she would go into a panic.

Next it became a terrible chore for Heather to walk: Her legs would slip out from under her, and she kept falling down in a heap, her legs flailing helter-skelter. At one point, she went into a spasm; her body was contorted into the shape of a "doughnut," as veterinarian Frank L. Earl's files described it. Her owner stood and watched helplessly for at least five minutes as the dog suffered a cramp that glued her nose to her tail.

Heather's walking problems became even worse: Her limbs were rotating outward at a grotesque angle, and her legs were slipping out from under her as if they were made of jelly. You may have guessed by now that Heather's body was becoming "unglued." As we discussed earlier, collagen is the body's "glue," and with Heather's disorder and other collagen disorders holistic veterinarians use natural ways to help the body produce enough of this glue.

Six orthodox veterinarians tried unsuccessfully to help Heather for almost two years while she kept deteriorating. Finally, she was scheduled for a dangerous decompression operation on her spinal cord, but her owners took her to Dr. Earl instead.

This holistic veterinarian started Heather on intravenous vitamin C, and after four days one of her many symptoms, bladder incontinence, had completely disappeared. The other symptoms took a bit longer to go away. The last I knew of her, she was taking several nutritional substances by mouth and had been totally without symptoms for more than a year and a half.

Dr. Long reported in 1981 that in treating cases similar to Heather's, he used acupuncture along with oral vitamin supplements, especially ascorbate zinc and B complex. He stated that this therapy resulted in "excellent results in four out of five of these 'wobbler' (or cervical syndrome) cases.

"Most of these animals," Dr. Long said, "have been previously treated with steroids with no improvement. Some have had myelograms showing narrowing of the cervical spinal cord—or a spondylolisthesis. There is usually a noticeable, sometimes dramatic, improvement after the first acupuncture treatment. Only six to eight acupuncture treatments are usually required. The pet is then maintained on nutritional therapy."

Dr. Long added that the four out of five pets who respond return to *completely normal* function.

For this new book, Dr. Long okayed his previous statements but added, "Some severe cases do better with gold bead implants."

Dr. Ralston reemphasized that wobbler syndrome usually has a strong component of a nutritional deficiency in the pet's diet. "Sometimes, though," he said, "the deficiency comes from the mother's diet while she was pregnant. And she passes that deficiency over to her babies. A deficiency that an animal gets in the uterus (what we call the water world) is hard to correct out here in what we call the air world. However, it can be done." (For instance, see the next chapter for how Dr. Ralston used holistic therapy to help an animal born with an incompletely developed eye.)

Posterior Paralysis (Spinal Myelopathy, Spinal Degeneration, Degenerative Myelopathy)

If your dog develops this disorder, your orthodox veterinarian might ask you how helpless you are willing to let your pet become before you put him permanently "to sleep." Yet, as long ago as 1981, Wendell O. Belfield, D.V.M., reported healing twenty-five out of thirty cases simply with the use of vitamin C and selected other nutrients.

As I list the symptoms of this devastating disorder, you will easily see why the orthodox veterinary medical profession often prefers to put dogs with this problem out of their misery.

If your dog gets this disorder, here's what she's in for: pain, progressive paralysis of the back leg muscles, curving of the spine, loss of control of her bowels, loss of control of her bladder. If you just touch her on her hindquarters, she may fall down as if you had hit

her with a baseball bat. As her back leg muscles deteriorate, your pet
will start pathetically trying to drag herself around on just her two
front legs. Simply picture your pet with that last symptom, and you
will see why owners seldom fight the suggestion of euthanasia for
this disorder.

You might think no one disorder could get worse than this; but
spinal myelopathy can progress farther, affecting the front legs, so
that the dog can no longer even try to drag herself along at all. Then
the disorder can progress even farther until it affects the brain.

With this grave disorder of posterior paralysis, modern holistic
veterinarians have good success by choosing what is best for the
specific dog from the large arsenal they have today to help crippling
disorders. These new therapies are detailed throughout this chapter
for similar disorders.

Dr. Long specified, as this book went to press, that "a wide range of
nutritional therapies, including certain amino acids and antioxidants"
are now recommended even by some conventional veterinarians. The
holistic veterinarian, commenting that he considers degenerative
myelopathy to be "a *major* nutritional and energy imbalance," wrote
me that he has good results with the following combination of nondrug, nonsurgery therapies:

- Vitamin C by intervenous injection for five days, then orally
  after that
- Vitamin E
- Vitamin B complex
- Vitamin B_{12} injections daily
- Amino acids, including amino caproic acid
- Acupuncture treatments
- Thyroid supplements if indicated

For a specific case history of posterior paralysis, I chose one from
this book's first edition. I thought you might like to know the kind
of success holistic veterinarians had in 1981, when holistic veterinary medicine was in its infancy, in an era when many of today's
therapies weren't available.

Bowzer was a seven-year-old beagle mix treated by Michael W. Lemmon, D.V.M. "Bowzer first came into my office with such extreme weakness in his rear legs," Dr. Lemmon told me, "that he could not walk at all. After five days on I.V. vitamin C and other nutrients—such as vitamin E, 400 units, and trace minerals—Bowzer began to walk well enough to be sent home on a regimen of oral vitamin C and a multivitamin/multimineral supplement." Soon thereafter, the dog was able to walk absolutely normally. The last I heard of Bowzer—many months later—he was still walking fine on his maintenance therapy of a few oral supplements a day.

Ruptured Discs

Symptoms of ruptured discs can include paralysis in the hindquarters and legs and inability to control bowels and urine. The daily addition of vitamins C and E, as suggested in chapters 2 and 4, will help prevent this problem. As long ago as 1981, Dr. Belfield reported that even in the more serious cases, it usually took only three to five days to bring an animal "back to its feet." He recommended that you try nutritional therapy before taking the pet for expensive and risky spinal surgery.

However, Drs. Robert and Marty Goldstein added a cautionary note: "We feel that this is a very delicate decision for an owner to make. In those cases in which the ruptured disc is putting a lot of pressure on the spinal cord (those cases in which surgery would definitely be beneficial), waiting days to see if a nutritional program helps could lead to permanent paralysis."

For this new book, Dr. Price reported that he finds chicken cartilage to be very helpful for ruptured discs. "I may also do a little spinal manipulation," he said. In the first book, vitamin C was reported as the treatment of choice. Dr. Price says he still uses this vitamin, usually orally.

Dr. Long recently wrote me he finds that "acupuncture is very effective along with nutritional therapies" in treating ruptured discs.

Dr. Ralston—who, like Dr. Price, was one of the pioneering holistic veterinarians—told me for this new book that he has a completely different idea about ruptured discs than he used to have: "Dogs will develop some gout along their spine," he said, "but it's usually deposits of toxins. And very often they are due to a deficiency in the thyroid gland." As mentioned earlier, Dr. Ralston finds that deficiencies in this gland are behind many cases of crippling disorders. He pointed out that in bringing this gland back to health, he doesn't use a synthetic thyroid drug. Instead he uses a prostaglandin. Prostaglandins are nutrients that act in the body as short-term hormones; the thyroid gland's major function is to produce the hormone thyroxin. The veterinarian notes that the prostaglandin "causes the gland to be able to work well on its own." He adds that "when we unnaturally supply something from outside that the body needs to be supplied from inside the body, we can get into trouble. We're *substituting* something for what nature had in mind. So we don't do that: Instead, we use the prostaglandin, which causes the thyroid gland to produce on its own what it's supposed to."

Summary

If you haven't found your dog's diagnosed crippling disorder mentioned in this chapter, this by no means indicates that holistic veterinary medicine doesn't successfully treat the problem. Instead, it indicates that holistic doctors use as guidelines for crippling problems the overall nutrients mentioned early in this chapter, and then they treat what's off base within the individual dog's body rather than basing the therapy solely on a diagnostic disease label.

To end this chapter, I'll add one more case history that focuses not only on the physical aspects but also on the emotional aspects of an animal's illness. For this book's companion book, *Keep Your Cat Healthy the Natural Way,* a number of holistic veterinarians told me that, while cats are strongly affected by their people's emotional problems, dogs will completely xerox them. (Some veterinarians have said that dogs, when dealing with strong feelings in their human loved ones, become "emotional sponges." We can use that, of course, in a positive way—by cuddling our dog more often, speaking to him in a reassuring voice, frolicking with him in a happy manner—when he may have had reason to pick up the idea from us that something is terribly wrong.)

I have even been told of dogs whose person had suffered an injury to a specific part of the spine in an accident and who a short time later developed similar damage to the same area of the spine although the dogs had been in no accident at all.

One veterinarian who particularly stressed to me the idea that "animals tend to somatacize the emotional imbalances that are going on in the family" was Neal K. Weiner, D.V.M. "Ted was brought to me with a bad back," he told me. "We found that the dog had spondylosis of the spine. Muscle testing [kinesiology] for Ted's *emotional* state indicated that the dog felt hopeless," Dr. Weiner said. "I don't think the dog was by nature hopeless. I think he had now found himself in a hopeless *environment*."

The veterinarian, who was a friend of the family, knew that Ted's guardians weren't getting along well and that Ted's female person had just had a heart attack. Commenting that sometimes heart problems come from a lack of joy in life, Dr. Weiner added that the dog's new hopelessness may have come from the fact that "he wasn't in a joyful home anymore."

The veterinarian's basic physical therapy was a chiropractic adjustment to the dog's spine. But Dr. Weiner told Ted's guardians— "respectfully"—that Ted seemed to be dealing with some hopelessness, and "I think it's coming from his home life." Dr. Weiner added that "within days that poor hopeless dog turned around and became much better."

This veterinarian commented that, as his experience in holistic veterinary medicine increases, he becomes more and more interested in "what has happened to somatacize the illness in the body." He increasingly finds that he is not dealing so much with a body getting ill, but "with a spirit *in* a body getting ill."

References

1. Wendell O. Belfield, D.V.M., and Martin Zucker, *How to Have a Healthier Dog* (Garden City, New York: Doubleday and Co., Inc.), 1981, p. 223.
2. M. J. Shively, D.V.M., M.S., Ph.D., *Dog Fancy*, December 1981, p. 17.
3. *Guide to Acupuncture for Animals*, The National Association for Veterinary Acupuncture, P.O. Box 5181, Fullerton, CA 92635, 1977.
4. *Veterinary Medicine/Small Animal Clinician*, September 1981, pp. 1307–12.
5. *Guide to Acupuncture for Animals,* op. cit.

Chapter 6

"I'm always amazed at the ability of the eye to repair itself, if you just give it the natural support it needs.

"I once treated an elderly dog who had been blind and deaf for six years. Acupuncture and nutritional therapy permanently restored both senses to him."

—*Norman C. Ralston, D.V.M.*

Problems of the Eye

"I find homeopathic phosphorus and the antioxidant glutathione to be of great help in treating glaucoma.

"Glutathione used with several other antioxidants also greatly improves the eyesight of most dogs with cataracts. Even if the cataracts are very advanced when I see the animal, his vision may improve. Seldom do dogs with very advanced cataracts get any worse."

—*S. Allen Price, D.V.M.*

"I just don't have a problem treating corneal ulcers, period."

—*Richard J. Kearns, D.V.M. (in 1981)*

A Plea Not to Put Your Blind or Otherwise Handicapped Dog "Out of His Misery"

Before we go into ways you can help your dog with eye problems, let me put in a plea on behalf of your blind or otherwise handicapped pet, who can't put in his own plea in words you understand: Please don't put him to sleep. (I dislike that phrase because I think it is a euphemism that sometimes lulls veterinarians and owners alike to do less than they might be able to do to help an animal.) I'm not in a position to tell you, of course, that there is never, ever a case where putting your pet "to sleep" isn't kinder than letting him suffer through a painful, hopeless existence. However, as this book shows over and over, there are countless pets deemed hopeless who can be easily and inexpensively helped by the newer field of holistic veterinary medicine.

To make that point as strongly as I can, let me start this chapter with two of the more dramatic case histories I've come across in over three decades of reporting on new medical techniques, orthodox and alternative, for humans and animals. Norman C. Ralston, D.V. M., recently told me of an elderly handicapped dog, Mark, who responded superbly to alternative therapy. What had been wrong with him? He had been both blind and deaf. And he had been blind and deaf for six years before holistic treatment. (Dr. Ralston commented that, while the dog had been getting along okay in his sightless and soundless world for six years, "When he found out he could see and hear again, this guy was like to have gone crazy with happiness.")

How did Dr. Ralston achieve this seeming miracle? He explained: "We started with an acupuncture technique called 'circling the dragon,' in which we circled the eyes with fine needles and left them in place for twenty minutes." Then the veterinarian used kinesiology to test Mark's body for the nutrients it needed and began giving them to the dog.

"Mark first began to respond to sounds," Dr. Ralston continued. "Before long, he started to be able to see things. He couldn't see them clearly, because he would gaze at something a long time, apparently trying to figure out what it was. But he progressed to the point where he could see fairly well."

Was this recovery some sort of a short-lived remission? Did Mark soon fall back into a world devoid of sound and images? "Mark lived to be twenty-one and a half years old, still able to see and hear," Dr. Ralston said. "And he was still a lively cuss."

The other case history also comes from Dr. Ralston. "A little girl recently brought in an abandoned puppy who had an incompletely developed left eye," he related to me. If an entity is born with half an eye, common sense dictates that nothing can be done, doesn't it? After all, you can't stick the deformed animal back in the womb to give it more developmental time under better nutritional conditions. And certainly an animal can't start growing body parts after he's born.

"We started that animal on the nutrients it tested out to be deficient in, primarily vitamin A," Dr. Ralston said, "and, by golly, that animal's eye has developed quite nicely. It will never be *exactly* normal, but nobody would know that dog had ever had an incomplete eye."

Even if your dog doesn't respond to treatment, remember that dogs are not devastated psychologically by handicaps such as blindness in the way that people often are. In addition, our pets actually *need* their eyesight less than we do. For instance, a dog put into a strange room will go about exploring his new surroundings not with his eyes, but with his nose. (Who cares what there is to *see* here; what is there to *smell?*)

As John E. Craige, V.M.D., put it in the first book: Blind animals "get along quite well. They can . . . do almost everything a sighted animal can do. They don't have any psychological traumatism as do blind people."

I would like to quote another statement pointing out that not only should you let your handicapped dog live out his life, you might even relax and stop feeling sorry for him. The following is a quote from a book by Pat Widmer, an animal nutritionist. Widmer has rescued numerous abandoned animals, so she has ended up caring for many handicapped dogs and cats.

"My so-called 'handicapped' pets have never demonstrated any overwhelming problems and have in many instances proved that they can be just as obnoxious as anyone else," Widmer said. "Blind dogs and cats have no difficulty, provided you don't move all the furniture every day. . . . Lameness or lack of a limb is meaningless to animals."[1]

I myself have often watched with dismay as a three-legged dog came hobbling in my direction, out on his walk with his person. However, I have watched these dogs go past me, walking as fast as any four-legged dog and enjoying their walk just as thoroughly. I came to realize that the animals' handicap didn't depress the animals—only me. If the owners had "kindly" put these dogs to sleep, they would not have been alive to enjoy this walk or many other moments they might tell us they enjoy tremendously.

I want to tell you about the dog called Sarah Bernhardt. Apparently she was named that because she milked her disability to get all the sympathy she could. That disability was the lack of two of her four legs, so we can understand her desire for sympathy. I recently saw Sarah featured on TV. Because of her plight, a new type of prosthesis was developed. Sarah had learned to walk well with the two devices, and the TV program showed her now struggling valiantly to learn to climb stairs with them. The program's host said the same thing I was thinking: That despite how hard she had to struggle, "She looks happy!"

Now Sarah, a dog that many owners would have euthanized, is making guest appearances all around and providing hope for other dogs.

Let me add one more thought before we go on to natural therapies for eye problems: I hope you always keep in mind, as you read about successful natural therapies anywhere in this book, that holistic M.D.s offer similar hope for us humans.

An Overview of the Holistic Approach to Eye Problems

A number of doctors have told me that they have found an ancient teaching of Chinese acupuncturists to be true: that liver problems play a prominent role in eye disorders. Thus, stimulating the acupuncture liver point often helps heal the eyes. As Marty Goldstein, D.V.M., once told me: In acupuncture, it is believed that the energy forces feeding the health of the liver are the same forces feeding the health of the eyes. "I believe," Dr. Goldstein said, "the majority of eye problems are not primarily eye problems, but rather secondary reflections of disorders of the liver. As a matter of fact," he added, "I have rarely seen a pet with a chronic eye problem who tested out to have a normal liver function." As we say elsewhere in this chapter, vitamin A has traditionally been known as "the eye vitamin." Dr. Goldstein commented that "in actuality, vitamin A is of great importance in preventing and treating eye problems because it helps the liver perform its detoxification chores." The liver's master plan in our animals' bodies, and in ours, is to filter out poisons from our system.

Interestingly, glutathione, a newly discovered nutritional substance that is now often used for eye problems, also helps the liver detoxify our bodies.

Agreeing that the health of the liver is of prime importance in eye health, Dr. Ralston recently added that "the eye also needs energy that comes from the brain stem. So do the ears." (The governing organ for ears is the kidney.) "Once we find out what's causing the problem in the individual animal, we can correct the organ problem or the brain stem energy by supplying the proper nutrients." The veterinarian added that often ribonucleic acid is very helpful.

Dr. Ralston added that testing the eye with kinesiology allows him to catch problems early, even if there are not yet any noticeable symptoms. "The eye should pulse at ten," he said. "If it pulses at anything less, then we know we have to start feeding it nutritionally."

Although we're covering here common therapies for eye problems, the bottom line—as always for holistic veterinarians—is to treat whatever tests out to be amiss in the individual animal's body.

"People ask me what do I use to treat so-and-so a disorder," Dr. Ralston told me, "and I say I really don't know. I have to ask the animal's body first. If you override what the body tells you, you're really just *guessing* what the animal needs.

"There were times when I felt sure the animal needed this or that nutrient," he added, "but when I tested the animal's body, it told me no. Then, maybe two or three weeks later, the body would say yes. In other words, when I first thought the animal needed the nutrient, it was attending to something else that was more important."

With all that in mind, the following covers therapies that most usually fill the individual needs of animals with one of several eye problems.

Glaucoma

Glaucoma is too much pressure behind the eye's cornea. The pressure is caused by a blocking of the normal flow of the fluid in the space between the cornea and lens (intraocular area). As you probably know, if not successfully treated, glaucoma will cause blindness.

Recently S. Allen Price, D.V.M., told me that to reduce intraocular pressure, he uses homeopathic phosphorus, at a strength of about 30C, usually once a week. "And I use glutathione," he added, "an antioxidant that is most abundant in the intraocular area when that

area is normal. I've found these two nutrients to be a big aid in dogs
with glaucoma."

Dr. Price told of two shih tzus "who used to have a glaucoma
problem. The treatment corrected the disorder in both the animals.
Now their owner, for maintenance therapy, just gives the homeopathic phosphorus once every six weeks."

Dr. Ralston added that "of course, vitamin A is our eye vitamin,
and we always check if the animal with glaucoma is deficient in it."
The relationship between healthy eyes and vitamin A has been established for a very long time.

Like Dr. Price, Dr. Ralston also uses the nutrient glutathione,
"which cleans the eye from behind." That doesn't mean this nutrient
has to be inserted behind the eye by surgery. If you put a natural
substance into the body, it will find its own way to where it's naturally supposed to go. And remember that glutathione naturally is
abundant in the space behind the eye. "As soon as you've cleaned up
that eye," Dr. Ralston said, "the animal's vision will improve."

He added that this use of glutathione is based on research going
back to the 1920s that has been validated and enhanced over the
years since.

"Once I've got the animals cleaned up and straightened out," Dr.
Ralston said, "I put them on a multivitamin/mineral supplement
that covers all the bases. And then I check up on them every two or
three months to make sure they're still doing all right."

Cataracts

I am often told that cataracts are the most common eye problem
in dogs.

Dr. Ralston told me the following case history: "We have one old
dog now, a little mixed terrier, who was almost blind because of
cataracts. We used nutrition and a homeopathic remedy, and now—
at the age of fourteen—she can see excellently." The veterinarian
added that "Actually, the owner was telling me recently that she
had the door to the yard open, but the screen door locked—so that

the dog could see into the yard, but couldn't get out. And the dog kept running back and forth, looking at something. The owner started looking herself, but she couldn't see anything. Finally, maybe 100 yards away, the owner saw that her dog was fixated on watching a squirrel in a tree."

John Fudens, D.V. M., recently sent me two case histories of dogs with cataracts, saying that the histories were closely representative of many more he could send me from his practice. I will give the less dramatic history first.

Mozart, a male wire-haired terrier, was brought to Dr. Fudens' clinic in November of 1993. Mozart had skin problems, as well as cataracts in both eyes. What Dr. Fudens saw as part of the disease process was that the dog "was highly toxic from heavy vaccination, commercial foods, cortisone given for skin itch, et cetera."

Dr. Fudens told me that basically what he did over four or five months was "to detoxify Mozart of the drugs, poisons, and the vaccines using homeopathy, nux vomica, and thuja. At the same time, I put him on a completely natural diet, and I gave him a liver glandular extract and a complex immune glandular to support all the glands of the immune system. I also put him on some Chinese herbs for a detox and some unsaturated fatty acids for his skin and coat." These fatty acids replaced the drug cortisone that Mozart had previously been given for his skin problems.

The veterinarian continued: "In early February—having cleaned out his body of the drugs, vaccines, and other poisons—I started him on a constitutional, silica, for the cataracts. My records tell me that in less than two months, the cataracts were almost gone."

Shortly after, Dr. Fudens started Mozart on another constitutional, sulfur. "By then," the veterinarian told me, "Mozart had no cataracts at all. But he still had some remaining skin problems, which cleared up immensely with the sulfur."

Dr. Fudens repeated the sulfur only once. "He has been totally cured since," the veterinarian told me more than three years later. "There are no cataracts, and his skin is still doing great."

Now I'd like to tell you about Casper, whose case history is a bit more dramatic. It might, therefore, give those of you whose dog is considered "hopeless" because of cataracts more hope and inspiration that your companion can be helped. "Casper is a Maltese," Dr. Fudens told me, adding a comment not common for veterinarians giving a case history: "a great little dog." The veterinarian said that, although Casper was only three years old, "he had very severe damage to his whole immune system, damage caused by drugs—cortisones, antibiotics for ear and skin problems—and heavy vaccination. He had had cataracts in both eyes for two years, and he was just about totally blind and ready to have cataract surgery."

When Casper came to Dr. Fudens' clinic, "the husband was very receptive," the veterinarian told me, "but the wife was extremely 'stiff' about the idea of alternative therapy and refused it. They left, and I thought I'd never see them or Casper again."

But the veterinarian did see Casper again, primarily, he thinks, "because of the husband." At the end of January 1995, Dr. Fudens began his program with Casper: "pretty much in the way I do with all of these cases. I started detoxifying him of the drugs, chemical toxins, poisons—following the detoxification after a while by the vaccine detox. It took about four or five months to clean out Casper's body."

During this time, Dr. Fudens also had the dog on Chinese herbs and liver and immune glandulars for his cataracts, and unsaturated fatty acids for his skin and coat (replacing the previously given cortisone and antibiotic drugs). Casper was also receiving high amounts of vitamin C and other antioxidants.

"Casper did very well during this period of detoxification," Dr. Fudens said. "At the end of May in '95, I started the constitutional, and the remedy I chose for his specific needs was homeopathic sulfur. Within one month, Casper's eyes were starting to clear. The right eye was almost normal. He was seeing out the window, responding to people. He could follow his owner's finger."

At this point, the husband-owner was, Dr. Fudens told me, "absolutely amazed." And the skeptical wife? "Totally flabbergasted."

Soon after, Casper's cataracts disappeared completely.

"Casper still has total health," Dr. Fudens told me three years later. "And his attitude and personality have improved—he is more friendly and social than he ever was. Actually, his owners asked me if I should consider toning him down: They were afraid he might have too much energy and spunk. And yet he is much, much calmer with people than he used to be, and he's not barky or growly anymore."

In short, "Casper's whole attitude and demeanor have changed. And his eyes are just perfect; his skin is perfect." Dr. Fudens, who doesn't like to give even natural remedies when a dog doesn't need outside help, said, "At this point, we're leaving Casper alone."

When, as this book went to press, I asked Dr. Fudens for a last-minute update on Casper, the dog was still doing fine. The veterinarian's only update was that "the wife is now one of the biggest believers and promoters of homeopathy and [other] holistic therapies."

A medical dictionary will tell you that cataracts are a filmy sort of substance in the lens of the eye that prevents animals and people from seeing clearly. As the substance grows thicker, it becomes opaque, so that the victim can no longer see at all. But what is this mysterious substance *made* of? "Cataracts are basically accumulations of toxins in the eyes," Richard J. Kearns, D.V.M., told me for the first book, reminding us that "a natural diet has few or no toxins."

For this new book, Dr. Ralston specified one of the toxins in an unnatural diet that can cause cataracts. "Dogs and people have several types of tears, and one type is an oil. Nowadays there are a lot of unnatural hydrogenated oils in our diets and those of our pets. And when these oils get broken down in the body, it doesn't know how to handle them. So eventually these unnatural oils make their way out into the eye and cause mutations in the lens that are known as cataracts."

Thus, as Dr. Ralston indicated some fifteen years after Dr. Kearns, the less unnatural food your companion eats, the less likely he is to get cataracts. Dr. Kearns also pointed out that if an animal has had cataracts successfully dissolved, they are likely to come back again if you keep your pet on toxic foods.

You will note that Dr. Kearns mentioned that natural therapy *dis-*

solves cataracts. The common cataract surgery *cuts* cataracts out after giving pets potentially dangerous anesthetics to cover the obvious great pain of having something cut out of their eye. Also, a cataract operation removes the lens of the eye (the cataract is in the lens, remember), so that normal eyesight is really never restored.

"I don't recommend the cataract surgery," Dr. Ralston said. "In my orthodox veterinary schooling, I was trained in that surgery, and I did it one time and said, 'That's enough; I'm not doing that anymore.' It was not successful, and when I later referred animals to veterinary ophthalmologists for the surgery, they didn't have the success I wanted, either." Dr. Ralston stated that using glutathione to clean up the eye has much more success than surgery seems to, and without the risks or expense.

Dr. Price uses glutathione and vitamin A (mentioned previously as "the eye vitamin"), as well as the antioxidants selenium and vitamins C and E, which were used for cataracts in the early 1980s.

"We've had a considerable number of dogs in which one or both eyes have substantially improved so they can see much better," Dr. Price said. "In most of the others—who have more advanced cataracts—they don't get any worse."

Let me talk a bit more about the use of vitamin E and selenium, mentioned above. Decades ago, veterinarian L. O. Brooksby reported, in the technical veterinary literature,[2] excellent results in three hundred dogs with cataracts and nuclear sclerosis. The doctor injected the nutrients intramuscularly and noted that improvement generally occurred by the third injection. A particularly dramatic recovery from cataracts was made by a ten-year-old shih tzu. She had lost so much of her eyesight that once, when she was left alone outside, she couldn't even see the swimming pool in front of her and fell into it. After only three injections by Dr. Brooksby, the little animal could see so well that she not only unerringly could sidestep the swimming pool, she was catching Frisbees in midair.

You might also check with a holistic veterinarian to find out if vitamin B_{15} drops might help your dog. When I researched the first edition, Dr. Kearns reported that these drops, along with, again, vitamin E, selenium, and a natural diet, helped stop the growth of cataracts 70 percent of the time—even in late cases. He added that this therapy actually *dissolved* advanced cataracts in some 30 percent of the cases.

I find it interesting that when vitamin B_{15} was first discovered and early researchers set to work to discover what health benefits it might have, they were discouraged—because the only benefit they could find was that it dissolved cataracts in dogs' eyes.

Macular Edema

Macular edema is an abnormal pooling of fluids (edema) in the macular area of the eye's retina.

"For this problem," Dr. Price said, "I've recently been using shark cartilage, about one gram daily for every ten pounds of body weight." He explains that cartilage contains a protein that "stops the production of new, unessential blood vessels that are getting in the retinal area, rupturing, and causing that edema."

Dr. Price added that in humans, macular edema "has been improved considerably with the use of shark, beef, or chicken cartilage."

Abscesses inside the Eye

Abscesses are holes filled with pus, surrounded by swollen tissue. They're caused by infection. Obviously, you don't want them anywhere on your dog's body—and certainly not inside her eye. Dr. Marty Goldstein once told me of a veterinary ophthalmologist (eye specialist) who asked him to help treat a dog with abscesses inside the eye. The dog had already lost one of his eyes to the same problem, and two years later the animal had developed abscesses inside his remaining eye. The ophthalmologist was aware that his orthodox medical approach was not helping the eye and asked Dr. Goldstein if acupuncture could help. Dr. Goldstein told me that it took only two acupuncture treatments before the problem was "completely controlled." The veterinarian added that he treated the dog at the acupuncture liver point.

Progressive Retinal Atrophy

This condition is a shrinking (atrophy) of the blood vessels in the retina. And it is called progressive because it does just that: It progresses, relentlessly, until the dog is blind.

Dr. Price recently told me that with standard therapy, most dogs with this disorder don't get well. Dr. Ralston stated that he has had "very good success" with holistic therapy. He said that, like other eye problems, progressive retinal atrophy is usually caused by not enough nutrition to the eye. "You can target the nutritional deficiencies in the individual animal and treat them." The veterinarian added that ribonucleic acid often proves to be of great help in treating this very serious eye disorder. So does glutathione, mentioned in the section on glaucoma as cleaning out the back part of the eye.

Drs. Marty Goldstein and Robert Goldstein, V.M.D., told me of Tina, a ten-year-old poodle who had progressive retinal atrophy. Veterinary ophthalmology specialists had found that there was "nothing to be done" for Tina. The holistic veterinarians simply "did an analysis of the dog's body, found out all the ways it was out of chemical balance, and restored the balance nutritionally." The last I heard of Tina, her progressive retinal atrophy had not progressed for a full three years, belying the first word in the disorder's name.

Corneal Ulcers

Ulcers on the cornea of the eye are a serious condition, and I have read books on orthodox veterinary medicine warning that without early treatment, the pet may end up having to have his eye cut out surgically. However, as long ago as 1981, holistic veterinarians such as Drs. Robert and Marty Goldstein were telling me that "a lot of times corneal ulcers that are incurable with standard drugs will heal

with natural therapy." And Dr. Kearns said, "I just don't have a problem treating corneal ulcers, period."

The veterinarians working on this new book indicated that the
earlier information is still valid, as long as you keep in mind the
newer nutrients also now in use.

The earlier veterinarians were using vitamin E and the herb eyebright. When the case called for it, Dr. Kearns would also sometimes
start off with an orthodox technique: a simple operation that brings
the third eyelid up over the ulcer. The third eyelid is that membrane
you can see in the inner corner of your pet's eye—if she'll let you
poke at her like that. Why bring this eyelid up over the ulcer? "There
is no blood supply to the cornea," Dr. Kearns explained. "That is
why corneal ulcers are generally so hard to heal, because there is no
way for any healing substance you put into the body to get circulated into the cornea. The third eyelid does, however, have circulation, and when placed over the ulcer, it will lend part of its
circulation to the ulcer." In other words, the third eyelid will help
bring the medicine to the ulcer.

John S. Eden, D.V.M., added that this simple operation also protects the ulcerated area from irritation caused by the outer lids passing over the ulcer when the animal blinks. As he stated: "This can be
of considerable value, when you consider that the lids blink thousands of times a day."

I once had occasion to learn too well, firsthand, what an animal
with an injured cornea can suffer. I was stupid enough to stick my
own finger into my own eye while gesturing dramatically to make a
point in an argument. I had managed to give myself an abrasion of
the cornea. You want to talk about pain? Orthodox eye specialists,
after admonishing me to try to learn how not to stick my finger in
my eye, simply taped an eye patch over my eye so I couldn't blink.
The pain immediately disappeared. You can see that the eye patch
was the equivalent of the simple third-eyelid operation. Why give
me an eye patch, and a dog a mini-operation? The doctors felt they
could count on me not to use my paws to scratch the eye patch off.

As a case history for corneal ulcers, Dr. Fudens recently told me
of Vladimir, a ten-year-old altered male dog that the veterinarian had

treated earlier for hip problems and skin problems. "And Vladimir had been doing very, very well for some two years," the veterinarian said. "But the owner brought him back in December of '97. For ten days his left eye had been watering a profuse clear-to-grayish discharge. He had a large corneal ulcer on the eye."

"So," Dr. Fudens said, "Vladimir had injured himself outside, some way, somehow."

The veterinarian used, basically, homeopathic euphrasia and the herbal extract eyebright, as well as some Chinese herbs. "A month later," Dr. Fudens told me, "Vladimir had started rubbing the eye, which had been better, again. Somehow, he had reinjured it."

Dr. Fudens then used homeopathic sulfur, Chinese herbs, and Nutriplex—a high-potency vitamin and mineral supplement for the eyes. "I also gave him Oxi-5000, which contains a number of antioxidants, and some shark cartilage." And in a few weeks, "there was much less discharge, and the red ulcerated areas were greatly reduced in size and less red and angry-looking. And the eye was not bothering Vladimir; he was not rubbing or pawing, or showing any sensitivity." Soon the eye was completely cured.

Other Problems of the Eye

In addition to the eye problems covered previously, holistic veterinarians have discussed with me successful natural therapies for other disorders, including dry eye, conjunctivitis, and chronic blepharitis (inflammation of the eyelid). Dr. Price also told me of several dogs who were considered "mysteriously" blind before they were taken to him. When he tested them for the level of lead in their bodies, he found it to be very high. He used the technique of chelation, which can remove a number of toxic substances from the body. The veterinarian reported that the dogs were then able to see quite well.

If your dog's problem falls outside this expanded list, keep in mind three facts: that I did not ask veterinarians about every conceivable eye problem; that all biochemical actions in the body are created by nutrients; and that even *if*, as I write this, there is no known successful therapy for a specific eye problem, the new explosion of research in alternative techniques may well have found a helpful therapy by the time you read this.

Also keep in mind that holistic doctors don't concern themselves basically with the diagnosed disease label, but with what their testing discovers to be *causing* the symptoms that led to the diagnosis.

References

1. Patricia P. Widmer, *Pat Widmer's Cat Book* (New York: Charles Scribner's Sons), 1981, pp. 49–50.
2. L. O. Brooksby, *Vet. Med./Sm. Clinician*, March 1979, pp. 301-302.

Chapter 7

Problems of the
Skin and Hair

"I suppose we veterinarians who do a lot of work with skin and hair problems ought to thank the commercial pet food manufacturers for all the business they create for us."

—*J. Keith Benedict, D.V.M.*

"For *some* dogs, just giving them the vitamin B complex is all they need to produce in their bodies a natural element that repels fleas.

"We can pretty well eliminate flea-bite allergy these days.

"For the infectious skin disease pyoderma, a good diet, a nontoxic shampoo, and a short round of antibiotics will usually be all that's needed. But if the animal is put back on a poor diet, the pyoderma will return—no doubt about it."

—*Nino Aloro, D.V.M.*

L*et me tell* you about Merlin, a five-month-old shih tzu who, Nino Aloro, D.V.M., told me in a recent interview, "came to me with the worst case of mange I've ever seen. The mange covered his face, feet, body, legs, and tail. You cannot imagine what that poor animal looked like." Another veterinarian had treated Merlin "without results." (To understand how grave orthodox veterinary medicine considers a case like this, see the section on red mange.)

"The first thing we did," Dr. Aloro said, "was to change the diet to one that is more natural for a dog, because very little works to help an animal if you don't give a good diet." (See chapter 2.) "Then we reinforced the immune system with a number of herbs combined for that purpose." These are specified later in this chapter.

But Merlin and Dr. Aloro weren't dealing only with a horrible case of a skin disease. "He also had rickets," the veterinarian told me, "and his joints were so weak that he couldn't stand up without pain." In addition to what we've already mentioned, Dr. Aloro gave the puppy various vitamins, including a number of antioxidants combined in one capsule for easy administration, and antibiotics.

"Within a month," the veterinarian said, "Merlin was able to walk around much better and climb steps with much more ease." But his skin disease wasn't responding the way Dr. Aloro would have liked. "So I used the parasiticide Ivomec." This is commonly used to treat internal and external parasites of cattle. "In other words," the veterinarian said, "it's strong stuff. But I gave Merlin only a fraction of a cc injected under the skin." That, in combination with the natural therapies, "really did the job" in ridding the puppy of his mange.

A number of months after this interview, I checked again with Dr. Aloro. How was Merlin doing? "Beautifully," the veterinarian said.

Dr. Aloro, who has been a holistic veterinarian for decades, said, "I could give thousands of successful case histories for skin and hair problems, but I consider Merlin to be one of my classics."

In this book's first edition—when holistic veterinary medicine was much less advanced than it is now—I told of Lorax, a golden retriever who suffered severely from a skin condition, moist dermatitis, for the first three years of his life. A battery of steroid shots offered him no relief. A specialist in allergies then discovered that Lorax had numerous allergies. But, after many months of allergy shots—and many hundreds of dollars—Lorax still had his skin problems.

He finally found help from a natural regimen prescribed by Robert Goldstein, V. M.D., and Marty Goldstein, D.V. M., that included a fast (with distilled water only) to allow the body to clear out accumulated toxins; and a change of diet, from one of the most popular "nutritionally complete" dog foods to grains, chicken, raw vegetables, and unsaturated fatty acids. Tests showed that Lorax had a deficiency of magnesium and the B vitamins, and he received daily supplements of those.

The doctors Goldstein told me that four years later, not only was the dog still free of skin problems, but he was also still free of the paralysis he had suffered at the same time.

As mentioned above, a major holistic therapy for all skin and hair problems is to start the dog—gradually—on a natural diet. If you have read chapters on other disorders, you've seen that a natural diet is a basic treatment for *all* disorders, since holistic veterinarians consider poor diet to be a prime *cause* of all disorders. Dr. Aloro said that a major dietary change he has to ask his clients to make is to stop feeding their dogs table scraps. Dogs' body systems never evolved to be the same as ours (see chapter 2). And, indeed, *our* bodies didn't evolve to maintain optimal health on a number of foods we may be eating and sharing with our dogs, such as foods containing sugar.

As detailed in chapter 3, the overuse of vaccinations has been found in recent years to be, along with poor diet, a major factor in just about every kind of chronic disease in dogs and cats. Michael W. Lemmon, D.V. M., stated that "no matter what skin or hair problem the dog has when he comes in, I start off by getting his history of vaccinations." The effects of overvaccinating can be helped by administration of a specific homeopathic preparation.

Many veterinarians have told me that problems of the skin and coat are the most common disorders they see. That would be good news if these problems were as inconsequential as they might seem to be: only "skin deep." But many veterinarians estimate that 90 percent of skin disorders are merely outward manifestations of something physically wrong *within* the body. And many skin problems are life threatening in and of themselves.

That's the bad news about skin disorders. This paragraph mentions some good news. Since natural therapies rebalance the total biochemistry, other, seemingly unrelated disorders often disappear along with the skin and hair problem. And as far back as 1981, Wendell O. Belfield, D.V. M., in his book *How To Have a Healthier Dog,*[1] stated that 70 percent of skin problems could be cleared up simply by putting a pet on a chemical-free diet and adding vitamins and minerals. Remember that holistic veterinary medicine was in its infancy in those days.

Some Basic Suggestions for Treating Skin and Hair Problems

See the text of this chapter for important details.

- Natural diet, as described in chapters 2 and 4, introduced gradually. Initially, a diet of lamb and *well-cooked* brown rice may be tried. (The lamb and rice should not be served at the same meal.) That diet is free of foods that commonly cause allergies in pets—and food allergies are frequent causes of skin disorders in dogs. Additional foods may be added to the diet one at a time; if any one addition results in a flare-up of the skin problem, it may be an indication that your dog is allergic to that particular food.

- A multivitamin/multimineral supplement formulated for dogs.

  Add the following to the supplement. (Dosages are for a 50-pound dog.)

- Additional vitamin C, 1,000–2,000 mg a day
- Additional vitamin E, 400 IU a day
- Additional B complex with B_{12}, 50 mg per meal
- Additional selenium, 50 mcg a day (not 50 mg)
- Additional zinc, 30 mg a day
- Cold-pressed oil (sunflower or sesame), initially, 2 tablespoons for each of the dog's two meals
- Wheat germ oil capsule, two per meal
- Kelp, 2 teaspoons a day
- Bone meal, 1 tablespoon a day
- Nontoxic shampoo

An initial fast, with distilled water only, may be helpful in aiding the body to rid itself of stored-up toxins. *A fast over twenty-four hours must be done under medical supervision.* Do not fast a dog—even for twenty-four hours—who has diabetes or any other chronic disorder without checking closely with a veterinarian who is experienced with fasting animals. Dr. Lemmon added that besides an initial fast, he will often suggest a 24-hour fast once weekly.

You'll note that the boxed information calls for *cold-pressed* oils. Dr. Lemmon warned that just because the label states that the oil is cold pressed does not mean that it has not been subjected to heat and light, which rob the oil of nutritional value. He stated that "manufacturers can call the oil cold pressed if it just starts out cold. But then the presses can be very hot, and of course they heat up the oils." A giveaway might be that if the product is not packaged in a dark or black container to keep out the light, the manufacturer may not have worried much about keeping the product from heat and light *before* packaging, either. If it is in a dark container and the label states the date on which the product was pressed, as well as the date by which you should use it, you can be more confident you're buying a truly cold-pressed oil.

Since most readers will study only the chapter on the disorder that concerns their dog, I feel that there are one or two facts I should repeat in every disorder chapter. Although this section offers suggestions (and remember they are only *suggestions*) that holistic veterinarians often give for skin and hair problems, these doctors will always tailor the therapy to the individual dog. So if you contact a holistic veterinarian who doesn't "do things" the way they're mentioned here, don't assume that the doctor is in any way wrong. (But, in line with the new communication people expect to have with doctors, you might want to ask *why* the veterinarian isn't doing something you expected.)

For instance, Dr. Lemmon said that the suggestions in the box "are important and certainly can be of help. So when a client comes in who has been using those suggestions, I'll say, 'That's fine.' But if the dog has not been completely helped, we'll modify that treatment. On the other hand, if the client has not been giving the dog any treatment, I won't necessarily use all those suggestions." Then, echoing the individual approach so central to holistic therapy, the veterinarian added that "it just depends on the case."

One way in which Dr. Lemmon would often use a different approach to get the same result would be in the suggested use of vitamin B complex in supplement form. "I'm not real big on the B complex in synthetic form," he said. "My own feeling is I'd rather give those vitamins in natural form: from the green concentrate herbs, such as spirulina or barley grass, or from the organ meats, or perhaps high-quality yeast—if the animal can handle that." (As stated elsewhere in this chapter, a number of dogs are allergic to yeast.)

Dr. Lemmon discussed other natural therapies he will often use for skin and hair problems, many of which have been added to holistic veterinarians' arsenals since the first edition. "Depending on the situation, I might use raw glandulars, such as raw adrenal concentrates," he stated. As you might expect, adrenal concentrates will be used when the dog's problem is traced in whole or in part to a malfunctioning adrenal gland.

"Another substance I might use is evening primrose oil, because it contains gamma-linolenic acid, which is helpful for inflammation, allergies, and other problems that go along with many skin and hair disorders," Dr. Lemmon continued. He added that for a 10-pound dog he might start with one-fourth of a capsule a day and increase to one capsule daily.

The veterinarian added that he may work on the specific animal's problem from a homeopathic standpoint, doing a classical homeopathic workup on the dog to find the best remedy. (These workups are painless and noninvasive.) Homeopathy, although by no means a new, untried field of medicine, was in very little use among holistic veterinarians in 1981 when I researched the first edition. Now it is in common use not only among holistic veterinarians but also among holistic M.D.s.

Depending as always on the individual case, Dr. Aloro will often use a number of herbs combined in one capsule that help rebuild the immune system. (This is the combination mentioned in Merlin's story at the beginning of the chapter.) Some of the herbs are propolis; barley green; echinacea; red clover tops; suma; American, Korean, and Chinese ginseng; ginger; chlorophyll; dandelion; goldenseal; burdock; spirulina; peppermint; and blue-green algae. Remember that these are all combined in one capsule; you don't have to get them into your dog in some twenty different "shifts."

Dr. Aloro told me that this combination of herbs has proven so useful that it has "greatly changed my practice in the last few years." The combination is prepared by an herbalist in the veterinarian's area.

The veterinarian added that he occasionally recommends regular Head & Shoulders for the shampoo. For tougher cases, he uses shampoos that are available only to veterinarians. His standard approach to skin and hair problems also includes testing for kidney function and, when he finds a problem, adjusting his prescribed diet accordingly. I say throughout this book that holistic veterinarians (and M.D.s) will use orthodox therapies if they feel they will aid in the optimal treatment of their patient. Dr. Aloro will occasionally use steroids, "but only a small amount. A few milligrams a day will not cause problems. I don't believe in large amounts of a steroid unless you're treating a dog who is in shock."

Before we discuss specific skin disorders, let me give just a brief "taste" of some of the medical research throughout the years that has shown how nutrition can prevent—and cure—skin and hair problems. While I might have chosen to list *new* research, I opted instead to give a sampling of studies from the 1930s and 1950s, so you'd have an idea of how long these problems have been linked with nutrition. The veterinarians I cite in this chapter have been using the *newest* research, which has often used this old research as a mere stepping-stone.

Human volunteers kept on diets just slightly lacking in one vitamin (B_2) developed overly oily hair and skin. The reverse problem, skin that is too dry, has been caused in humans by giving too little vitamin A or C, linoleic acid, or any one of several B vitamins.[2]

Imagine the following "mysterious thing" happening to your body and you might conclude that only a miracle could help you. You're a fair-skinned person, but your skin begins turning dark. (This condition can be caused by exhausted adrenal glands, as in Addison's disease.) Eventually, your skin becomes nearly black. It was shown many years ago that an adequate nutritional program could reverse this process and restore your natural skin tone.

In 1950, a study showed that 4 to 8 tablespoons a day of the natural food substance lecithin healed even the most severe cases of the skin disease psoriasis within five months.

Gray hair? Once you've got it, the only way you can get rid of it is with dye, right? It's just God's or nature's will. Or it's just part of growing old. Yet, gray hair was produced in various studies before 1965 by giving too little copper, too little folic acid, too little pantothenic acid, or too little PABA—all nutrients. And hair was restored to its original color sometimes by giving only PABA.

So much for a sampling of how medical research has been linking skin and hair problems to nutrition for at least six decades. Now for information about how all these decades of research can help your dog.

Fleas

Some Suggestions for a Do-It-Yourself Nontoxic Flea Treatment

The following is a nontoxic treatment suggested by a number of holistic veterinarians for a dog with a moderate case of flea infestation. (See the text for important details.) *If your dog is bleeding or is chewing excessively, consult a veterinarian, at least by phone.*

- In some cases, just the use of the B complex vitamins will help the body produce a natural flea repellent.
- Bathe your dog in a nontoxic shampoo and dry him thoroughly.
- Apply a natural healing ointment (vitamin E, A, or D) to the reddened areas and deter your pet from licking it off.
- Give a 50-pound dog 1 tablespoon of brewer's yeast a day.
- Add one or two cloves of fresh garlic per day to your dog's food. Use a garlic press or chop the garlic finely.
- Flea collars? See text of this section for details.
- Sprinkle brewer's yeast onto your pet's coat and skin every two to three days during heaviest infestation. Then use once every two weeks.
- *Gradually* change the diet to a chemical-free diet. See chapters 2 and 4.

Putting your dog on a natural diet, supplemented with a multi-vitamin/multimineral pill, will help rebuild the total health of your pet. Fleas are parasites, and as such their role in life is to scavenge the blood of sick bodies—and sick bodies only. (Remember we said earlier that more often than not skin problems are a sign of internal sickness?) When you have rebuilt your companion's overall health, he will no longer fit the category of a sick host. At that point, your dog will probably be able to come into contact with fleas many times (from other animals, from the yard, from newly hatched eggs hidden in your house), and the fleas will snub his body as being an unfit place to live.

To the abbreviated suggestions in the boxed material, Dr. Lemmon added that you should try to make sure the brewer's yeast is of high quality. And remember always that a number of dogs are allergic to yeast. Indeed, Doggie, whom I picked up as a stray (hence the generic name), once came down with an awful-looking problem of the hair and skin from which she completely recovered soon after I replaced her multivitamin/multimineral pill containing yeast with a pill that was yeast-free.

Commenting on the suggestion of using garlic, Drs. Aloro and Lemmon stated that it sometimes is very helpful and sometimes doesn't help at all. Again, we're back to the fact that, while specific nutrients often help certain disorders, dogs have individualized biochemistries. My own experience with my high-strung dog, Mr. Sandman, who seemed likely to go crazy with scratching his ears for several weeks, was that garlic didn't help him. A combination of several fatty acids (mentioned in this chapter) did. (Because of illness, I'd gotten lax in feeding a fully natural diet, and he had developed ear mites.)

One very simple method of flea control was offered by Dr. Lemmon, who said that if your dog is short haired, a flea comb can be of help. "First of all, it can be an easy way to find out if the dog *has* fleas," he said. "And it can be useful in helping to get rid of them."

Dr. Aloro stated that in some cases just giving your dog a B complex supplement will be all that's needed. While he has found that to be true over the years in terms of actual results, he doesn't believe the biochemical rationale has been discovered yet. His theory is, though, that some bodies produce a substance that is a natural repellent to fleas. "As you know," he said, "some people are eaten up by fleas, while others in the same yard or room are unaffected. I think some of my patients don't have that particular element in their bodies, and the B complex given on a daily basis helps to produce the natural repellent."

Dr. Aloro pointed out that brewer's yeast, mentioned in this chapter as being helpful in controlling fleas and in aiding other skin and hair problems, is a good source of B vitamins.

Nontoxic rinses are also helpful for controlling fleas. Holistic veterinarians point out that unlike unnatural, chemical rinses, you can use nontoxic ones every day, thus increasing their effectiveness. These rinses can not only help get rid of fleas but can also soothe irritation from the scratching that fleas cause. And, since they don't contain poisonous chemicals, your dog won't be harmed while she does "her thing" of grooming her hair to keep it pretty.

What about Flea Collars?

In some cases it's possible to bypass flea collars, whose drawbacks we discuss below, with the simple, inexpensive use of brewer's yeast and/or raw grated fresh garlic in your pet's food. Both these substances give the dog's skin a smell that nobody notices—except fleas, who can't bear it. The garlic and yeast also contain nutrients that are extremely healthful for our pets—provided, as always, that your dog isn't allergic to yeast. As a matter of fact, some veterinarians recommend that brewer's yeast and garlic be a part of your pet's daily diet—fleas or no fleas.

Or you might dust brewer's yeast directly onto your pet's body. In grooming himself, your dog will lick up the yeast on his coat and will thus benefit not only from the good external effects, but also the good internal effects of the yeast.

It's best to take your dog for a walk or let him in the yard for a while after the "dusting," because the yeast is not a poison and therefore does not kill the fleas (or your dog), as poisonous flea collars can. It merely sends the fleas scampering off your pet's body.

Regarding flea collars, Dr. Aloro said: "As far as I know, there is no flea collar that is effective, including the ones that the companies guarantee will kill fleas for months. I had one that guaranteed to keep working for a full year; but when I saw that the fleas were just, say, having a nice time frolicking right there under that collar, I gave up the idea of dispensing any flea collars."

In the first edition, veterinarians recommended herbal flea collars as being not only safe but also much more effective than the poisonous collars. They work not by killing fleas—and therefore potentially killing the dog—but by giving off an herbal aroma that fleas hate. So they abandon the pet's body in search of another dog who doesn't smell so awful.

Dr. Lemmon, however, recently stated: "I don't push herbal flea collars. I'm not opposed to them if the client has already used one, and it's worked well for the dog. But I have found that some pets do have problems with these collars."

For another basic suggestion of what you might use for your dog instead of flea collars, see the next section.

New Flea Controllers

Dr. Lemmon believes that many veterinarians are turning away from flea collars in favor of several new products called flea controllers. These products came out only a few years ago.

"Apparently they work quite well," Dr. Lemmon said. "And when a client tells me he or she has already been using one of the products, and the animal has shown improvement and hasn't had any side effects, I say, 'Sure, go ahead using it.' But I'd prefer not using them if I can avoid them." Dr. Lemmon's concern is that not enough time has elapsed since they were put into use for us to have full knowledge of any possible long-term harmful effects.

Dr. Aloro added that these new products "are supposed to be nontoxic. But until millions and millions of dogs use them without any problem, how can we really be sure that they're not toxic?"*

However, both veterinarians see indications that these new products work to control fleas. Dr. Lemmon said that he has had some clients tell him, "My pet used to have problems with fleas all the

---

* The two products the veterinarians were discussing here are Advantage and Program.

time. I just put one drop on his skin, and he doesn't have any problems any more."

Dr. Aloro suggested, though, that you read the labels thoroughly. One of the products specifies "in the small print that even some doctors don't read" that you must still use shampoos and treat the house. "If you can't eliminate the source of fleas in the dog's environment, you will have an endless flow of fleas onto the dog, and the product will be just a worthless added expense."

It's impossible for me to know how long after I write this book you will actually be reading it. Let me suggest that you call one or two holistic veterinarians from the list at the back of this book to get updated information. Ask how these products have withstood the test of time regarding effectiveness and lack of toxicity.*

Getting Rid of the Source of Fleas by Cleaning Up the Environment

If you have successfully gotten rid of fleas that were tormenting your dog, yet they have come back, first make sure you have been maintaining your pet on a natural diet. Second, consider that the fleas that left your dog's body simply took up residence elsewhere in your house until their "medical threat" was over. You may have to take steps to get fleas out of your dog's domicile. (Actually, as mentioned previously, some flea products say you have to do this as a matter of course.) Dr. Lemmon told me that "very often, just really good cleanliness can be enough to get rid of the source of fleas: really good vacuuming, cleaning up the beds, getting rid of hair and other debris, that type of thing." When that doesn't work, Dr. Lemmon has recommended cleaning with 20 Muleteam Borax or Flea Busters because they are relatively nontoxic and have worked very well over the years for his clients. These two products consist basically of boron, an essential nutrient.

* Late note: As this book went to press, Dr. Lemmon wrote me that he has now seen a few cases of increased skin inflammation from two of these products. And John Fudens, D.V.M., wrote me a strongly worded blanket objection to all these new flea controllers.

Fleabite Allergy
(or Flea Allergy Dermatitis)

Fleabite allergy is an extension of the general problem of flea infestation. This disorder shows itself in bald spots and in swollen, inflamed (and painful) skin, the result not only of the fleabites but also of the afflicted dog's sometimes desperate biting and scratching to try to make things better. Just as we do when we are in constant discomfort, your dog may lose her appetite and change from a sweet, happy being to an irritable, mean one.

"We can pretty well eliminate fleabite allergy these days," Dr. Aloro said. He specifies, of course, that changing to a natural diet is of crucial importance. "And we have to ascertain that the kidneys are in good working order and use natural therapies as necessary if they're not. Also, now we have better shampoos than we used to have to treat fleas and other skin conditions."

Dr. Aloro will often use Advantage or Frontline. "You just put a little on the back of the neck, not the entire body," he noted. "And that kills about 98 percent of the fleas within twenty-four hours and will keep working effectively for the next month. Then you just keep repeating as directed."

Dr. Lemmon added that acupuncture is sometimes helpful for fleabite allergy.

Hair Loss

"You have to determine what is *causing* the hair loss," J. Keith Benedict, D.V.M., once told me. "But no matter what is causing it, it is imperative that you improve the animal's nutrition." George M. Thue, D.V.M., like Dr. Benedict, stated that he will check for such things as hormonal deficiency, parasites, and pressure wounds that might be causing the hair loss. "When there is no indication for specific treatment, I will occasionally use cider vinegar, in addition to a natural diet plus supplements," Dr. Thue told me. "Daily application of cider vinegar rubbed in thoroughly on small areas of hair loss can do wonders to stimulate dead or weak hair follicles and restore natural hair growth."

Years ago, Dr. Thue sent me before-and-after pictures of a dog that had come to him with a large bald spot on her back and with hair that had turned gray around her eyes and mouth. Within about two months, the "after" picture showed the bald spot completely grown in, and the gray hair was now dark. Dr. Thue treated the dog with a liquid B complex, vitamins C and E, lecithin, unsaturated fatty acids, and Viokase (a mixture of natural pancreatic enzymes).

Dr. Lemmon told me that a lot of what he does today is similar. He particularly stresses the importance of the unsaturated fatty acids. As always, they should be cold pressed. Dr. Lemmon added that flaxseed oil and primrose seed oil are particularly helpful in treating hair loss.

To sum up: Hair loss in your dog should be checked out by a veterinarian to find its exact cause. Remember that skin and hair problems are very often signs of something amiss within the dog's body. However, no matter what the cause is, you can help your companion by making sure his nutrition is optimal, as detailed in chapters 2 and 4.

Skin Ulcers

In the first edition, holistic veterinarians reported success with vitamin E. One case history, reported in a personal communication to Dr. Wilfrid E. Shute (one of the world's major pioneers in research with vitamin E), told of a young dog with skin ulcers whose coat was restored to beautiful condition after about ten weeks on the vitamin. This was despite the fact that the dog had been in such trouble that literally half his body was bald. The owners had dragged the animal to half a dozen veterinarians, none of whom could help him, for two years. You can imagine how much that cost the owners in dollars—and how much it cost them and the pet in stress. At the end of those two years, the owners had been told to give up and put their companion to sleep. (By the way, the owners were able simply to give the vitamin E by mouth at home.)[3]

The breeder who had suggested they try vitamin E reported: "When I saw the dog again I couldn't believe my eyes. The coat was long and the dog was in beautiful condition, with no trace of ulcers or rash."

Other veterinarians working with me on the first edition reported success with vitamins C and A—depending, as always, on which of the nutrients that are generally helpful for a disorder are most deficient in the particular animal's body. Jan Bellows, D.V. M., specified that he often found the mineral zinc to be helpful.

Dr. Thue added that he used a medicated shampoo and ointment for skin ulcers and shaved the affected area to keep it clean. He also gave B complex and vitamin C. Then he had the owners continue giving their pet multivitamins with additional C and E.

Advising me for this new edition, Dr. Lemmon said, "That information is certainly fine. But I'd like to add that I will also usually investigate the animal's problem from a classical homeopathic point of view."

Red (Demodectic) Mange

This skin disorder usually affects dogs under two years of age. At first, hunks of hair disappear from around the muzzle and the eyes. The bald areas are red and a bit swollen. If you see these symptoms, you should obtain immediate veterinary aid for your pet. Red mange can spread quickly. A chemical insecticide may be needed to kill the mites that cause the disorder. Be absolutely certain to increase your dog's nutritional supplementation at this point to help detoxify the insecticide.

For *generalized* red mange (that is, red mange that has already spread over the body), every source I turned to—whether orthodox or holistic—while working on the first edition offered mainly despair. (Merlin, the dog whose story led off this chapter, suffered from generalized red mange.) I persisted, however, until I found holistic veterinarian Dr. Bellows, who gave details of a combined orthodox-nutritional therapy which, he said, "works on almost all cases." The veterinarian stated: "First the pet must be supplemented with vitamins to get him in a positive nitrogen balance, using mega-doses of the B complex, C, and E. Also, any infections must be cleared up with antibiotics. Then Amatraze (an insecticide) must be used as a rinse."

Animal nutritionist Pat Widmer added that in her clinic all animals with generalized red mange tested out to have very low levels of zinc in their bodies. "With the use of zinc," she said, "we have seen the entire coat grow back within a week." Widmer also stated that relieving stress is very important. "When I find a pet has a very stressful home situation," she told me, "I persuade the owner to let the animal stay with me at the clinic, where I make sure to give him a calm environment and a lot of loving attention."

Dr. Lemmon, reviewing the above for this new book, said: "Now, beyond that, we have other natural substances that are very helpful. It's very important to support the liver. You can use either the herb milk thistle or a good-quality raw liver concentrate. One that I find helpful in mange cases—and a number of other holistic veterinarians have been using it, too—is called Liquid Liver. Or sometimes I'll use a product called Livaplex from Standard Process Laboratories."

Adding that it's important to improve the immune system so it can perform its natural job of fighting the disease, the veterinarian said, "I usually like to give the animal a product called Immunoplex, also from Standard Process Laboratories."

I don't generally like to recommend specific products. Between my writing of this book and your reading of it, the company may have gone out of business, or an even better product might have come out. So if the holistic veterinarian you consult in person or by phone doesn't use one of the above products, just ask if he or she knows of them and why the doctor isn't using them.

Dr. Lemmon added that he will always consider treating the dog with red mange homeopathically. "And of course sometimes we'll treat the dog externally. Depending on how bad the mange is, we'll give him support with various herbs or various gentle emollient rinses and shampoos." Emollients soften the skin. "Sometimes I'll use oatmeal," he noted, "and in some cases stronger herbs, to kill the mites externally."

You may have noticed that Dr. Lemmon's major thrust is to treat the dog's skin problem according to what is going on *inside* the body. This leads us back to something I said early in this chapter: Skin problems usually are not just "skin deep."

Pyoderma

Pyoderma, a staph infection of the skin, attacks young dogs. Eruptions appear on their bodies and start oozing pus. The standard treatment is antibiotics and steroid cream, but this treatment works slowly for pyoderma—when it works at all. It is not uncommon for dogs on this standard treatment to end up having to be destroyed.

For the first edition, Dr. Benedict stated that antibiotics used alone are not the best way to treat pyoderma. "You've really got to get the nutrition up," he said emphatically. "As a matter of fact, there is no contest between the standard antibiotic treatment and the combined antibiotic-and-nutrition therapy." He stressed high amounts of vitamin E, which helps promote healing and prevent scarring.

One reason antibiotics used alone are not the best solution for pyoderma was given by Drs. Robert and Marty Goldstein. The substances that come out through the skin in the pus "are built-up toxins within the body. Antibiotics stop the elimination of these toxins. This, of course, causes a buildup of toxins within the body and eventual recurrence of the pyoderma. Therapy must include some detoxification in order to achieve a cure. This detoxification is a nutritional program."

Since I, like you, am a person owned by animals, I can well understand that if antibiotics used alone stopped that awful pus from oozing out of your dog's body, you would consider the dog cured. And, if the dog came down again with pyoderma, you would consider this a "normal part of the disease." But, for holistic veterinarians, a return of any disease is not normal.

John S. Eden, D.V.M., many years ago stated that he used antibiotics "only in severe or intractable cases." Besides diet and supplementation, Dr. Eden stressed cleansing of the skin, using either an iodine-based or chlorhexidine shampoo. "I recommend that the owner, while bathing the pet, open the pustules and remove scabs to allow the shampoo (surgical scrub) to get at the bacteria," he stated.

Commenting on the preceding paragraph for this updated book, Dr. Lemmon said, "To treat the animal externally, I might use iodine or chlorhexidine, but only if the problem is very severe. Otherwise, I would treat the animal with herbs. There are a number of herbal bases, including goldenseal and witch hazel, that have the power to disinfect and to kill the bacteria." He added, as he did elsewhere for skin and hair disorders, that homeopathy can also be helpful.

As Dr. Thue once told me, vitamin C is especially valuable in helping skin to heal. "For instance," he told me, "I've done surgery on animals whose bodies simply couldn't heal the skin. Two whole weeks after surgery, there would be no healing whatsoever. Then I've given vitamin C, and in another week or two the skin was completely healed."

For this new edition, Dr. Aloro said, "We're still using antibiotics for severe cases of pyoderma. But diet is crucial for treating pyoderma, as it is for any type of skin disorder. Because if the diet is the kind that causes allergy, any skin outbreaks will become infected, will become pyodermic. So a round of antibiotics lasting from a few days to a few weeks usually takes care of the pyoderma—as long as people change the diet." The veterinarian added that you should give a probiotic when a dog is given antibiotics.

"But," Dr. Aloro added, "if they put the dog back on a harmful diet, the pyoderma will come back. No doubt about it." You may note from earlier in this section that in 1981 the doctors Goldstein, expressing themselves a bit differently, gave the same warning that pyoderma will tend to recur if antibiotics are given without nutritional therapy.

Dr. Lemmon recently told me of one of his toughest cases ever of a skin problem. It included pyoderma. "Lucky is an Akita who was found as a stray when he was a three-month-old puppy. At that time he just had very itchy skin. When I first saw him, he was about eighteen months old and he had been to other veterinarians, who treated him with antibiotics. His skin problems would clear up and get worse, clear up and get worse all over again." The veterinarian said that Lucky had a "very severe allergic dermatitis and a suppressed immune system. He was always getting pyodermas, or scab infections on the skin. He had a lot of hair loss and a lot of pruritis, or itching and redness."

Perhaps one fact that prolonged Lucky's illness was that his owners took him, variously, to orthodox veterinarians and then back to Dr. Lemmon. "We worked on Lucky at various times with nutrition, homeopathy, and herbs. And we, too, would get improvements and then relapses—even though I've been able to turn around a lot of dogs like this with a good diet and a homeopathic." Finally, when Lucky was brought once again back to Dr. Lemmon, the veterinarian put him on probiotics and on a raw thymus product to help the immune system.

"That combination worked to cure Lucky," the veterinarian said. Dr. Lemmon added that the dog is still doing very well and has not had one of the previously frequent relapses for several years.

References

1. Wendell O. Belfield, D.V.M., and Martin Zucker. *How to Have a Healthier Dog* (Garden City, New York: Doubleday and Co., Inc.), 1981, p. 205.

2. V. Ramalignaswami, et al., *Brit. J. Derm.*, 65, 1, 1953; F. Bicknell and F. Prescott, *The Vitamins in Medicine* (Milwaukee, Wisconsin: Lee Foundation for Nutritional Research), 1953.

3. Personal communication to Dr. Wilfrid E. Shute, cited by Wendell O. Belfield, op. cit., pp. 205, 206.

Chapter 8

Infectious Diseases: Pneumonia, Parvo, Kennel Cough, Distemper, and More

"The only time I use an antibiotic for respiratory diseases is when the client insists on it. With drugs, the animal has less of a chance of being cured than he has with natural therapy. Also, even in those cases where the drug does cure, the poor dog can be suffering for a week or two; whereas with vitamin C and other nutrients, he can be well in three days."
—*Richard J. Kearns, D.V.M. (in 1981)*

"For Lyme disease, we have a homeopathic remedy that works wonderfully.

"Dogs with kennel cough respond very well to homeopathic treatment. If the guardians really want antibiotics, I'll honor that wish. But if they let me use the homeopathics, I don't need the drugs."
—*Neal K. Weiner, D.V.M. (in 1998)*

"Bacteria and viruses do not attack a healthy body. Most doctors worry about the bacteria and viruses. I do not treat them. I treat the animal."
—*Numerous holistic veterinarians (from 1981 to 1998)*

When dealing with infectious diseases in your dog, you *must* watch for emergency situations. One of the most serious problems in these diseases is dehydration, the loss of body fluids.

Several holistic veterinarians have told me that to save pets and owners the stress of separation, and to spare owners expense, they will send some dogs home with an IV drip kit after teaching the owners how to use it. Since some infectious disorders overtake a dog so quickly, you might want to ask your veterinarian for one of these kits even though your dog is not sick. Ask the doctor when it would be appropriate for you to start using it on your own, before you can get the dog to a veterinarian. (If you pull up the hair and skin at the back of your dog's neck, and the resulting wad doesn't go back down almost immediately, your pet is most likely dehydrated.)

I said in the introduction that for many problems, if you don't live near a holistic veterinarian, you can try consulting directly on the phone with such a doctor or, better yet, have your own veterinarian consult. But since time is so crucial with some infectious diseases, you can't risk taking an unnecessary step. *If your dog has a high temperature, get to your own veterinarian immediately.* As a matter of fact, that might be amended: *Get to the nearest available veterinarian immediately.* Show the doctor these pages and ask— or if necessary, demand—that he or she consult with one of the holistic veterinarians listed at the back of the book.

If, for any reason, holistic consultation is not quickly available, let the orthodox veterinarian take complete charge until holistic therapy can be added. (Holistic veterinarians and M.D.s rely on their orthodox training most heavily for emergency situations.)

If you're starting this chapter as a die-hard skeptic, you will read some facts that may seem much too good to be true. But I believe that if you read with an open mind, you will finish this chapter with new knowledge that can save your dog's life.

For instance, you will read that even if your veterinarian has told you that there is nothing to be done for your dog in the final stage of an infectious disease, your pet may be back to all her old mischief within days after administration of a natural therapy.

No, I am not claiming that holistic veterinarians can work miracles. Although the recoveries may often *seem* like miracles, the therapies these doctors use are built virtually always on modern medical research—or at the very least hundreds, sometimes thousands, of years of actual proof.

For instance, you will see that vitamin C—rather than antibiotics—is often basic to the therapy for infectious diseases. As we will detail shortly, the "miraculous" results of this vitamin in dealing with these diseases have been documented in medical studies since at least 1937.

Keep in mind that every disease was once incurable—until medical science found a cure for it. Keep in mind also that it took a number of years for many of today's totally accepted cures to come to the attention of most doctors and even more years before most doctors accepted them. This book covers new cures and controls for pet disorders that are presently caught in that unfortunate limbo.

The following are just a few instances of how long it sometimes can take for new medical knowledge to become known and generally accepted. They focus on the use of vitamin C.

For about two centuries (the late 1500s to the late 1700s), some sailors cured themselves of "incurable" scurvy by eating foods containing a high amount of vitamin C, the nutrient in wide use today by holistic doctors for infectious (and other) diseases. No one paid any attention to these cured sailors, while for some 200 years the still-"incurable" scurvy often wiped out 50 percent or more of the sailors at sea. Finally, in 1747, Dr. James Lind, who had been compiling data for years, ran a controlled scientific study. Dr. Lind concluded that a bit of lemon or lime juice (both found to be high in vitamin C when the vitamin was discovered many years later) should be given to crews. The medical community attacked him. The navy officials attacked him. After all, how dare anyone suggest that an incurable disease was curable? Doesn't common sense tell you otherwise? *And with something as simple as a food??*

It was about half a century later that Dr. Lind's recommendation was finally taken. Lemon juice (at that time called lime juice) was prescribed as part of the regulation diet for British sailors—and the "incurable" scurvy disappeared. (The fact that the sailors drank lime juice to protect themselves from scurvy led to their being nicknamed "limeys," which they are still called.)

The general acceptance of the fact that foods high in vitamin C could help scurvy came some 175 years after a John Smith wrote advice to ships' captains detailing what "victuals" they should have on board before sailing. The required "victuals" included "the juice of lemons for the scurvy." Apparently, Smith thought this fact was so well known among sailors, because of actual evidence, that it needed no explanation.

Today the fact that scurvy is due to a deficiency of vitamin C—and that the disease can be *cured* with the vitamin—is accepted by every medical student as very primitive medical knowledge. But consider how many hundreds of years it took for that knowledge to start to "take hold"—and how many lives were needlessly lost in that limbo period.

I hope this book will help cut down the time otherwise needed for some of the *newer* uses of vitamin C to become generally known.

I know of medical studies going back to 1937 that show the "new notion" that vitamin C can kill bacteria.[1] Dr. Fred R. Klenner, chief of staff at the Memorial Hospital in Reidsville, North Carolina, began his work in the late 1940s, and as I researched the first edition in 1981, was still continuing it. Dr. Klenner's work, published extensively in the medical literature, was often done with human patients who were by all rights supposed to die. Many of them had been previously treated with penicillin, Aureomycin, and other antibiotics with no success. Often these terminally ill people, with fevers of 103 to 105 degrees, had a normal temperature within a few hours after administration of vitamin C—and were able to enjoy the next meal offered at the hospital. Two or three days later—when they otherwise would have been lowered into the earth—they walked out of the hospital in good health.[2]

The diseases Dr. Klenner successfully treated with vitamin C included hepatitis, herpes simplex, measles, chicken pox, mononucleosis,[3] meningitis, encephalitis, polio, viral pneumonia, and lockjaw.[4]

Nutritionist Adelle Davis published several books in the 1950s and 1960s that were so popular with the public that, the last I checked, they were still in print. I believe she was the first strong voice in getting information about nutritional therapies out to the public. Her books were popular despite the fact—or maybe because of the fact—that they were heavily weighted by her fervor for giving proof of every fact with details from technical medical research. Backing up Dr. Klenner's work, Davis cited a number of other studies, conducted in the years from 1938 to 1960, which reported that vitamin C is deadly to all types of bacteria and viruses.[5] Why *all*? Because vitamin C doesn't waste its time racing through the body trying to attack the viruses and bacteria per se; it rebuilds the immune system. And the rebuilt immune system kills the viruses and bacteria, just as it does, when it is strong, many times in the course of a normal day.

A Basic Therapy for All Infectious Diseases

So many advances have been made in alternative medicine since my first book that holistic veterinarians now have numerous therapies in addition to those I reported in 1981 from which to choose the optimal treatment for your dog. Both Neal K. Weiner, D.V.M., and Nino Aloro, D.V.M., for instance, agreeing that high amounts of vitamin C are still in common use, specified that they now also use homeopathic remedies and a lot of herbal medications—particularly echinacea, goldenseal, and garlic. Echinacea, for instance, as Robert Goldstein, V.M.D., pointed out, stimulates the immune system by increasing the number of white blood cells and phagocytes.

Dr. Aloro commented that in addition to herbs, he stresses the use of the B complex vitamins and amino acids, "because, especially in commercial foods, these nutrients are deficient, or of poor quality." Dr. Weiner told me that he relies heavily on glandular therapy, using natural substances to strengthen organs found to be functioning poorly.

In times of crisis, vitamin C will be given intravenously, often at the rate of ½ gram or more per pound of body weight, twice a day. The difference between intravenous vitamin C and a vitamin C tablet can very probably be *the* difference between life and death for your dog with a serious infectious disease. Nutrients given intravenously, rather than through the mouth, bypass the digestive system. This allows them to go directly into the blood and begin circulating immediately throughout the body. Also, because intravenous medicines bypass the digestive system, you can give much higher amounts without toxicity.

The preceding paragraph gives only one reason that I urge you not to make up your own treatment for your dog with a severe infectious disease. (Maybe you would never dream of doing that, but I worry about the people who believe that natural therapies can always be used without the help of a doctor.) Once your dog is past the crisis, lesser amounts of the nutrients will be needed, and you can administer them orally.

Often, in crisis cases, intravenous fluids (a standard orthodox treatment) also will be administered to offset existing dehydration, a common killer for humans and animals alike in acute illnesses. And solid foods will be withheld.

Holistic veterinarians also will often use thymus extract for infectious diseases. The thymus gland is a major part of the all-important immune system; and, as Richard J. Kearns, D.V.M., once told me, "The amount of thymus gland hormone in the blood can be just about destroyed in twenty-four hours by infectious problems."

Dr. Weiner told me in a recent interview that holistic veterinarians who have glandular therapy as one of their specialties will use blood work or kinesiology testing to determine weaknesses in other glands besides the thymus. "Then," he said, "we'll use the appropriate glandular extract, herb, or homeopathic to support that gland."

Calcium and the B complex and other vitamins also are often used as part of the natural therapy for infectious diseases.

To combat phlegm, discharge, and lung congestion—common problems with many infectious diseases—various herbs and homeopathic remedies are helpful. However, holistic doctors point out that *if these discharges are not adversely affecting the dog*, they should not be stopped, because they are the body's natural way of getting rid of toxins. In other words, what's coming out of the body in these gunky discharges are substances that *should* be coming out; and holistic veterinarians believe it's not their job to hamper an animal's body as it uses its innate wisdom to try to heal itself.

Vitamin A not only helps rebuild the immune system but also helps directly in problems of the mucous membranes common in a number of serious infectious diseases. While the original form of vitamin A is fat soluble (which means it can accumulate in the body and be toxic if used in extremely high doses), a newer form of the vitamin is water soluble and does not accumulate in the body. Dr. Kearns pointed out in 1981 that up to 200,000 units a day of this nontoxic form can be given to an animal weighing 10 pounds or more. The ability to use such massive amounts helps the body to flush out poisons very quickly, "much more quickly than with drugs," Dr. Kearns added. The reason for this is that, obviously, huge amounts of toxic drugs can't be used without killing the dog.

Unlike many orthodox veterinarians, holistic veterinarians often will not try to fight the symptom of fever, unless it is extremely high. Fever is a sign of increased body metabolism; the high metabolism results from the fact that the body is in the middle of intense activity fighting off its invaders. Also, heat kills bacteria. As you know, that's why we boil contaminated water.

Actually, some holistic veterinarians have told me that if a dog is brought to them in the final stage of a disease that usually produces a fever and the dog doesn't have a fever, they have much less hope of curing him. They consider fever a sign that the dog's life force is still strong enough to fight.

What about antibiotics? While these are the mainstay of orthodox treatment for infectious diseases, holistic veterinarians often do not use them; these veterinarians treat the dog instead with natural substances that do the same work as antibiotics without the potential for harmful side effects. However, as I stress throughout this book, holistic veterinarians were trained as orthodox veterinarians before specializing in alternative fields of medicine, and they won't deny a dog orthodox therapy if that is part of what the dog needs to get well quickly. When a holistic veterinarian uses antibiotics, however, the accompanying use of natural therapies helps protect the dog against the usual side effects of these drugs.

Parvovirus

Parvo is an infectious disease that can overrun your puppy's body and kill him even before you have a chance to notice any symptoms. It is also extremely serious in the adult dog. Jack Long, V.M.D., tells me that the parvo virus is almost identical to the virus that causes feline distemper and that the symptoms it produces are virtually the same. To give an idea of just how dangerous this is, some books on orthodox veterinary medicine have referred to feline distemper as the most deadly of all cat diseases. In contrast, Dr. Long told me in a recent interview that "with holistic therapy, parvo is certainly a treatable disease, and we pull most dogs through it."

I will give you a specific example, from my personal experience, of how desperately sick a dog with parvo can get: Once a huge stray dog looked at me with sad eyes, and I brought her home just to keep her warm overnight. (She's sitting at my feet as I write this many years later.) Days after, she became violently ill. It was 3:00 A.M. when I realized Doggie was in the midst of an emergency. As I say elsewhere, holistic veterinarians have recommended that in an emergency you get your dog the nearest available veterinary help, so I rushed her off to the nearby twenty-four-hour orthodox veterinary center, which happens to be considered one of the best orthodox centers in the country. (I hold that belief, too.) She had bloody diarrhea and was vomiting blood. It didn't take long for the center to diagnose parvo. (Parvo is thought to be spread through the feces of an infected animal, and I suspect that while Doggie was homeless, she had eaten feces in a desperate attempt to keep herself alive.)

The center kept Doggie in isolation in the intensive care unit for weeks. For most of that time, I was told that there had been no improvement; Doggie was still "touch-and-go," still "fighting for her life." At one point, when these reports had gone on and on, I shared my despair with the veterinarian in charge of Doggie's case. She responded, "Don't you give up. Doggie hasn't given up. She's a real tough fighter—if she weren't, she wouldn't still be here."

Eventually, this orthodox veterinary center that bears the highest respect in this country did deliver Doggie back to me, no longer with bloody diarrhea or bloody vomiting. She was, however, still depressed and without energy; she was still vomiting. I consulted by phone with a holistic veterinarian, who told me that now the task at hand was to help Doggie rid her body of the negative residual effects of the antibiotics she had been given for so long without any backup of a natural therapy. It took two weeks of therapy with a homeopathic and a probiotic until Doggie's digestive system healed. (Antibiotics unbalance the digestive organisms. Probiotics contain these organisms in balanced amounts.)

Actually, holistic veterinarians have been curing parvo since at least 1981. And back then, holistic veterinarians reported to me that they usually controlled parvo within two days. The only dogs they have told me of losing were those who were left too long without any treatment, or those who were first treated unsuccessfully by orthodox means. For instance, in 1981, Dr. Kearns told me, "I have lost only one dog to parvovirus. That was a puppy who had been treated by another veterinarian. When the puppy was brought into my office, he was literally one hour away from death. He did not have enough time left for the vitamin C to take effect."

If, as I have said, parvo can sometimes overwhelm a puppy so fast that there may be no time to notice symptoms, what can you do to help save him from the disease? You can make sure his mama has been fed a natural diet with preventive amounts of vitamin C during her pregnancy, as detailed in chapter 4. And you can give the puppy a natural diet and preventive C, as recommended in the same chapter. A number of veterinarians have told me that they have never seen a dog with parvo whose owner had followed those recommendations. A few have specified that this fact was true of dogs who had not been vaccinated against the disease, but I would follow the recommendations of more cautious holistic veterinarians and vaccinate a puppy as soon as possible. (See chapter 3 for holistic veterinarians' recommendations about vaccinations.)

Symptoms of Parvo

The principal signs are high fever and protracted vomiting. There is diarrhea, with grayish or yellow-gray stools. Later the stools become bloody.

Holistic Treatment of Parvo

A basic part of the therapy is, as it was in 1981, intravenous vitamin C in the sodium ascorbate form. However, in more recent years, many holistic veterinarians have added homeopathy to their arsenal to fight this disease.

Because of the swiftness of parvo, a holistic veterinarian may use four times the amount of vitamin C in treating it as he or she might use for some other viral diseases. Recovering patients are sent home with vitamin C to be taken by mouth.

Holistic veterinarians will also administer a high volume of fluids to prevent or treat dehydration, a life-threatening condition that results from the body's loss of fluids through vomiting and diarrhea. Depending on the individual case, a holistic veterinarian may use an antibiotic at the beginning of treatment, as an adjunct to the natural therapy. (The fluids and antibiotics are, of course, orthodox treatments. As I stress throughout this book, holistic veterinarians do not deny animals orthodox care when it can help them.)

According to the individual dog, holistic veterinarians may add herbs such as garlic. This herb contains built-in antibacterial agents— that is, built-in *natural* antibiotics.

Holistic veterinarians will also use natural therapies, such as vitamin E, to help prevent scarring of the heart. This scarring kills some dogs even after they have recovered from parvo.

Since parvo viciously attacks the intestines, holistic veterinarians will often add probiotics, a product developed only in recent years that contains all the natural organisms, in a natural balance, that occur in the intestines of a healthy dog.

When the dog is well enough to eat again, veterinarians are careful not to let her go right back to her normal foods. She may be kept for a few days on a liquid diet, such as chicken and vegetable broths. Then she may be switched for several days to a diet of rice and cottage cheese. These two foods are easily digested and therefore "go easy" on the intestines.

TREATING THE DOG'S SPIRIT Dr. Weiner and I were talking about parvo when I mentioned I had initially experienced some difficulty in getting case histories of specific diseases. The veterinarian suggested that this may have been a reflection of the fact that over the years, holistic veterinarians have increasingly tailored their therapies to the individual animal, not to the disease label. So a veterinarian may clearly remember a dog and even the therapy he was given, but may not remember the dog as a "case" of parvo, or a "case" of arthritis. Elsewhere in this chapter, I explain how Dr. Weiner individualizes nutritional therapies. He also tests for the dog's specific emotional state.

"We may have two patients at the same time who have parvo. One of the dogs may be very hot-blooded and nervous," Dr. Weiner said. "The other may be cold-blooded, and lonely, and angry. So the energetic imprint of that disease in the second being-in-a-body is different from parvo's energetic imprint in the first being's body." In other words, the two dogs have the same disease, with the same symptoms, but their bodies have different unbalanced energies, which must be treated along with the disease symptoms.

Dr. Weiner uses kinesiology to alert him to the dog's basic emotional state and then will try to find out what is going on in the animal's home that may be causing the fear or hopelessness or anger in the dog. The veterinarian often discovers that the dog's spirit is reacting to fear, hopelessness, or anger among his guardians. (Dr. Weiner has often talked to me about the fact that dogs somatacize the emotional issues of their people. Other holistic veterinarians have mentioned that while cats also react strongly to their owners' emotions, dogs tend to absolutely "xerox" them.)

Dr. Weiner finds that explaining to the pet's guardians "in a respectful manner" how their emotional interactions may be contributing to the dog's physical problem often leads the people to reevaluate those interactions and often results not only in a more peaceful spirit in the animal, but also more peace among his guardians.

You will find a specific case history of the effects of owners' emotions on their pet in chapter 5, where Dr. Weiner tells of a dog suffering from both a serious crippling disorder (spondylosis) and a spirit of hopelessness who responded very well within days basically to one chiropractic treatment and to the guardians' reevaluation of the way they related to each other.

Kennel Cough (Infectious Tracheobronchitis)

Kennel cough is characterized by a harsh, dry, "honking" cough along with retching and gagging. Early in the disease, your dog may also produce varying amounts of mucus. This disorder is called kennel cough because it usually strikes dogs who have come in close contact with other canines at boarding kennels or at grooming parlors, shows, or pet stores.

Robert Goldstein, D.V. M., sent me a copy of *Love of Animals* (a newsletter he and his wife, Susan, write) that discussed how you might help protect your companion against kennel cough if you have to travel and leave him behind. First, try to find a pet sitter who visits or stays at your home and cares for your dog on his own territory. Not being ripped away from his familiar environment will help alleviate stress—another common factor behind kennel cough. And, of course, the dog will not be in close proximity to other dogs that may be carrying the virus. I must add, from my own experience and that of others, that you should very stringently check the references of anyone to whom you entrust your pet's care.

Dr. Goldstein pointed out that if you must leave your companion in a kennel, you may find yourself facing the "sticky situation" that the kennel won't accept him without proof that he has been vaccinated against kennel cough. The veterinarian then covers several points, given in more detail in chapter 3, as to why he calls standard vaccinations a "sticky situation."

"If," Dr. Goldstein said, "you are forced to vaccinate, select the intranasal vaccine that contains only *Bordetella* and *Parainfluenza*. Do not go the route of the injectable vaccine that also includes distemper and hepatitis (adenovirus)." Echoing information given in more detail in chapter 3, Dr. Goldstein added that "this way you are not overloading the immune system with five to seven different vaccines at the same time. The immune system can focus on the two challenges at hand and not be spread thin."

Dr. Goldstein went on to recommend that you vaccinate, if you have to, "about seven days before boarding; and begin twenty-four hours after the vaccine administration the homeopathic remedy *Thuja occidentalis* 12X or 30C five to seven days. Or use 1 teaspoon Viratox, a detoxifying homeopathic tincture, daily for seven days."

The veterinarian recommends the following amounts of *Thuja occidentalis*: For a dog up to 14 pounds, one pellet a day; dogs 15 to 34 pounds, two pellets a day; dogs 35 pounds and over, three pellets a day.

Dr. Weiner told me that the common orthodox treatment of antibiotics and cortisone has approximately the same high success rate
in treating kennel cough as does the homeopathic remedy and vitamin C that he uses unless clients insist on antibiotics. But those of
you who aren't already aware of the potential side effects of antibiotics and cortisone might have a rude awakening if you glance
through any book listing drug side effects.

Dr. Weiner, who told me that kennel cough is one of the more
common infectious diseases he sees in dogs, will use either drosera or bryonia (both homeopathic remedies). "If the dog's cough
is worse with motion," he noted, "I'll use bryonia. If the cough is
worse when the dog is resting, I usually will use drosera." The
veterinarian adds that he will "certainly also use vitamin C."

Canine Distemper

Canine distemper and the secondary bacterial infections that accom-
pany it were, when I researched the first book, estimated to kill 90
to 95 percent of the dogs brought to veterinarians. At the same time,
holistic veterinarians who had a lot of experience in treating infectious diseases in dogs were reporting an 85 percent cure rate. And
in those days, most holistic veterinarians weren't using acupuncture, homeopathy, or numerous other therapies they use now.

Symptoms of Distemper

Early symptoms of distemper are loss of appetite, depression, and
fever. Often these symptoms disappear for a few days, and then the
disease manifests itself again with a vengeance. There may be watery
or puslike discharge from the eyes and nose. The dog's eyes may become sensitive to light, and he may try desperately to keep himself
in a dark place. There may be diarrhea and a skin eruption on the
abdomen and on the insides of the hind legs. There may be a hard-
ening of the foot pads.

Holistic Therapy for Distemper

To start, I would like to share with you the true story of probably one of the earliest cases of diagnosed terminal canine distemper treated with what is today considered the most primitive natural therapy: vitamin C used without any other treatment. If this puppy's story doesn't interest you from the standpoint of historical medical interest, you may find in it inspiration to believe that your dog has a good chance of surviving with holistic therapy—no matter how sick your dog is, or how hopeless an orthodox veterinarian has said he is—especially since holistic therapy is now far more advanced.

I heard R. Geoffrey Broderick, D.V. M., talk passionately about this puppy in a speech at a convention on alternative medicine in the late 1970s. He didn't mention the dog's name, but I would like to call him "Lucky," and I think you'll see why.

"When the puppy was brought in to me," Dr. Broderick said, "he had been given up on by orthodox veterinarians. He had a temperature of 105 degrees. He was foaming at the mouth. He had not eaten in a week. He had not touched water in two days. He couldn't stand up. The other veterinarians who had seen him were quite right: He was dying.

"The question was," the veterinarian continued, "should I follow all the rules of orthodox veterinary medicine? If so, I too was going to have to put this little guy permanently to sleep. Or was I going to try a treatment for which there were at the time few or no precedents?"

Dr. Broderick asked the owners: "Will you be willing to try a bit of medical pioneering with me? Will you let me try vitamin C?" The owners agreed—quite possibly not out of any belief in the treatment, but because this was the only glimmer of hope any veterinarian had offered them for their puppy.

"As I filled the needle to inject the vitamin C into the dog," Dr. Broderick said, "I could just hear all my colleagues uttering, 'Preposterous! The dog is dying, by all rules of medicine—and you are going to cure him with a vitamin?'

"Nevertheless, I couldn't take the easy way out and destroy this dog. I gave him 25,000 milligrams of vitamin C, intravenously, main line. Then, with perhaps more hope than I really felt, I put a bowl of food in front of this dog who had been too sick to eat for a week—and left him alone for an hour in quiet.

"An hour later, I came back to see what I would find. The puppy, who had come in an hour before in a crumpled heap, was now standing up. He had his head in the bowl of food and was eating away ravenously. His tail was wagging up a storm. The tail wagging is not a scientific indication, but it certainly affected *me* at the time."

The veterinarian concluded: "There *was* a scientific barometer, though. His temperature was now absolutely normal. The doomed puppy had been cured in an hour."

I have named this puppy Lucky for three reasons: He was obviously lucky that his parents (as Dr. Broderick likes to call pet owners) didn't accept the suggestions of the other veterinarians to put him permanently to sleep, and he was lucky that he ended up in the offices of a doctor who was willing to try an uncharted therapy. He was also lucky that he responded so well to a therapy now considered very primitive by holistic veterinarians (including, I'm sure, Dr. Broderick).

You might want to call this puppy's luck karma, or a strong spirit, or an indomitable life force, or God's will. But the fact remains that this puppy did end up in Dr. Broderick's office and did serve as a starting point for other holistic veterinarians to investigate the long-ignored vitamin C research of Dr. Klenner and others in humans—and to put it into general use for dogs. Maybe that's another reason to call this puppy Lucky?

While vitamin C is still a mainstay of holistic treatment for infectious diseases, Dr. Weiner gives further details of how a dog with distemper today might be treated. "If the dog has clinical signs of distemper, or another virus," the veterinarian told me in a recent interview, "I'll use kinesiology to help diagnose and to help find the best therapy for that individual dog." He explains that there's a point on the body that deals with viruses, "and if the surrogate's arm drops—becomes weak—at that point, that indicates we are indeed dealing with a virus."

Then Dr. Weiner will, as other holistic veterinarians who use kinesiology do, test various natural substances known to help treat viruses by placing them on the dog's back. If a substance weakens the arm of the person touching the dog, the substance is discarded as a potential therapy. "I might test Chinese herbs or the herb goldenseal," the veterinarian told me. "I might test Noni juice and various homeopathics." When he has found the substances that give strength to the dog's body, he combines them—"and that combination becomes the therapy for that specific dog."

HOLISTIC TREATMENT FOR THE AFTEREFFECTS OF DISTEMPER With orthodox treatment, dogs who survive distemper have traditionally often been left with debilitating neurological problems if the disease progressed to the central nervous system. Michael W. Lemmon, D.V.M., once told me of two dogs presented to him that had been having chomping fits for several days. A dog with chomping fits will look as if he is chewing gum furiously, and often a bubbly froth will come from his mouth. (In chapter 3, veterinarians discuss the shortcomings of standard vaccinations. These two dogs are examples of these shortcomings: They both came down with distemper shortly after receiving the distemper vaccine from other veterinarians.)

Dr. Lemmon used a single fifteen-minute acupuncture technique on each dog, and both dogs were free of the chomping fits within twelve hours. The dog who had been more severely afflicted had a relapse after a week. "I feel another treatment would have helped the animal to a total cure," Dr. Lemmon told me, "but the owners . . . chose to have their dog euthanized. I know that other veterinarians, using acupuncture for this 'incurable' neurological aftereffect of distemper, have very high success—when the owners cooperate."

Robert Goldstein, V.M.D., and Marty Goldstein, D.V.M., have told me that "acupuncture is very successful in the alleviation of seizures secondary to distemper—even when permanent damage has been done to the central nervous system."

Dr. Kearns, who also dealt successfully with the neurological aftereffects of distemper, once gave me the following case history: "I first saw the German shepherd when he was a nine-month-old puppy. He had been treated at one of the most prestigious animal hospitals in the Northeast for distemper and, while they saved his life, he was left with encephalitis and massive seizure activity." Dr. Kearns started the dog on 30 to 40 grams of intravenous vitamin C daily, "and within ten days the seizures had stopped." The veterinarian added that "the dog never again had a seizure—although he lived to the rather ancient age of fourteen."

Lyme Disease

Lyme disease is spread by ticks. Symptoms vary but often include muscle and joint pain, high fever, and swollen lymph nodes. Since it hurts so much to walk, you may note that your dog chooses not to move around very much—and when she does walk, she has a stiff gait.

Dr. Weiner noted that orthodox treatment includes antibiotics, "but in homeopathic medicine, we have a remedy that works wonderfully for Lyme disease." In addition to the homeopathic, the veterinarian adds supportive therapy of a better diet and whatever herbs, vitamins, or other nutrients the dog tests out to need.

Although Dr. Weiner, when we talked, had not himself yet treated many cases of Lyme disease, all the dogs "have responded very well," he said.

Respiratory Diseases (Including Pneumonia and Pneumonitis)

As long ago as 1981, Dr. Kearns reported that he had approximately 95-percent successful results in treating respiratory diseases if the animal had not been given antibiotics before being brought to him. Other holistic veterinarians reported that they had approximately a 90-percent cure rate in early cases of upper respiratory tract diseases but added that if the animal had already been treated with antibiotics and other drugs, their success rate dropped to about 75 percent.

Symptoms of Pneumonia and Pneumonitis

These diseases are characterized by high fever, coughing, rapid breathing, and rapid pulse. In severe cases, there will be a blue cast to the lower eyelid. This is due to the fact that your dog is suffering from oxygen starvation. You may notice your pet trying hard to avoid lying down. He may take up an odd new sitting position, with his neck extended forward and his elbows turned out. This strange behavior is his instinctive attempt to give his constricted chest cavity literally *more room to breathe*.

Holistic Therapy for Pneumonia and Pneumonitis

In 1981, Dr. Kearns reported better results than the other veterinarians I talked with, so I printed the therapy he used. Veterinarians helping me to update told me that today basically the same therapy is used, with some changes because of new knowledge in holistic medicine. Following is the updated basic therapy.

Vitamin A (perhaps 10,000 units daily) and vitamin C were and remain mainstays of the holistic treatment for respiratory diseases. The B complex is considered very helpful also, and occasionally *Arsenicum album* (a homeopathic remedy) is used at a low potency for dogs that have a lot of nasal discharge and painful inflamed eyes.

Sometimes holistic veterinarians in 1981 used the herb garlic, which has a great mucus-destroying effect. Mucus in the lungs, of course, is a prime problem in respiratory diseases. While today many more herbs are in common use, garlic has withstood the test of time. Dr. Weiner, in a recent interview, told me: "One general statement I can make is that garlic is an excellent herb for lung problems."

Dr. Aloro also relies heavily on herbs to treat pneumonia and pneumonitis. He once treated a dog who had been taken to an emergency clinic the day before "with lung congestion so severe that the dog was turning blue." (This means that the lung congestion was stopping blood from flowing freely to and from the heart, and the dog was on the brink of dying from oxygen starvation.) "They managed to get the dog out of the immediate risk of dying, and the next day her owners brought her to me," Dr. Aloro said. "I started her immediately on herbs that are known to support the lungs and the heart, which now had a valvular defect." Dr. Aloro told me that since then "the dog's lungs and heart have been functioning fine." The only problem this dog who was snatched from death now faces is that "she will have to be on the herbs for the rest of her life." Since herbs, at least if prescribed by someone trained in their use, don't have dangerous side effects, as drugs do, I think we might consider this dog lucky.

Holistic veterinarians will, of course, use the typical conventional treatment of keeping the dog hydrated. And they will get calories into the dog the best way they can—orally if the dog is ready for that, or by stomach tube if he's not.

Other Respiratory Diseases

With rhinotracheitis and other respiratory tract diseases, the holistic veterinarians I worked with in 1981 reported a 90-percent cure rate in early cases, but if the animal had been treated with antibiotics and other drugs before they saw him, their success rate dropped to about 75 percent. Why should the antibiotic-treated pet have a lesser chance of being cured? Dr. Lemmon explained: "While antibiotics may inactivate or kill bacteria, they also suppress the immune system." Since the immune system is the body's *natural* way to kill bacteria, the therapies used by holistic veterinarians improve it, rather than weaken it.

Then why in certain emergency situations will some holistic veterinarians use antibiotics? The veterinarians I just quoted were talking about pets who had been treated with antibiotics before coming to them. If a holistic doctor feels he or she must resort to antibiotics, the veterinarian knows which natural therapies can off-set the negative effects of the drugs.

For this edition, several veterinarians specified that they will never use an antibiotic for a viral infection. Contrary to popular be-lief, antibiotics, while they can be effective against bacteria, do not tend to have an effect on viruses. Viral infections will cause clear nasal and ocular discharges, while bacterial infections will cause cloudy or thick yellow discharges.

In treating infections of the upper respiratory tract, Dr. Weiner re-lies heavily on homeopathic remedies, as other holistic veterinarians have told me they do in treating animals with these infections. For herbs, he most often finds that dogs respond best to either echi-nacea or goldenseal—"particularly goldenseal, which is very good for inflammation of the mucous membranes."

Dr. Aloro added that one reason he uses herbs is to prevent the infection from turning into pneumonia.

Septicemia (Blood Poisoning)

Septicemia is blood poisoning throughout the entire body of the dog. The definition tells you that it can be a very serious disease that is often fatal. Septicemia, for instance, is said to kill many more new puppies than does any other disease. However, even back in 1981 numerous holistic veterinarians were reporting to me excellent re-sults with septicemia.

Since septicemia can kill very quickly, I urge you to look at the earlier sections of this chapter for suggestions on how to deal with serious infectious diseases as quickly as possible.

Symptoms of Septicemia

It is imperative that an owner keep a sharp eye out for symptoms of septicemia, especially in a newborn puppy, because once the dis-ease gets hold of the baby, it can spread like wildfire. The puppy may have started out his new life looking well and nursing well. But then, perhaps a week after birth, he may withdraw from the rest of the litter and even from his mother. His cries become piteous and grow fainter. The nontechnical name given to septicemia in puppies is descriptive of the symptoms: fading pup syndrome.

When the symptoms start, the animal should get immediate veterinary help, or he will die within twenty-four to forty-eight hours.

Symptoms in the adult dog will be listlessness, poor appetite, and fever.

Holistic veterinarians add a point that they make for all other disorders covered in this book, and if you've read other sections, you may be sick of hearing this: This dread disorder can be prevented by the natural diet and supplements detailed in chapter 2. However, to stop septicemia from striking your newborn pet, prevention must begin with the mother at the start of pregnancy or before (See chapter 4).

Holistic Therapy for Septicemia

I am told that the therapy detailed in the first edition is still in common use among holistic veterinarians today. That therapy started with—you won't be surprised to hear—intravenous vitamin C (½ gram per pound of body weight).

Also having withstood the test of time, garlic and other herbs known to purify the blood are still relied on. Purifying the blood is, of course, the task at hand in blood poisoning. Garlic, for instance, is one of the few foods containing inulin, which helps the kidneys remove soluble materials from blood.

All solid foods are withheld until the dog is cured; only liquids are given. Enemas will sometimes be administered to help clear the system of toxins faster, especially if the poisoning is thought to have come from foods.

When blood tests and acupuncture testing reveal an accompanying problem in an internal organ such as the liver or kidneys (both of which filter out poisons from the body), a holistic veterinarian may use vitamin B_{12} injected in the acupuncture trigger point for that organ. Why B_{12}? You may know that Hollywood and sports stars sometimes get B_{12} shots for energy. While this is a gross oversimplification of all that B_{12} can do, the vitamin does act as a stimulant on acupuncture points that are deficient in energy. And obviously, if your dog is being treated for blood poisoning, you want her liver and kidneys to have a lot of energy so they can accomplish their natural, appointed mission of getting poisons out of her body.

Dr. Weiner noted that he can achieve the same result for septicemia by using chiropractic care. (You might see my personal story of my miniature poodle, Shiki, at the end of the introduction. A one-second chiropractic adjustment restored to her the full use of her back legs, a use my husband and I thought she had lost forever because of her advanced age.) Dr. Weiner explained that specific vertebrae along the spine supply nerve impulses to specific organs of the body. Using chiropractic, Dr. Weiner often finds the vertebrae corresponding to the liver or kidney to be out of alignment and readjusts them chiropractically.

Other Infectious Diseases

If the disease you're concerned about isn't specified in this chapter, check the index at the back of the book to see if it is mentioned in another chapter. If it isn't, this is by no means any indication that holistic veterinary medicine can't successfully treat it. See the list of holistic veterinarians at the back of this book and phone those in your area. I specify in your area because infectious diseases tend to die down or reappear in clusters in different areas of the country. For instance, a number of veterinarians told me that they had not seen cases of parvo for years, but veterinarians in other parts of the country reported that parvo is a major infectious disease they treat in their practices.

Also remember, as detailed throughout this chapter, that holistic veterinarians tend to treat what's off base in the individual dog's biochemistry—so the "name" of the disease sometimes fades in importance.

I didn't cover AIDS in this chapter because as I wrote it, this disease had not yet hit the dog population. (It had, however, started to strike cats; and I detailed successful holistic therapy for feline AIDS in this book's companion book, *Keep Your Cat Healthy the Natural Way*.) But, as Dr. Weiner told me, "We don't know why AIDS hasn't hit dogs—or if it's going to happen." You probably know that AIDS initially seemed relegated to only one segment of the human population and soon spread to other segments, before spreading to strike cats. So it's possible that by the time you read this, AIDS may have infected your dog. If it has, don't despair. Again, call holistic veterinarians in your area.*

References

1. C. W. Jungeblut et al., *J. Immunol.*, 33, 203, 1937; see also I. J. Kliger, et al., *J. Path. Bact.*, 46, 619, 1938; and C. W. Jungeblut, *J. Expt. Med.*, 70, 315, 1939. Cited by Adelle Davis, *Let's Get Well* (New York: Harcourt, Brace and World, Inc.), 1965, p. 141.
2. Adelle Davis, *Let's Eat Right to Keep Fit* (New York: Harcourt, Brace and Co.), 1954, p. 142.
3. Adelle Davis, *Let's Get Well* (New York: Harcourt, Brace and World, Inc.), 1965, p. 142.
4. Ibid., p. 141.

* A successful therapy detailed in my book on cats was used by Jack Long, V. M.D.

Chapter 9

Some Problems of Internal Organs: Diabetes, Cystitis, Stones, Kidney Inflammation, Intestinal Worms, and More

"Many times veterinarians react to diabetes by starting the dog immediately on insulin. Often, if they had just changed the diet to the one that's natural for dogs, the animal would never have *needed* insulin shots. Typically, when holistic veterinarians first see a dog with diabetes, the pet has been to one or more veterinarians and he is already insulin-dependent. Now we have to treat not only the diabetes but the dependency on insulin. We still can get the dog's diabetes controlled—to the point where he doesn't need insulin at all—within six weeks or six months, depending on how long he's been on the insulin.

". . . I have close to 100-percent success in treating urinary problems, unless there's a tumor in the bladder. . . . Natural diet is the key."
—*Ihor John Basko, D.V.M.*

"I have very good success with chronic kidney inflammation. Even if we don't get to see dogs until they already have the usually fatal uremia, we typically give them a much-extended life that is comfortable and happy.

". . . You can rid your dog of any type of intestinal worms if you restore his normal intestinal balance of bacteria, flora, and fauna by adding a natural probiotic to his food. . . . Probiotics were developed first as a natural therapy for humans. They can help people with such 'mysterious' disorders as chronic fatigue syndrome."
—*Neal K. Weiner, D.V.M.*

"Probiotics can help greatly in treating not only worms but also other problems of the intestinal tract, such as inflammatory bowel disease and colitis. . . . Since intestinal health is so important to the *overall* health, probiotics can help with many other problems in addition to those of the intestines."
—*Jack Long, V.M.D.*

I*n this chapter,* holistic veterinarians discuss therapies for a number of serious problems of internal organs, including the pancreas, bladder, kidneys, and intestines. These therapies involve little or no surgery or drugs and are often much more successful than the more toxic therapies that are in wider use.

If your dog's disorder isn't mentioned in this chapter, or in any chapter of this book, don't despair. As I repeat often, nutrients are behind every biochemical reaction in the body. Call a holistic veterinarian listed at the back of the book and discuss your companion's disorder.

Not included in this chapter, for instance (for reasons of space), are successful holistic therapies for problems as diverse as hepatitis, a serious liver disorder, and Cushing's syndrome. The latter syndrome comes from a tumor in the pituitary gland, which causes the gland to secrete too much hormone to the adrenal gland, which in turn becomes overactive. Neal K. Weiner, D.V. M., recently told me of a dog with Cushing's syndrome to whom he gave a short-term holistic treatment. "Orthodox blood testing before our treatment and after it," the holistic veterinarian told me, "revealed that the dog is 75 percent better. . . . And all the symptoms have disappeared."

Diabetes

Diabetes overtakes your dog if her pancreas becomes unable to secrete enough insulin to maintain a normal blood sugar balance. Diabetes can cause convulsions and death. Traditional treatment can be successful in controlling the diabetes, at least for a time. But, as will be discussed, this traditional treatment has drawbacks that often lead orthodox veterinarians to suggest that owners consider euthanasia. You will see that the newer therapies detailed here do not have these drawbacks.

Symptoms of Diabetes

It is imperative that you don't ignore the symptoms of diabetes. Not only can diabetes be a killer directly, it can also lead to liver enlargement (the liver can actually double in size), kidney damage, and cataracts, among other serious problems.

Your pet's appetite can be a symptom: He may become a glutton. At the same time he's eating more, however, he may start losing weight. (This does not mean an obese animal cannot develop diabetes. The disease is as common in obese pets as it is in obese people.) He may also develop increased thirst, spending more time at his water bowl, lapping furiously. If these symptoms appear, don't think of them as "odd changes in habits." They could be the only warning you'll ever get that your dog has diabetes.

The Difference between Orthodox and Holistic Approaches to Diabetes

Standard medical treatment involves introducing insulin from *outside* the body for the lifetime of the dog. Holistic veterinary treatment involves rebuilding the total health of the body, particularly the pancreas, so that it can again naturally produce enough of its *own* insulin—*inside* the body—just as it always did before the dog "got" diabetes.

Insulin shots are expensive and have to be maintained throughout the pet's life. They do not always work. (Some veterinarians have told me it would be more accurate if I wrote that "they *many times* do not work.") Their rigid scheduling can make an owner a slave to the pet's sickness. (Scheduling of nutritional supplements is not so crucial and allows the owner more freedom.) For these reasons and others mentioned in the next paragraph, some orthodox veterinary books for the public have stated that you might be better off putting your diabetic companion permanently "to sleep."

Insulin introduced artificially into your dog's body makes him continually vulnerable to diabetic shock, which can be fatal. This is called an insulin reaction: If you are not around to give your pet immediate emergency help, he may die. (If your dog is on insulin, *please* be sure to have your veterinarian tell you when insulin shock is most likely to occur, what signs to look for, and what emergency help you can give.) This is another fact that leads an owner either to become a slave to a diabetic pet, sometimes rearranging work and sleep schedules to be nearby when diabetic shock can be expected, or to dispose of the pet entirely.

Once a natural therapy allows the dog to be weaned away from insulin, of course, the owner need no longer worry about the possibility of insulin shock.

At its best—when insulin controls diabetes without side effects—it does only that: It controls the diabetes. It does nothing for the degenerative changes in the body that caused the diabetes in the first place, that are still preventing the body from creating its own insulin naturally, and that are probably causing other health problems as well. An overall holistic approach will attack the cause of the diabetes (a chemically imbalanced body), rather than just trying to control the diabetes, which is only a *symptom* of the imbalance. In this way, the body usually will again be able to form enough of its own insulin. You may also very well find that your dog suddenly recovers from other, seemingly unrelated, health problems as well. A number of case histories in this book tell of dogs who recovered not only from the problem their people were concerned about, but also from disorders they had no idea could be connected, disorders that were coming from the same imbalances in the dog's body.

Holistic Therapies for Diabetes

In this section, I will focus on therapies presently used by two holistic veterinarians. In some details the approaches may seem different, but in those details the two doctors are using therapies that have the same results: changing the biochemistry of the body back to its original ability to produce enough insulin on its own.

Ihor John Basko, D.V. M., summarizing his basic therapy for dogs with diabetes, said in a recent interview, "I use individualized diet change, acupuncture at the points on the body known to stimulate insulin production and healing of the pancreas, pituitary, and digestive system, and Chinese herbs." The latter two therapies have thousands of years of empiric evidence behind them, and have recently undergone scientific study on Western terms. Dr. Basko adds that exercise is extremely important, supervised by a veterinarian knowledgeable in endurance training in health-compromised dogs.

"We put the dogs on a natural diet," Dr. Basko continued, echoing the words of every holistic veterinarian over the years who has spoken to me about prevention or treatment of any disease. "We give them foods that help stimulate the natural secretion of insulin within the body. We try to get fresh pancreas from the butcher and give it to the dog. We use other fresh raw organ meats, such as liver, and other meats and some fish. We also give the dogs vegetables that help stimulate insulin, such as string beans, yams, and squash." John Fudens, D.V. M., adds that alfalfa and whole grains also stimulate insulin.

For the herbal part of his treatment, Dr. Basko uses ginseng. "I don't use ginseng straight," he said, "but in combination with other herbs, which I choose individually according to the animal." The veterinarian adds that Noni, a Hawaiian herb, is used to treat diabetes "with good success."

Dr. Basko said that the typical dog he treats for diabetes "has been to conventional veterinarians and has been having to receive increasingly higher doses of insulin. And with the increasingly high doses, his people have been getting more and more alarmed." The need to give more and more insulin to keep the dog "where he used to be" is common when insulin is introduced into the body from outside. As mentioned in the introduction, the higher success of holistic veterinary medicine can be seen as particularly amazing in light of the fact that these veterinarians often don't get to see a pet until he's very far along in a disease.

The typical diabetic dog brought to Dr. Basko is being fed commercial dog food. He added that "in many cases, if the previous veterinarians had just changed the diet and used exercise, the dog would never have needed insulin shots."

"With the typical dog I get to treat," Dr. Basko continued, "we are dealing not only with advanced diabetes, we are dealing also with a problem of insulin dependency. It can take us anywhere from six weeks to six months to mollify the insulin dependency. Often, with the acupuncture, the new diet, and the ginseng combination, we are able to *start* lowering the insulin dose after a week or two, lowering it 30 percent every two weeks until the dog is on about one-fourth of what he had been on when he was brought to us. And then we gradually keep on lowering it, until his dependency is completely over. Then we stop the insulin entirely."

Dr. Basko added that at that point the dog's body is back to producing the normal amount of insulin that it produced before he came down with diabetes—and any need for insulin shots is only a nasty memory for the dog and his owners. You might want to know if the continuing holistic therapy that replaced the insulin is as expensive as insulin. There *is* no continuing holistic therapy except a natural diet, which, as detailed in chapter 2, can be actually less expensive than a diet of toxins.

Remember that the previous discussion was about Dr. Basko's typical patient—a dog treated by insulin before being taken to a holistic veterinarian. Remember also that Dr. Basko's typical case history of an animal treated early by a *holistic* veterinarian would be of a dog receiving a recommended change of diet and being sent home without any other therapy except herbal and mineral supplements.

An important warning: As holistic veterinarians warn elsewhere for other disorders, do not take it upon yourself to remove your dog from an orthodox therapy. Note, for instance, that Dr. Basko *gradually* withdraws dogs from insulin shots as holistic therapy increases the animal's ability to produce her own insulin.* It is crucial that there at no time be either too much or *too little* insulin introduced from outside the body, to balance the new amount your pet's body is producing. Monitoring insulin levels requires periodic scientific testing.

Norman C. Ralston, D.V.M., once pleaded with me to reemphasize the previous point. "I just lost a wonderful cat," he said, sounding almost as pained as if the cat had been his own. "The owner decided to treat her animal herself because what I did seemed so simple. And it *was* simple—but she depended too long on her own treatment, without having the cat's insulin level professionally checked. The cat was rushed to emergency and died."

Complementing Dr. Basko's information, Dr. Weiner said, "I certainly try to persuade all owners to get our patients on fresh-food diets; and I know what basic vitamins and minerals have been proven to work best for diabetes, but beyond that I tailor my protocol to my individual patient." This is, actually, a prime approach of holistic doctors in treating any disorder; and Dr. Basko, like Dr. Weiner, began his interview with me by saying: "We don't treat one diabetic dog like all diabetic dogs. We treat them like individual animals."

"For the herbal part of my treatment," Dr. Weiner told me, "I'll often use Essiac tea, which is a combination of four herbs often used to treat cancer. It's a powerful detoxifier and immune-system strengthener. I show my clients how to brew the tea, and they mix it in with the dog's food. Or I may use a combination of herbs called Noni juice, which is specific for pancreatic functions and is very, very wonderful for diabetes." Both these products are available, as I write, at some large health food stores. By the time you read this—if the present explosion of knowledge about natural therapies continues—you may well be able to go to the nearest drugstore and get these products. This has certainly become true of a number of products that were little known when I wrote the first edition.

---

* This is monitored by blood and urine testing.

"What I do before I choose my specific herbs," Dr. Weiner continued, "is to test the dog to find which herbs known to help diabetes have the most beneficial effect on the energy pattern of my individual patient's body, especially the pancreas and kidneys." (The latter organs are often damaged in diabetes.) To test how various substances affect energy patterns, Dr. Weiner uses kinesiology, which is relied upon heavily these years by a number of other holistic veterinarians.

Dr. Weiner defined kinesiology—at least as used by holistic veterinarians: "I put the food or other substance I'm testing on the dog's back, and I have a surrogate touch the dog. The person tries to keep his or her arm straight. If the arm goes down—that is, if it is weakened—the energy of the food is drawing energy out of the dog's body."

Continuing his discussion of how he treats diabetes, Dr. Weiner added: "Minerals are really important for insulin metabolism. I use a product called Sea Meal, which contains nineteen different seaweeds that are ground into a powder." This product, he says, "has a vast array of minerals that help in proper insulin metabolism." He recommends that Sea Meal, which is made by a company called Solid Gold, be given "at ⅛ a teaspoon for every 15 pounds of the dog's body weight."

Dr. Weiner added: "Since diabetes deals with problems of the pancreas, I may put my patient on a pancreatic enzyme supplement to take the stress off the organ." (These enzymes were popular among holistic veterinarians even in 1981.) He specified that he often uses a product called Prozymes. He also uses digestive enzymes, which, he says, help the pancreas work better.

Dr. Weiner almost always puts dogs with diabetes on vitamin E, generally about 200 IU a day for a small dog and 400 IU for a medium to large dog. He will give 500 mg of vitamin C daily to a small canine and approximately 1000 mg to a medium to large dog. He will usually also give cod-liver oil. And he uses kinesiology to see which homeopathic remedy affects the dog's body energy most positively.

Dr. Weiner's reference to vitamin E leads us back to the first edition, in which I cited a number of studies that found this vitamin allowed 80 percent of people with diabetes to go off insulin entirely or to drastically curtail its use. I think taking your time to detail this information here would be unnecessary. Any holistic veterinarian or M.D. should know of this research, as well as updates. For the same reasons I warned earlier about taking your dog off insulin and self-treating, I make the same strong warning here in reference to when vitamin E is used. *Consult a holistic veterinarian before cutting down at all on your dog's insulin.*

For some suggestions for a basic diet for diabetes, see the following section on pancreatitis.

Pancreatitis

Dr. Basko told me that dogs who eat commercial foods, "especially the canned foods, which tend to contain a lot of overcooked and rancid fat, are very prone to pancreatitis."

Pancreatitis—inflammation of the pancreas—can kill. If your dog doesn't die, she may, with standard treatment, have recurring bouts of the disease, any one of which might kill her. With holistic therapy, dogs do not tend to have these recurring bouts.

Drs. Robert Goldstein, V.M.D., and Marty Goldstein, D.V.M., have told me that "pancreatitis is the root of many, many other conditions. Once the pancreas starts to deteriorate, other organs often follow." These veterinarians, too, considered an improper diet the usual cause of pancreatitis.

Symptoms of Pancreatitis

The acute form of pancreatitis manifests itself in sudden vomiting, depression, abdominal pain, and fever. These are symptoms of a number of other problems also, and only a veterinarian can give a differential diagnosis. Since pancreatitis can kill very rapidly—as can some other diseases with the symptoms of vomiting, depression, and fever—get your dog quickly to the nearest available veterinarian, holistic or orthodox. As mentioned often in this book, holistic veterinarians rely heavily on their orthodox training in emergency situations.

Chronic pancreatitis (or pancreatic insufficiency) is frequently marked by voluminous putty-colored stools. These stools have a rancid odor. Your dog may have a great appetite but lose weight. Why? He may be losing weight because his diseased pancreas is not digesting (that is, not allowing his body to use) the food; he may have a large appetite for exactly the same reason.

As we have said, the unfortunate animal with chronic pancreatitis is subject to bouts of the acute form. Indeed, chronic pancreatitis *is* the "recurring bouts" that are common when acute pancreatitis is treated by traditional means. Chronic pancreatitis is very uncommon when the acute form is treated holistically. As long ago as 1981, holistic veterinarians such as Dr. Kearns were telling me: "As long as my clients keep their pets on a natural diet, with pancreatic enzymes, we just have no further problems."

Therapy for Pancreatitis

Orthodox therapy may be used initially for acute pancreatitis. This includes antibiotics, steroids, and fasting with water only. Once the medical emergency is over, the dog will be shifted to a diet of *real* foods tailored specifically to support the pancreas. (See the accompanying boxed information.) Supplements of pancreatic glandulars and digestive enzymes may also be prescribed, also to support the pancreas. Vitamin C and other natural supplements that strengthen the immune system will be added.

A Basic Diet for Diabetes and Chronic Pancreatitis

The following diet is recommended by Drs. Basko and Weiner, as well as other holistic veterinarians. They make changes in this diet according to the individual dog's needs.

- 50 percent complex carbohydrates, such as cooked brown or wild rice, millet, buckwheat, rye, and oatmeal. Organic and flaked for easy digestion.

- 25 percent finely chopped green vegetables, carrots, and sprouts.
- 25 percent protein, including organic organ meats, steamed fish, soy granules, and seaweed.

     How foods are combined in each meal is extremely important for pancreatic problems. Acceptable combinations are
- Grains and vegetables
- Grains and fruits*
- Protein and vegetables.

To the information in the accompanying box, Dr. Basko adds that root vegetables such as sweet potatoes should be cooked, but vegetables like sprouts should be given raw.

Dr. Weiner believes that feeding more frequent, smaller meals can be helpful for the dog with pancreatitis. This was a view held by some holistic veterinarians back in 1981, who stated that these smaller feedings allowed the pancreas to do its job of digesting food on a more even keel throughout the day, rather than performing with sudden bursts of energy. Dr. Basko believes, however, that this recommendation is more appropriate for diabetes and is "not necessarily true" for pancreatitis. You might want to discuss this point with a holistic veterinarian as it relates individually to your own dog.

Case Histories of Pancreatitis

John Fudens, D.V. M., sent me several detailed case histories of dogs he has recently treated for pancreatitis. All the dogs also suffered a number of other health problems. Kate, for instance, a wirehaired terrier, also had arthritis and diagnosed chronic progressive lung disease, among other disorders, when Dr. Fudens first saw her. As the veterinarian summed up, Kate's disease state "had gone from the

---

* Dr. Basko recommends that only Noni and papaya be used as the fruits on this diet.

eyes and ears into the lungs, digestive tract, bones, and joints." One month after starting holistic therapy, Dr. Fudens wrote me, Kate—whose personality had been altered by all her physical problems—was "acting like a wirehaired terrier again: sleeping with the owners and just in general being belligerent and bossy." Her physical symptoms had also greatly improved in that month. After that, Kate had some minor setbacks; but when Dr. Fudens wrote me several months later, Kate was doing "very, very well, greatly improved over just a short period of time as far as her overall health is concerned."

Fluffy, a seven-year-old female Peke-a-poo, suffered from not only pancreatitis but "a mixed bag of seizures (which she had been having for five years), spinal disc problems, corneal ulcers, and cataracts. Her health was a total mess." Fluffy's recovery was so speedy and relatively easy that it surprised even Dr. Fudens, who called it "amazing." Fluffy now remains free of disease on no therapy at all, just a natural diet.

I will give this next case history in detail more closely approximating the depth Dr. Fudens gave in the other histories he sent. "Pumpkin is a Yorkie, female, spayed, eleven years old when I first saw her," Dr. Fudens wrote me. "That was in January, '94." You will see in the veterinarian's following list of what was wrong with Pumpkin that he alternately mentions diseases and drugs and surgery. I was reminded of the holistic veterinarians who have told me over the years that they wished more veterinarians would recognize commercial pet foods as a disease.

Here is Dr. Fudens' list of what was troubling Pumpkin when he first saw her: "severe chronic degenerative disease, vaccines, multiple surgeries for many things, pancreatitis, bloody gastroenteritis, cortisones for the skin and digestive tract every day for years, many of the intestinal drugs, antibiotics, spinal disc problems, cataracts." Although the years of treatments with surgeries and drugs indicate a long history of serious health problems, when Pumpkin first met Dr. Fudens "she was going downhill very fast." That is, she was now going downhill very quickly on a dangerous descent she had begun long ago.

Dr. Fudens related to me his program for saving Pumpkin: "I

started with my usual detox programs over many months—first the homeopathic nux vomica and after several months thuja. I had her on bitter Chinese herbs and on my liver glandulars and my immune complex glandulars. We put her on natural foods, and on Chinese herbs for the diarrhea."

Pumpkin did very well on the detoxification program, and in July of 1994, Dr. Fudens started her "on her first homeopathic constitutional, which was sulfur. I have repeated the sulfur a total of three times over about a year and a half," he continued, "and it has worked very, very nicely. She has gravitated to a much higher plane of health."

Pumpkin is now about sixteen years old, some five years older than she might ever have gotten to be without holistic therapy. Although she is free of all the disorders she suffered when her karma (if you will) brought her to Dr. Fudens, the very advanced age she had lived to by late 1996 opened her up to some heart problems. For almost two years, Dr. Fudens has been treating Pumpkin as a heart patient, with homeopathic digitalis, an herbal diuretic, a heart glandular extract, and some Chinese herbs that are known to help the heart. And the veterinarian told me that Pumpkin has been doing "quite well—especially considering that the fact that she's sixteen and still alive is amazing in the first place. When Pumpkin was first brought to me, I never thought she'd go this far."

For more information on alternative medicine and heart problems in animals (and humans), see chapter 10.

Urological Disorders: Cystitis, Bladder and Kidney Stones, Urinary Blockage

"Urinary tract diseases respond very well to holistic therapy," Dr. Weiner told me, echoing the ideas expressed by Dr. Basko on the covering page of this chapter. "About 85 percent to 90 percent of the dogs do quite well—and never have the recurrences that are considered somewhat inevitable."

While urinary tract problems are less common in dogs than they are in cats (I cover the dreaded feline urological syndrome in this book's companion, *Keep Your Cat Healthy the Natural Way*), Dr. Weiner noted that they pose the same serious dangers in dogs once they strike. Dr. Basko added that another similarity between urinary disorders in dogs and in cats is that the basic cause is commercial foods. (For more details, see chapter 1.) Dr. Basko also added that "just eliminating commercial foods, and substituting fresh foods, can go a long way toward healing urinary disorders."

Holistic veterinarians have been telling me since 1981 that it is when owners *keep* their dogs on a natural diet—after the dogs are healed—that the common recurrences just don't happen.

Urological problems involve the kidneys and bladder, because urine is secreted from the former and stored in the latter. These disorders are painful and often life-threatening. They pose a particular danger to male dogs, Dr. Basko told me, and dalmatians are more prone than other breeds to suffer the very serious problem of urinary blockage.

With conventional therapy, these problems are expensive to treat. As Dr. Basko pointed out, the expense comes from the fact that "with traditional treatment, the problem doesn't clear up. The dog is put on antibiotics and various other drugs—and when the drugs are withdrawn, the problem just comes back." He said that orthodox veterinarians do recommend a low-ash diet, which is a correct recommendation, "but all too often people keep on giving the dogs dry foods," which are high-ash diets.

As we see in this section, dogs treated holistically for urological problems can often be helped easily without drugs, surgery, or great expense. And there are seldom the relapses considered almost inevitable with conventional therapy.

If you have read the early chapters on prevention, you already know *why* holistic veterinarians believe many diseases don't strike animals eating their natural diet in the wild—and seldom strike domesticated animals eating their natural diet even though the rest of their environment (a human's house) is unnatural. Adding information specific to urological disorders and dry diets (kibble), Dr. Weiner said that investigators studying dogs in the wild have found that these dogs "get almost all their moisture from the animals they eat, and so they drink very little water. A dog in the wild who drinks a fair amount of water, they say, already has a weakness in his body."

Dr. Weiner continued: "So when domesticated dogs eat a dry-based diet, they're getting very little moisture. This lack of moisture may weaken the kidneys." Dr. Basko explained further that dogs can't drink enough water to supplement what's lacking in dry foods, and the kidneys attempt to work harder to accomplish their natural job of flushing out wastes from the body.

The veterinarian stated strongly that "dry food is not an appropriate food for dogs. I'd say that 95 percent of the holistic veterinarians I know acknowledge that fact." You may have an obvious question here: Then why in the world are there so many dry foods out for dogs? Dr. Basko had a succinct answer: "Because most of the research is done in veterinary colleges that are supported by money from big pet food companies."

Dr. Basko's strong words about dry foods, which echoed those of the veterinarians who worked on this section in the first edition, led me to a question I asked Dr. Weiner in a later interview: What about the top-quality purer prepared dry foods recommended (reluctantly) by some holistic veterinarians to owners who for various reasons don't feel they can give their dog his natural diet? Would these foods be as likely to lead to urological problems in a dog? Dr. Weiner's answer indicated that, while they certainly are less detrimental to the dog's general health than commercial dry foods are, they still have the same problem of lack of moisture.

Dr. Weiner added another reason, besides moisture, that a natural diet prevents urological problems: "Those dogs out there in the wild are eating their kill; they're eating a lot of meat. Meat creates an acid urine, and bladder and kidney stones rarely form in an acid urine." (Dr. Kearns once pointed out that there are a few forms of bladder stones in dalmatians and several other breeds that can form in an acid urine.) In the chapters on prevention, we pointed out that the healthy pH of a dog's body—to help keep *all* problems away—is acidic. Dr. Weiner continued: "But many commercial foods have a lot of grains, and grains create an alkaline urine." An alkaline urine will allow stones to form. In addition, Dr. Weiner pointed out that, of course, "commercial dog and cat foods have more debris and toxins that the kidneys have to filter out, which can also weaken them."

Symptoms of Urological Disorders

Your dog may strain, trying hard to pass urine—and yet many times he may pass little or none. The reason for this behavior is that the itching and burning of the urethra, which carries urine out of the body, make the dog think he has to urinate extremely often, when in reality he doesn't.

If this symptom of cystitis is left untreated, the urethra will plug up, and your pet won't be able to urinate even when he has to. Or your dog may forget all his manners about where you have taught him he is supposed to urinate and start urinating wherever he happens to be at the time. (Veterinarians warn that the latter symptom may be misconstrued as "psychological" in origin—for instance, an attempt to get back at you for introducing a new pet or baby to the dog's territory.) There may be blood in the urine. As Dr. Ralston emphasized for the first book, these last symptoms "may be an emergency, and the pet should be rushed immediately to a veterinarian." These symptoms indicate urinary blockage. (For more on urinary blockage, see page 227.)

Male dogs, because of body structure, may exhibit the earlier signs mentioned above for only a day or two before they advance to the emergency state of urinary blockage. So, if your companion is a male dog who has been on a commercial diet, try to keep an eye out for the early symptom of straining without urinating and treat that symptom as an emergency.

Cystitis

Vitamin C can be very helpful in curing cystitis. This disorder is caused by a virus, and the secondary infections accompanying cystitis are caused by bacteria. As covered in the chapter on infectious diseases, vitamin C is effective against virtually all, if not all, types of viruses and bacteria. Also, vitamin C, in the form of ascorbic *acid*, makes the urine *acidic*, which we have explained is what dogs need.

Dr. Basko warned that vitamin C alone will probably not be enough to prevent recurrence of cystitis indefinitely. "Dogs have to have Chinese herbs," he told me, referring to a combination of these herbs, which, he said, "remove the problem from the kidney, not just the bladder. They remove predigested products that eventually form stones. They help acidify the bladder and heal the bladder's lining." The veterinarian added that these herbs, plus a small maintenance level of vitamin C, will result in a permanent control.

Many holistic veterinarians have expressed concern to me that some owners don't keep up prescribed maintenance doses of nutrients. In 1981, Dr. Ralston made this strong warning about cystitis and other disorders: "An owner can become too confident that everything is all right, discontinue maintenance—and end up with a dead animal."

Another word of warning: Do not treat your dog yourself until your veterinarian has established that your companion has cystitis and cystitis only. For the dangers involved, see the section later on urinary blockage. Also, consult at least by phone with a holistic veterinarian about a specific therapy for your companion.

Dr. Weiner gave us his therapy for cystitis. Like Dr. Basko and other nutritional veterinarians, he will get the dog off dry foods and on a low-ash diet and will try hard to convince the owner to use the dog's natural diet. "And I definitely get dogs on vitamin C, 500 mg a day for a small dog, 1000 mg for a medium to large dog. I use cod-liver oil and vitamin E, 200 IU or 400 IU." Cod-liver oil is a good source of many nutrients, especially vitamin A. Vitamin E, known to prevent scars, is helpful in cystitis because it aids in preventing and healing scarring of the bladder. "I will often give a product called Rentean," Dr. Weiner noted, "which has a number of different herbs that are very good for restoring health to the kidneys." The veterinarian will also use various homeopathic remedies chosen for the needs of the specific patient.

Dr. Basko's initial therapy for cystitis includes the Chinese herb combination he spoke of earlier for maintenance therapy. He said that this combination "works like a charm with or without antibiotics and with or without acupuncture." He added that he uses antibiotics "very rarely, maybe 10 percent of the time." Acupuncture helps to heal and also eases the pain that cystitis causes. The veterinarian noted an additional treatment: "I use oral vitamin C to flush out the kidneys and bladder. I recommend Ester-C." Dr. Basko also uses antioxidant nutrients.

The veterinarian said that if the dog is refusing to eat, he makes a kind of "milk shake" of raw liver, tomato juice, and purified water. "I put that in a blender," he said, "and the dog will usually drink that straight out. I may also mix a little bit of fresh carrot juice in there. Carrot juice has a lot of vitamin A, which is good for the bladder lining."

In the first edition, J. Keith Benedict, D.V. M., pointed out that a liquid diet, which of course the previous is, "allows the system to clean itself out."

Bladder and Kidney Stones

Both Dr. Basko and Dr. Weiner said that they use the same therapies for stones that they do for cystitis, covered previously. However, the first step now must be to flush out the bladder or kidney by giving a large amount of liquid intravenously. Dr. Basko stated that instead of using painkillers, as orthodox veterinarians do, he uses herbs and acupuncture. He also massages the area of the bladder and kidneys. Acupuncture and massage are well-proven techniques to help pain without dangerous side effects.

Vitamin C (in the form of ascorbic acid) helps keep the urine acidic. And an acidic urine can actually dissolve stones, which are alkaline. Keeping the dog on a small amount of ascorbic acid after recovery—that is, keeping the urine acidic—is one reason holistic veterinarians don't have the recurrence of stones that is so common with drug therapy.

Urinary Blockage

Complete urinary blockage is an emergency situation. The retention of urine, and its waste products, causes poisoning throughout the body that results in death in forty-eight hours *or less*. The bladder can be so swollen with trapped urine that it is as hard as a stone— and as large as a big orange. (Imagine how much space that would take up in your dog's body.) A badly swollen bladder can rupture.

The preceding explains why I said earlier that you must have a solid diagnosis of cystitis before you try a simple home treatment. If what you are really dealing with is urinary blockage, you will have a dead dog within two days.

The first step in treating urinary blockage, as with stones, is to flush out the bladder. This removes the "sand" collected in the urethra (the canal that carries urine out of the body) and allows the urine to flow again. This release of the urine also relieves pressure on the kidneys, which is a problem with urinary blockage. The "sand," by the way, is caused by bits of bladder stones passing out of the bladder.

Dr. Weiner said that when he is dealing with *complete* urinary blockage, "I have a dog with an immediately life-threatening situation. So I unblock him the fastest way possible—which is surgery." Once the surgery has released the stored-up urine and debris from the body, "then I try to convince the owners to put the dog on a fresh-food diet, and I give the animal vitamin C and cod-liver oil. I add Sea Meal for minerals. And then I'll test the dog's body. Depending on what I find the individual animal's body needs, I may use the herbal combination Noni juice or the herbal formula Rentean. And I'll use whatever homeopathic remedies the dog needs."

Dr. Basko recently told me that the recommendations made in 1981 by Michael Kreisberg, D.V.M., for a diet for a dog recovering from urinary blockage still stand. That diet would include fresh raw beef liver, kidney, or heart several times a week. Also included would be cooked chicken, cottage cheese, raw egg yolks (no whites), and whole-grain cereals. Do not give dry food, milk, or any food containing fish. Sharp-eyed readers will see a bit of a difference here (*no* fish, and *cooked* chicken) from the recommendations made in chapter 2, but remember that the diet covered in that chapter is to prevent disease. When a disease has developed, holistic doctors may have to modify the preventive diet according to the new needs of the animal's body.

Ask your dog's doctor if you should give your recovering pet distilled water. A number of holistic veterinarians have told me it can help leach out of the body the harmful debris that may be clogging up the bladder. Others have pointed out that it also is free of the impurities in tap water, which can cause even further harm to an already weakened animal. I ask you to question a holistic veterinarian before using distilled water because several doctors have warned me that if it is used too early in the treatment of a highly toxic animal, its leaching effect may create stone formation as the body rids itself—perhaps too fast—of toxic wastes.

Kidney Problems: Chronic Interstitial Nephritis, Uremia, and Renal Failure

The preceding section also discusses therapy for some kidney problems.

Chronic interstitial nephritis, a serious kidney inflammation, is common among older dogs not raised on natural diets. It is so common that many veterinarians believe that testing for kidney function should be run routinely on the older animal.

The most common symptom is that the pet drinks increasingly more water and excretes increasingly more pale or colorless urine. As the disease progresses, the animal may have bouts of vomiting, constipation, or diarrhea. When these latter signs appear, your pet may have uremia and may be struggling to get along with only 30 percent kidney function. Uremia is poisoning of the entire body caused by accumulation in the bloodstream of waste products that are normally helped out of the body by healthy kidneys.

Drs. Basko and Weiner told me that the basic diet recommended in 1981 in my first book is still the one to use in treating kidney inflammation: a low-residual diet with less animal protein than the dog should have when he is healthy. Dr. Weiner specified: "While a dog in normal health should get a third to 50 percent of his diet in the form of protein, for a dog with kidney inflammation, I would reduce it to about 25 percent."

Richard J. Kearns, D.V. M., once explained that the reason for the two dietary changes (less protein and less residue) in an animal with kidney inflammation is that you now must give the animal food that will take as much strain as possible off the kidney. "You have to help the body produce as little waste as possible, so that the kidney is asked to do the minimum of work to reduce that waste." He added that in cutting down the protein, you must make sure that the protein you do give is of very high quality. If you have read any other part of this book, you won't be surprised that at this point in checking over the manuscript many veterinarians wrote that most, if not all, commercial pet foods have very low-quality protein.

Dr. Kearns also explained that a low-residual diet includes such foods as chicken and turkey, well-ground and well-cooked grains, rice, squash, and greens.

In a recent interview, Dr. Basko stressed that you must take your dog off all dry foods, because dogs with kidney problems need a lot of moisture. He recommended a vegetarian diet with a boiled kidney soup. "Soak the kidneys overnight in cold water, and then wash them out thoroughly before you start cooking them," he said. "Make a broth along with some Oriental (shiitake) mushrooms. That broth will give dogs with kidney problems all the protein they need at this point."*

Dr. Weiner recently gave me his therapy for chronic interstitial nephritis: "I use a homeopathic remedy, nux vomica, that helps detoxify and cleanse the kidneys. I put these dogs on a 30X dosage of it, one pill a day. I also give them a product called Renafood, made by Standard Process, which is a glandular extract that goes in and helps not only to detoxify, but to rebuild, the kidneys. The dogs

---

* Dr. Fudens disagreed, saying that you should "never, ever make a dog a vegetarian."

get one tablet a day. I also use a product called Rentean," Dr. Weiner added, "an herbal formula made by Christopher Ortz that helps rebuild and strengthen the kidneys. Or, according to the particular needs of the individual dog, I may use the herbal formula Noni juice.

"We usually have the owners administer fluids underneath the skin two to three times a week at home, to help the kidneys flush out the toxins," Dr. Weiner added. "We give them an intravenous set with lactated Ringer's, and we teach them how to use it." Dr. Weiner is talking about that bottle of clear liquid you often see turned upside down and attached to the arm of hospital patients. This was the first time I had heard that lactated Ringer's therapy, traditionally relegated only to hospitals (and therefore expensive), could be used at home.

For animals who already have the often fatal uremia when brought to them, Drs. Robert and Marty Goldstein told me in 1981 a few details of what they used, including orthodox therapy and kidney extract, a form of glandular therapy. When a diuretic was necessary, they used herbal diuretics rather than drugs. For this new book, Dr. Basko said that he uses the same technique today, "along with intravenous fluids, vitamin C, B complex, and acupuncture."

For uremia, Dr. Weiner recently said: "I use the same treatment as for chronic interstitial nephritis, except that I administer fluids more frequently."

I asked Dr. Weiner for a case history of a dog with uremia that he treated with holistic therapy. Please keep in mind here that uremia is often fatal when treated by orthodox means. Instead of talking about a specific dog, Dr. Weiner said, "The case histories of these animals are almost always the same, because usually, with uremia, we find that three-quarters of both kidneys are no longer functioning. The dogs come in to us on the brink of death, but we can get them comfortable and happy again and give them six months to a year and a half of an extended life—and a nice one."

Worms and Other Problems of the Intestines

As we will see in this section, an exciting new set of natural products, called probiotics, has made the treatment of intestinal problems—as well as disorders that we may not think of as stemming from something wrong in the intestines—much easier to treat successfully. This is true not only for our beloved dogs and cats but for ourselves.* And the reason these products work so well makes supreme common sense medically.

Intestinal Worms

Intestinal worms sap your pet's strength by "gobbling up" his food and thereby robbing his body of nutrients. These worms also feed on your dog's blood and can damage intestinal tissue. A heavily infested dog can die.

An animal can become infected by intestinal worms through the mouth or through the skin. He may swallow a worm egg, or he may eat a "transport host" that is carrying worms. Worms can enter the skin by way of blood-sucking insects such as mosquitoes or ticks. A puppy can be born with worms passed on by his mother, or he may become infected by her while he is nursing. (If you are owned by a pregnant dog as you read this, see chapter 4 for information on how to help prevent her from passing on worms to her babies.)

SYMPTOMS OF WORMS It is imperative that you have your veterinarian make regular fecal checks, since the most dangerous worms cannot be seen by the eye. However, you can also take a look at the feces every several days. If you see squiggly things moving around, or if you see what look like grains of rice, those are roundworms or tapeworms. (Of course, if you have recently fed your dog rice, which we recommend in the early chapters as a healthy food, those things that look like grains of rice may actually *be* grains of rice. So, in order not

---

* My husband, Joe, and I have recently experienced results with these products that we would consider magical if we didn't know better.

to give yourself an unnecessary scare, make your "inspection" some days after Prince has had rice.)

You will not be able to see hookworms or whipworms in the stool. These two types are the most dangerous. Dr. Ralston warns that hookworms can kill very quickly. *So if you see any of the FOL-LOWING symptoms—and DON'T see the signs of worms in the feces—take a sample of the feces to your veterinarian immediately for microscopic testing.*

In puppies, a common symptom of worms is a skeletonlike little body accompanied, peculiarly enough, by a potbelly sticking out of the skeleton. The entity is a skeleton because the worms have been gobbling up his nutrients. The potbelly comes from the direct damage the worms do physically, which causes weak muscles, gas, and fluid buildup.

A puppy or adult dog with worms may also suffer from diarrhea and/or convulsions. There may be loss of appetite, or there may be a huge increase in appetite.

WHAT YOU SHOULD *NOT* DO FOR YOUR DOG WITH WORMS Don't buy a chemical dewormer and use it yourself. If you give your dog such a dewormer, let it be at least by prescription of a veterinarian who supervises its administration. Even then, Dr. Ralston once warned: "Please be sure you inform the doctor if you have been giving your pet any medication whatsoever—for worms or for any other problem. Because what your veterinarian might give your pet for worms, in combination with whatever drug you may have been giving him, might kill him."

In the first edition, Wendell O. Belfield, D.V.M.,[1] gave a heartbreaking example of why you should never give a chemical dewormer to your companion without working with a veterinarian. He told of the frantic woman who called him one Sunday morning about her puppy, saying, "It's just lying there." Saying that the puppy had developed worms, she went on: "I went to the supermarket and bought a preparation and used it according to the directions. Now my dog is dying."

The puppy was beyond help when she was brought to Dr. Belfield, and the only procedure he got to perform was an autopsy. What the woman didn't know, because she had not been working with a veterinarian, was that with worm infestation there may be malfunction of organs outside the intestinal tract. In this puppy's case, autopsy found that she had a swollen liver. Dr. Belfield said: "Apparently the swollen liver had been unable to cope with the chemical dewormer." The product had indeed done its job of killing the worms that were infesting the small intestine. "But the damaged liver was unable to detoxify the chemical, which circulated through the system and caused the death of the animal."

Other veterinarians have told me that they have seen many similar tragic cases.

Until now, we have been talking about why you should not use chemical dewormers yourself. Are the chemical dewormers used by orthodox veterinarians also dangerous? Yes. They are poisons, too. And any poison strong enough to kill a lot of healthy worms is strong enough to kill a dog whose health has been weakened by those worms. (However, your veterinarian's individualized prescription and follow-up should help decrease the risks of treating your dog on your own.)

You can help your dog's body detoxify itself of the poisons in standard dewormers by giving him vitamin C before, during, and for two or more weeks after the deworming, according to some holistic veterinarians. Pancreatic enzymes can also be very important.

One veterinarian for this new edition said he thought the chemical dewormers have become less poisonous in recent years, but a poison is still a poison. In researching this new book, I personally had trouble finding chemical dewormers in supermarkets. Maybe one reason they have become less poisonous is that they have become less available for the public to administer without the advice of a veterinarian? I much more easily find herbal dewormers in health food stores, but even they might cause a problem for your dog unless you at least call a holistic veterinarian and discuss your individual dog.

Now let's see how holistic veterinarians get rid of worms without poisoning them—and therefore without risking the poisoning of your dog.

THERAPY FOR WORMS When I researched the first edition, I came upon only one holistic veterinarian (H. H. Robertson, D.V.M.) who reported success in treating all four types of intestinal worms naturally. Others seemed to have success with natural techniques only for one or two types of worms. For this new book, I didn't find a veterinarian who knew about the successful product reported to me long ago (Fossil Flour, available at the time from Agri-Tech in Kansas City, Missouri), but I found Dr. Weiner, who gave me exciting information about a newer therapy.

Dr. Weiner told me he has in recent years found a natural product, a probiotic called Nature's Biotics, "that works to get rid of all types of intestinal worms."

If you're extremely skeptical of natural medicine, you may be saying right now: "Oh, sure, a miracle product." As I say often in this book, although the results of holistic medicine may often *seem* like miracles because they are results we have been led not to expect, they are based on solid medical knowledge.

Dr. Weiner began our interview on this subject with an accepted medical fact: "A healthy intestinal tract has a certain known balance of the proper bacteria and flora and fauna." The idea of *proper* bacteria may seem jolting, because all we ever hear about are "bad" bacteria. But if you took a course in biology in high school, you may remember that there are some bacteria, called "friendly" bacteria, that are necessary for good health.

"The only time worms can get into the intestinal tract," Dr. Weiner continued, "is when these bacteria and other organisms are out of balance." So how do probiotics like Nature's Biotics get all these organisms to be balanced in the intestines? Very quickly, very simply, and by way of supreme common sense: This product *is* the organisms in proper balance—combined with, as Dr. Weiner said, "all the right trace minerals and vitamins needed to make these organisms grow properly."

Dr. Weiner continued: "When you get the intestinal flora working properly, the worms just get flushed out—no matter what type of worm they are." Actually, since this natural product gets rid of the underlying *cause* of the problem (which, as I've often pointed out, is always the goal of holistic medicine), it can not only rid the dog of intestinal worms but of other intestinal problems as well, as we discuss a bit later.

When Dr. Weiner first described this product to me, I had a fleeting bizarre vision of having to deal with a bunch of horrible wiggly entities and trying somehow to get them into my dogs' intestines. If you had the same thought, you may have realized quickly that these organisms are microscopic, so you don't even know you're looking at them. And, of course, all food goes through the intestines. So, as Dr. Weiner explains, owners simply put a certain amount of the product on the dog's food once a day.

Other Intestinal Problems—and Beyond

"The single most common problem of internal organs I have been seeing in dogs recently is chronic diarrhea," Dr. Basko told me in a recent interview. With this disorder, the veterinarian explained, "The dog's lining of the stomach and intestines are swollen, so he can't absorb food—and the animal is basically starving to death."

Dr. Basko said that the common orthodox treatment for long-term diarrhea is antibiotics. "And sometimes this treatment will help the symptoms, temporarily, because it kills some of the bacteria that are causing the diarrhea," he added. However, one of the basic reasons behind the overall harmful side effects of antibiotics is the fact that they tend to kill not only the "bad" bacteria in the intestinal tract but also the "good" bacteria that are necessary for health. "So, in the end," the veterinarian stated, "antibiotics make the dog with chronic diarrhea worse."

However, "if the dog is lucky enough to find an alternative practitioner, he or she will usually get completely well," he said.

Dr. Basko indicated that holistic testing will often find that the diarrhea stems from a food allergy. Removing the food or foods from the diet, and treating the dog to his natural diet (chapters 2 or 4, depending on his time in life), is of course a necessary step. But the veterinarian warns that often owners, although maintaining the dog's natural diet, find that the long-term diarrhea recurs. "They will say, 'Well, I didn't change anything in the natural diet except one little thing.' That one little thing may turn out to be commercial dog biscuits or a rawhide chew bone." Dr. Basko stressed: "It can take only one time, one dog biscuit or one chew bone, to make everything change in the dog's digestive system—and the dog has a severe allergic reaction and another three or four weeks of diarrhea."

For actual therapy for the allergic reaction, Dr. Basko often will use acupuncture, homeopathy, and Chinese herbs. He may also use probiotics or l-glutamine. The veterinarian added: "Some veterinarians will use steroid drugs. They work to cover symptoms, but they have side effects, and they don't really do anything for healing. They actually slow the healing down."

As I mentioned, since Nature's Biotics and other probiotics restore the natural balance of organisms to the intestines, they can take care of other intestinal problems besides worms. Also, as Dr. Weiner pointed out, "there's a basic holistic belief that the *overall* health of a dog, a cat, or a human is very dependent upon a properly functioning intestinal tract. And if you get the proper balance of organisms back in the intestines, many health problems will be eliminated, and a lot of time and money can be saved by not using other therapies that now become unnecessary."

Dr. Weiner told me about Donna, a mixed-breed dog who was brought to him with several health problems, including diarrhea and vomiting, that had plagued her a long time. Actually, unlike the other case histories in this book, Donna is not a specific dog but a composite case history that, Dr. Weiner said, "details how my treatment commonly goes with dogs with problems like this.

"Kinesiological testing told me that Donna had chemical toxicity and weakness in her large intestines. It also told me which vitamins and minerals she was deficient in. So I gave her a homeopathic remedy to detoxify the chemical toxicity. In this case I used nux vomica, as I often do. But, according to the needs of the individual dog, I may use the herbal combination called Noni juice." (These products are discussed earlier in the chapter.) He chose Donna's nutritional supplements, of course, according to what his testing had revealed she needed.

"We found that the weakness in Donna's large intestines was due to the fact that she was on a commercial dog food." (No big surprise there for any of you who have read chapter 1.) "So we recommended a more natural diet, adding digestive enzymes and probiotics. Often, we find that dogs' symptoms can be traced, at least in part, to a sensitivity to the standard vaccines they've been given. But in Donna's case, this didn't turn out to be true. If it had, I would have given her a homeopathic remedy that can detoxify these effects." (For more on vaccines, see chapter 3.)

"Donna's long-standing bout with vomiting typically occurred very shortly after she ate," Dr. Weiner continued, "a fact that made me strongly suspect that the dog was allergic to something she was commonly being fed. We found that Donna was allergic to a couple of common allergens, and we changed her diet to one that didn't contain them.*

"So, after my testing, I gave Donna's people my recommendations for the treatments they could give her themselves at home, and Donna was on her way out of my office. As is typical, Donna's owners called me six months later, saying, 'God! Her hair coat is shiny, and she's more alert and active than she's been in years.' "

Since I have spent several decades working closely with holistic doctors and using holistic therapy for myself, my husband, and our animal companions, I was not at all surprised to hear that Donna's people were reporting resolution of problems they didn't even ask Dr. Weiner to treat. After all, Donna had been sick for so long with

---

* Dr. Fudens believes that allergies are caused by a damaged immune system, and that if classical homeopathy is used to rebuild it, the dog can eat anything natural without getting diarrhea.

vomiting and diarrhea when they took her to Dr. Weiner that they weren't worried about "little" problems like an unhealthy-looking coat and a lack of joy of life.

I knew what Dr. Weiner's answer would be, but to give you an official answer, I asked him anyway: "But what about the long-standing diarrhea and vomiting?" Dr. Weiner answered, "Oh, that, too, of course. They said that Donna's been free of those problems for quite some time now."

Dr. Long wrote me that he, too, uses probiotics—although unlike Dr. Weiner, he didn't stress any specific product. He did add the information that plain yogurt can provide probiotics but that powdered preparations are more concentrated. In other words, a small amount of them is likely to work better and faster.

Dr. Long also provided further details on how and why probiotics help many health problems, not only those of the intestines. "Probiotic (or 'friendly') bacteria produce enzymes that help digest food material and kill pathologic bacteria and viruses, which might otherwise be absorbed from the intestines into the body as a whole."

Specific to this section, Dr. Long commented, "I have found probiotic supplements to be helpful in inflammatory conditions of the intestinal tract, such as inflammatory bowel disease and colitis."

He will give supplementary enzymes and dietary fiber along with probiotics.

Dr. Weiner pointed out that, like many of the "really powerful health-promoting products," probiotics work well for both animals and humans. He mentioned chronic fatigue syndrome in humans, for instance. "When you get the intestines back to a normal balance, the person no longer has the puzzling array of symptoms known as chronic fatigue syndrome."

References

1. Wendell O. Belfield, D.V.M., and Martin Zucker, *How to Have a Healthier Dog* (Garden City, New York: Doubleday and Co., Inc.), 1981, pp. 122, 123.

Chapter 10

*Heart Problems
and Hypertension*

"I estimate that, using natural therapies, I successfully treat dogs with early to moderate heart disease 97 to 98 percent of the time.

"In treating hypertension, I have almost complete success."

—*Norman C. Ralston, D.V.M.*

"I've had cases of heart disease that were absolutely given up on by other veterinarians, because the cardiograms indicated there was no hope. Natural therapy has improved the animals' health greatly and has given them years more of life."

—*Michael W. Lemmon, D.V.M. (in 1981)*

"By far most of the dogs I treat for hypertension get well. . . . I really haven't seen much improvement in dogs treated with orthodox therapies. Most of them are too nervous, too hyperactive.

"Natural therapy, such as coenzyme Q10 and vitamins A, C, and E—along with orthodox therapy, such as sodium carpalstete—have been a successful treatment for heartworms. There are very few side effects."

—*S. Allen Price, D.V.M.*

Heart Problems

I'd *like to* tell you about Snuffy, a female spayed Yorkie-poodle mix who was brought to John Fudens, D.V. M., with, the veterinarian told me, "*significant* cardiac failure and severe chronic disease due to all the commercial foods, vaccinations, et cetera." She also had cataracts in both eyes and deep behavior, or emotional, problems. "She was very aggressive and hostile to other animals and to people," Dr. Fudens told me. "She had bitten her owners a number of times and was extremely territorial, very jealous of her toys and bones and her food.

"She had been coughing almost constantly for several weeks," the veterinarian added, "a dry harsh cough both at rest and excitement. And her heart was extremely rapid, muffled. The valves were leaking very badly.

"With cases like this," Dr. Fudens said, "I do a more emergency type of approach. I gave her a heart glandular, the Chinese herbs ginseng and Tang-Kuei and herbal diuretics. I also put her on a homeopathic digitalis—and, of course, I put her on natural foods."

Soon, Snuffy was put on a much less intensive maintenance therapy, and two and a half years later "Snuffy is doing extremely well," Dr. Fudens told me. "This is a dog that's now about sixteen years of age. Her energy and appetite are extremely good, stool and urine are absolutely normal." She rarely if ever coughs. And her emotional problems are a thing of the past.

Dr. Fudens summarized: "So this is a very old dog with severe chronic disease that now is extremely stable, and she has quality and quantity of life. And at this point she will go on until she decides that she wishes to drop the body."

This ancient dog's recovery from severe heart failure—and everything else that plagued her—may seem like a sort of miracle, as I said in the introduction that many of this book's case histories might seem. But Dr. Fudens told me: "I chose Snuffy to talk to you about because her response to the holistic approach was one of the usual cases that I run into."

Dr. Fudens added that, after thirty-seven years of practice, it "never ceases to amaze" him how well animals heal with a holistic approach.

Norman C. Ralston, D.V.M., who worked closely with me for this chapter—and who reports some 97 to 98 percent success in treating early to moderate heart disease in dogs and cats—gave himself as an example of the success natural therapy can have with the *late stages* of heart disease. "In 1976," he said, "I was so ill with congestive heart failure that I couldn't walk across the street and back without sitting down to rest. Now I can work in my clinic, standing up, for twelve hours without stopping." Dr. Ralston talked to me about this some twenty-two years after he probably "should have" died. When we talked, he was seventy-eight.

"In recent years, heart disease in dogs has been very prevalent—much more prevalent than people might think," S. Allen Price, D.V.M., told me in a recent interview. "We have a lot of congestive heart conditions," he said, "and we have a lot of secondary heart conditions due to other disorders, such as kidney and liver problems."

Dr. Ralston warned of another heart problem that he says affects many dogs he sees in his clinic. "Their hearts are pulsing at 30, 37, 40," he told me. "They should be pulsing at 12." (As we'll detail, the heart's pulse is not to be confused with its beat.) "I'd say that most of the dogs I see are pulsing at 20 or above," he said. "I had a cat the other day whose heart was pulsing at 42. That told me he was close to having a convulsion."

What makes a heart's pulse race? "The heart takes over when something is not functioning somewhere else," Dr. Ralston explained, "say the thyroid gland or the adrenal gland isn't working right. When the heart takes over the pulse effect, that increases the blood pressure, which of course can cause a stroke."

The veterinarian stressed that, unlike the *beats* of a heart, the *pulses* cannot be picked up by listening through a stethoscope. "You have to find some other way to detect the pulsing. I use kinesiology."

Dr. Ralston added that "all dogs' and cats' hearts should pulse at 12. So should yours and mine."

Symptoms of Heart Problems

Even if your dog seems healthy, he should have periodic examinations. Heart problems can't always be properly diagnosed without sophisticated diagnostic tools. But trouble can develop between examinations. So that you will know when you should report any possible problems to your veterinarian, this section discusses some symptoms you can watch out for.

Check your dog's legs. Swelling may indicate a heart problem, the swelling being a sign of accumulation of fluids. You might listen to your dog's heart for signs of trouble. (Again, the following information is not to be used as a substitute for periodic examinations by your pet's doctor.)

Just put your head on her chest and listen. Or make yourself a sort of stethoscope by putting a drinking glass over your dog's heart area and listening through the open end—if this strange device doesn't freak her out. If her heart skips a bit around the fifth or sixth beat, don't panic. Dogs and cats are naturally prone to irregular rhythms, dogs more so than cats. As a matter of fact, if your pet's heart rhythm is completely regular, you should bring this to your veterinarian's attention. At the same time, if the heart seems to be skipping an entire beat, you should tell the doctor about that.

Is the heartbeat confined to the immediate heart area? Good.

(Sounds that can be heard all over the chest area may mean an enlarged heart.) Do you feel a buzzing or vibration over the heart? This may be due to a narrowed valve or a hole in the heart. Do you hear a hissing sound? This may be due to a leaky valve. Does the heartbeat sound muffled? This also should be brought to your veterinarian's attention.

Jan Bellows, D.V.M., once vividly described to me the progressive outward symptoms of congestive heart failure:

- The dog coughs and has a slight decrease in exercise tolerance.
- The dog's gums start to become blue. Exercise tolerance becomes even less.
- The dog comes into the office puffing. If he takes more than several steps, he coughs hoarsely.
- In the last stage of congestive heart failure, the dog can't walk into the office at all. He is carried in on his side.

"In this last stage of congestive heart failure," Dr. Bellows said, "the animal is literally drowning in the excess fluids accumulated in his lungs. Even at this stage, we can save a few animals, but they have to be put on oxygen and given drugs." Nutrients were used only as supportive therapy, to help increase the pet's chances of surviving.

Remember that the previous information from Dr. Bellows refers specifically to congestive heart failure.

Treatment for Heart Problems

What can be done to get those speeding heart pulses Dr. Ralston talked earlier about down to the normal rate of 12? "You have to find out what malfunctioning organ the heart has taken over the pulsing effect for," Dr. Ralston told me. "Usually you'll find it's the thyroid gland. That gland provides energy for the brain, heart, kidneys, and the adrenal gland." The latter gland pumps fluids through the body.

Some Basics of Treatment for Heart Problems

These are some of the basics of treatment shared by the holistic doctors who worked on this section in 1981 and those who worked on this new edition. See text for important additional details.

- **Vitamin A.** Depending on the size of the dog or cat and the severity of his condition, up to 400,000 IU a day of the water-soluble form of the vitamin may be used. (This form does not accumulate in the body the way the "usual," fat-soluble form does, and so it can be used in much higher amounts without causing toxicity.)
- **Vitamin C.** As you may know, drugs called diuretics are routinely used in the orthodox treatment of heart problems, both for people and for animals, to rid the body of accumulated excess fluids. Vitamin C is a natural diuretic, with no side effects when used properly. (Up to 20 to 25 grams a day may be used, again depending on the size of the dog and the severity of the illness.)
- **Vitamin E.** Up to 4,000 to 6,000 IU a day of the water-soluble form may be used. This is another natural diuretic. It also enhances circulation; a damaged heart has trouble fulfilling its major function of circulating blood through the body. Vitamin E also has been well proven to strengthen all the muscles of the body—and the heart is a muscle. (Some holistic veterinarians have warned me that while vitamin E is quite safe for less serious heart problems, it can be very dangerous if used indiscriminately for a very weak heart. They recommend that an animal with a serious heart problem be stabilized first before adding vitamin E and that it be prescribed for a pet with a very weak heart only by holistic veterinarians.)
- **The elimination of salt (sodium).**
- **Moderate exercise.**
- **Weight reduction in an overweight animal.**
- **And, as with any disorder, a natural diet as detailed in chapter 2 (or chapter 4, depending on the dog's age).**

To the basic regimen sketched in the boxed material, holistic veterinarians will add other natural substances. We'll cover those additional aids after a closer look at some of the recommendations mentioned in the box.

VITAMIN C We say elsewhere in this book that holistic veterinarians often use the sodium ascorbate form of vitamin C, rather than the more widely known ascorbic acid form. But for heart problems, they use ascorbic acid. They don't use sodium ascorbate because it contains sodium, more commonly known as salt. As we cover in this chapter, the elimination of salt is very important in treating heart disease.

VITAMIN E As stated in the boxed material, vitamin E can strengthen a weakened heart and can function as a diuretic, helping the body to remove dangerous excess fluid. (Let me reemphasize that in congestive heart failure and in animals with very weak hearts, vitamin E must be used only under the supervision of a holistic veterinarian.) This vitamin also reduces the body's need for oxygen. Oxygen starvation is a major problem in heart disorders.

Richard J. Kearns, D.V.M., back in 1981 said of vitamin E: "This vitamin will cure many heart problems without using the drug digitalis at all. When the animal is in really bad shape, you may have to use a little digitalis." Even in those very advanced cases, however, "if you use enough vitamin E, you can cut the drug down to about 10 percent of what you'd have to use normally."

In the first edition, I cited a number of studies going back as far as 1945 that showed that undersupplying animals with vitamin E produced abnormal electrocardiograms and heart degeneration. I also cited studies from the same era that found that people who had already had heart attacks showed improved electrocardiograms and more regular pulses after taking vitamin E. I think that in this new era of enlightened knowledge about nutrition, I don't have to prove that E helps the heart by citing individual studies.

I will, though, mention again very early research on vitamin E used directly on more than twelve hundred dogs and cats with heart problems. Dr. N. H. Lambert began his work in 1945 and published it ten years later.[1] He had good results with everything from angina to valvular murmur to congestive heart failure. Dr. Lambert's very first case was a nine-year-old dog who was dying; previous treatment had not helped her. With vitamin E, the "dying" dog lived another six years, to the ripe old age of fifteen.

Please keep in mind here something you should always remember if you read of studies involving only one nutrient. Vitamins and minerals act synergistically, so the effects found for one nutrient may well be strengthened when other nutrients are added.

THE QUESTION OF EXERCISE While vigorous, *regular* exercise is a good preventive for heart trouble, once the heart is damaged, you must take a middle-of-the-road approach to your pet's exercise. (Of course, if your dog is in an emergency situation, you won't try to exercise him at all.) Holistic veterinarians have told me that if you just let your dog sit around all day, he will tend to get worse. If you try to get him to do vigorous exercising, he will get worse, too.

LOW-SALT DIET A low-salt diet is so important in treating heart disease that some veterinarians have informed me that in the early stages of a heart problem, simply cutting out salt alone can sometimes dramatically help the animal.

Low-salt foods include corn grits or farina, oatmeal, lima beans, squash, dried beans, sweet potato, black-eyed peas, egg yolks (not whites), beef, chicken, turkey, lamb, corn kernels, and white rice. (We have said in this book that white rice has fewer nutrients than brown rice. That's true, but it also has less salt.) Feed these animal foods, vegetables, and grains in the proportions given in chapter 2.

Dr. Bellows reported sadly in the first book that many well-meaning people keep their pets on a special low-salt diet, then—perhaps feeling sorry that the animal isn't getting any "treats"—give them beef jerky or bologna, both saturated with salt. "Such foods," Dr. Bellows said, "totally defeat everything." Some other *not*-permitted foods are cornflakes, wheat flakes, cheese, margarine, cottage cheese, frankfurters, canned stew, and bacon. "Foods like these," Dr. Bellows said emphatically, "can get the animal into *big* trouble."

We do not have the space here to list all the permitted and

not-permitted foods on a low-salt diet. So please check with your veterinarian before adding a food the doctor has not already recommended. In this instance, a small detail that you don't know might kill your pet. Many packaged and canned foods, for instance, are loaded with salt. And even tuna fish, recommended in chapter 2 as a good food for a healthy dog, weighs in at a stupendous 700 milligrams of sodium (salt) per three ounces! So you see, even the addition of an apparently "safe" food might be lethal to your pet. Again, always check with your veterinarian before adding any food to the low-salt diet the doctor has already recommended.

VASCULIN AND CARDIO-PLUS I asked Dr. Ralston if these two natural products, used in 1981, were still used for heart disease. "You'd better believe it," he said. "Those are very good products." He found a bottle of one of the products and enthusiastically began reading me the list of ingredients, which included bovine heart extract, bovine liver powder, choline, calcium lactate, and numerous other natural factors that can help the heart.

Michael W. Lemmon, D.V.M., was just as enthusiastic about Vasculin and Cardio-Plus in 1981. "I've had cases that were absolutely given up on by other veterinarians," he told me, "because the cardiograms indicated there was no hope. These two products, though, improved the animals greatly and are giving them years more of life."

Dr. Ralston added in regard to giving products such as Cardio-Plus: "I have the clients mash the pill up in the dog's food, so he can feel he is still in control of what's going on in his life. I don't want the person he has come to love and depend on grabbing him and shoving things down his throat."

MAGNESIUM AND ENZYMES In the first edition, H. H. Robertson, D.V.M., stated that "one major cause of heart problems—in dogs and in cats—is that proteins don't get broken down by the body into amino acids. Therefore, it is complex proteins that are circulating in the system. And of course the body cannot utilize complex proteins.

"When these complex proteins reach too high a level in the circulatory system, the heart rate is increased. Eventually, the heart wears itself out." When testing revealed that the proteins were indeed not being broken down, Dr. Robertson gave magnesium to the animal. "Magnesium will cause the desired release of the nonprotein nitrogen in the body," he said. In other words, it will help the body to get rid of the undigested protein.

Dr. Robertson and Dr. Kearns reported that they also used pancreatic enzymes to help improve the breakdown of protein. Dr. Robertson added that "pepsin and trypsin are particularly important."

LECITHIN This is a natural substance occurring in some foods, such as soybeans and eggs. Holistic doctors often add lecithin to their therapy for heart problems. Lecithin emulsifies—that is, cuts through—fats. By emulsifying the plaques of fats adhering to the walls of blood vessels, lecithin also helps improve the animal's circulation.

COENZYME Q10 All the previous therapies were used by the holistic veterinarians who worked with me in 1981 for the first book. As I said in this new edition's introduction, none of the earlier therapies has been found to be invalid, but the explosion of nutritional research in recent years has given holistic doctors a much larger arsenal of weapons to fight diseases. One of these new weapons is coenzyme Q10, which, Dr. Price said, he uses for "any and all heart problems."

What is this newly discovered and studied nutrient with the strange name? I researched it before starting work on this book and was so convinced of its helpful effects that I added it to the basic supplementation regimen for myself and my husband, Joe. Because this book has a strong practical focus, I won't go into the textbook facts I found involving lipids, mitochondria, the collection of hydrogen atoms removed during cellular oxidations, and oxidative phosphorylation that describe the biochemical processes by which this coenzyme works.

The long and the short of it is that cells require energy to live, and coenzyme Q10 supplies that energy. Research has found deficiencies of this nutrient in human patients with heart disease such as congestive heart failure and angina and in older people with high blood pressure, subjects covered in this chapter. And, not surprisingly, supplements of the nutrient have been found to help people with these problems. Coenzyme Q10 has also been found to bolster the immune system and in that way to help people undergoing standard cancer therapy to fight the side effects of radiation and chemotherapy. The nutrient has been used in Europe for patients with soft tissue cancer, including breast cancer.

As is true of nutrients in general, no side effects have been found when used as recommended.

Dr. Price gave one specific way coenzyme Q10 has been of help in recent years for his patients with heart disease: "If the dog has excess fluid in the chest cavity, and you don't drain it out, traditionally you had to use diuretics," he said. "But I don't have to use them nearly so often since I've been using the coenzyme."

RAW HONEY? I have read several recommendations for raw honey as a natural heart stimulant for the dog with heart problems. Holistic veterinarians have told me, however, that honey can *seem* to help the dog because, being sugar, it gives the animal an immediate boost of energy that makes him seem better for a little while. But honey also causes more fluid to be retained—the last thing needed by heart patients who are already retaining too much fluid.

I began this chapter writing about Snuffy, a dog with severe heart problems who, in recent years, was restored to good health through holistic therapy. But such "surprising" recoveries aren't surprising to holistic veterinarians, who have been achieving them for decades. For instance, in 1982, Dr. Price told me about Duchess, a German shepherd mix who was only three years old in 1977 when she was given her "death sentence" by an orthodox veterinary center.

Duchess was vomiting blood. She was retaining so much fluid that her stomach had to be drained every week. (This problem is called dropsy.) She was extremely anemic.

The orthodox center diagnosed a leaking heart valve and an abnormally slow heartbeat. Their prognosis: Duchess might live another six weeks. She might last as long as six months.

The last I heard of Duchess, she had beaten her death sentence by half a decade. And she was not only still "surprisingly" alive, she was, Dr. Price told me, "a completely normal, healthy dog with no symptoms of dropsy or any other heart condition."

SOME SPECIAL WORDS ABOUT THE LAST STAGES OF CONGESTIVE HEART DISEASE As hopeless as this problem sounds, all of the holistic veterinarians I have talked to since 1981 say they can save some of these seemingly doomed animals.

Dr. Ralston recently added information I found very interesting. When I asked if his therapy for this end-stage heart problem differed from his therapy for milder cases of heart disease, he answered "Yes." I expected to hear him tell me of a more intensive nutritional therapy or that he might have to use drugs as well as natural substances. Instead, he said, "You have to be even more careful than ever to avoid stressing this already traumatized animal. For instance, many dogs, even when healthy, get terrified when you try to draw blood from them."

Dr. Ralston stated that the medical facts a veterinarian needs to know at this point "show up in the blood last. Also," he said, "the more stressed a dog is when you're trying to examine her, the more she can change her blood count." So, this holistic veterinarian asked rhetorically, "If a blood test is not that accurate at this point, why don't you try to look for something else—and be kind and be gentle?"

Heartworms

Heartworms are worms that congregate in the heart. They can damage not only that organ but also the lungs, kidneys, and liver, and can eventually cause death.

Since heartworms are transmitted by mosquitoes, to prevent heartworms you must protect your dog from these insects. Dr. Price noted that brewer's yeast and garlic are still used to repel mosquitoes, as they were in 1981.

What about the drugs out to prevent heartworms? He generally doesn't use them, he said. "I might consider recommending them for a dog living in a swamp area or a part of the country where there's a tremendous amount of heartworm at the time." He uses Heartguard, which has "a very low level of drugs."

For therapy, Dr. Price may use one of two common orthodox treatments along with nutritional therapy.

The antioxidants Dr. Price uses include coenzyme Q10 and vitamins A, C, and E. He also uses "a minute amount" of selenium because in recent years it has been found that this nutrient helps the action of vitamin E. "I may add supportive treatment," he says, "such as the vitamin B complex and liver extract."

As noted in the covering pages of this chapter, Dr. Price has good results treating heartworms.

When I asked if he felt that in general natural therapy had a much greater success with heartworms than orthodox therapy, he said, "It sure does—for me, anyway. It's just a lot more fun when you get good results, and the dog doesn't have any side effects."

Dr. Fudens takes a somewhat different approach to treating heartworms. As stated often in this book, holistic veterinarians have many different nutrients—and even many different modalities (acupuncture, homeopathy, and so on)—from which to choose. They select from these according to their own areas of training and expertise. However, differing specific choices are all geared to producing the same healing biochemical changes within the dog's body.

"I have had some fifty to seventy cases of heartworm that I've treated so far with this basic approach," Dr. Fudens told me, "and to my knowingness there have been only two or three cases that I have failed to clear of heartworms. And the reason was that the dogs' *general* health was just so bad. They came to me near death."

So these two or three dogs died? No. With holistic therapy, Dr. Fudens said, "what has happened is that their overall health has dramatically improved, so that they have quantity and quality of life." He considers these dogs his few failures in treating heartworms because "they still retain some of the heartworm infestation."

Dr. Fudens contributed his standard treatment for heartworms by way of the history of a dog on whom he used the therapy. "Wu is a mixed golden retriever who came to me as a youngster of a year and a half," the veterinarian told me. "She had been a stray. She had heartworms, poor appetite, low energy, pale mucous membranes, and some coughing. Wu also had ear mites and in general was run-down, with serious immune system damage.

"I gave Wu my standard heartworm program," Dr. Fudens continued, "which includes the homeopathic *Arsenicum album*, one or two times a day, at 12X. I also use the black walnut herbal extracts, choosing the dosage depending upon the weight of my patient. I also give some Chinese herbs and a liver glandular, and I use my general immune glandular. The latter protects the immune system and heals the damage that the heartworm disease is doing to the immune system."

Dr. Fudens added that recently he has started to use an orthodox drug to prevent reinfestation with heartworms while the natural therapy has time to take effect—"if there is a heavy infestation of heartworms in the area where the dog lives."

The veterinarian adds that, when Wu was free of heartworm disease, he "went further and detoxified her from the drugs, vaccines, et cetera she'd previously been given. Now she's a wonderful-looking dog; you would never believe by looking at her that she'd ever had any health problems at all."

And, half a decade after treatment, Wu remains free of heartworms.

Hypertension

As seen in the quotations on the covering page of this chapter, both Dr. Ralston and Dr. Price report extremely high success rates in using natural therapies to treat dogs with hypertension.

Discussing symptoms of hypertension, Dr. Price said that the external symptoms that he looks for include extreme nervousness, "often to the point where the dog has ceased to be a good pet." Indeed the hypertensive pet can sometimes be so nervous that he makes his owner a nervous wreck. "Also, animals with high blood pressure have about two or three times the amount of skin problems that other pets do. If the animal has a painful condition, the pain is three times worse than it would be for another pet. "In short," Dr. Price said, "nothing seems to go right for the poor animal with hypertension."

Therapy for Hypertension

Dr. Ralston commented that hypertension is often due basically to a malfunctioning thyroid gland. "Treating hypertension more as hyperthyroidism than as pure hypertension," he said, "I can almost always successfully treat high blood pressure."

Dr. Price told me that scientific tests find that "most of these animals have an extremely high lovel of sodium." We have previously established that sodium (salt) is a primary cause of high blood pressure. So, of course, he puts the animal on a low-salt diet as detailed earlier in this chapter.

The veterinarian relies heavily on the nutrient coenzyme Q10, also discussed earlier. And of course, he will, as all holistic veterinarians do in treating any disorder, try to persuade the dog's person to put her on a natural diet.

As a matter of fact, Dr. Price stated strongly: "Almost all—if not, indeed all—cases of hypertension can be traced, I believe, to the processed foods, most particularly those 'meaty-looking' products." He added a poignant fact: "Sometimes you can even see a courageous little dog who has heart and/or circulatory problems, but whose body is managing to compensate for the problems so that the animal has no symptoms. Then the owner puts him on one of those fake meat products, and in three weeks' time the little fellow has dropsy."

Dr. Price added that he may also use Aspartate, something he's used "down through the years on any circulatory problem." Aspartate is in part a combination of magnesium and potassium, and the veterinarian also finds it invaluable in treating congestive heart conditions. "Magnesium is a very mild natural tranquilizer and helps the nervous hypertensive calm down naturally, without the side effects of drug tranquilizers," the veterinarian said. "It also is an excellent support for producing enzymes that digest blood clots." The possibility of blood clots is one of the major dangers of high blood pressure. (Dr. Robertson once stated that, while potassium should always be used for hypertension, magnesium should be used only if the nonprotein nitrogen in the blood tests out to be too high.)

"Potassium," Dr. Price explained, "balances the high sodium level present in the hypertensive." Sodium and potassium work together in a crucial balance in the body. Most people and animals upset this balance by taking in much more sodium than potassium. This overload of sodium tends, in turn, to rob the body of much of the potassium it does take in.

Animals in the wild, of course, don't know about the decades of research on the body's need for a balance between potassium and salt. As nutritionist Adelle Davis once pointed out, when an animal in the wild "overdoses" on eating leaves and grass—which contain high amounts of potassium and no salt—he'll walk hundreds of miles, if he has to, to find the nearest salt lick. This is an instance of something we say often in the book: An animal in the wild instinctively eats what is best for his body. And of course he never eats the fake foods the ads tell us are "best" for him.

References

1. N. H. Lambert, *Proceedings of the Third International Congress on Vitamin E*, September 1955, pp. 611–617.

Chapter 11

"When we get a dog or cat with a prognosis of living only six months because of cancer diagnosed as terminal, which has not been over-vaccinated or subjected to chemo or radiation therapy, we have a 50 to 60 percent chance of restoring good health and achieving a remission. When the animal is only one to three months from certain death our chances of remission drop, but we can often greatly improve the day-to-day quality of these animals' lives and in about a quarter can achieve a lasting remission."
—*Robert Goldstein, V.M.D.*

"In treating cancer, the number one thing I do is to suggest that the dog or cat doesn't get any more vaccines. The number two thing I do is try to get the owner to put the animal on a natural diet. Then I find the holistic therapy that seems best for the individual pet.

"For most dogs with cancer, there are any number of natural therapies you can choose from to help them."
—*Michael W. Lemmon, D.V.M.*

Cancer: Terminal *Often Doesn't Mean Terminal Any Longer*

Mike, *a standard* poodle, had been diagnosed with cancer of the abdomen, spleen, and bone marrow when he was brought to Robert Goldstein, V.M.D. The type of cancer destroying his spleen and bone marrow was lymphosarcoma, the most deadly form of cancer—and it had been diagnosed as grade 3 in his bone marrow. (Grade 4 is as high as cancer gets.) Mike had received numerous drugs, chemotherapy, and three surgeries. It might seem obvious that any hope to save Mike had run out a long time ago.

When the poodle came under Dr. Goldstein's care, the veterinarian wrote me, "he had been anemic and refusing to eat. Whenever he moved his bowels, the pain was so great that he fainted." Mike showed an immediate response to Dr. Goldstein's Immuno-Augmentative Therapy (detailed later in this chapter): Within twenty-four hours, Mike was eating again, and he was no longer fainting. Within five months, Mike was in clinical remission. Mike died some four years later, still with no evidence of cancer of any type in any part of his body.

Before continuing this chapter, you might want to read, in the introduction, my personal story of Shiki, my miniature poodle who nicely survived diagnosed terminal cancer. She was treated many years ago by holistic techniques that might be considered primitive today. In particular, I know that the veterinarian who successfully treated her, Marty Goldstein, D.V.M., has long since gone on to work with the same very sophisticated natural cancer therapy used by his brother, Dr. Robert Goldstein. This is the therapy that saved Mike and that has saved thousands of other dogs and cats diagnosed as having terminal cancer, as I will detail a bit later.

In my first book, researched in 1981, I posed two questions that were even then rhetorical: Can holistic veterinarians successfully treat cancer? Can they do this often without any surgery or drugs? I asked five holistic veterinarians to estimate their success rate. The best reported results were 95 percent for early cancer and 25 percent for diagnosed terminal cancer. None of the other veterinarians reported total failure with terminal animals, although the diagnosis of terminal means, by definition, that the animal is deemed certain to die. The other estimates ranged from 5 percent to 20 percent. Even at the low of 5 percent, there were a lot of animals' lives being saved in 1981 that weren't "supposed" to be.

In those days, holistic veterinary medicine was in its infancy. As you saw from the statement by Dr. Robert Goldstein on the opening page of this chapter, the earlier high of 25 percent success with terminal cancer is now substantially higher. Since, like orthodox medicine, holistic medicine continually seeks and finds new answers to treating diseases, those statistics will hopefully be even higher by the time you read this.

I asked readers another rhetorical question in 1981: Were the veterinarians who were reporting some success with terminal cancer miracle workers? I pointed out that a miracle is something wonderful that is worked by means we cannot understand—and that definition didn't qualify these doctors as achieving any miracles whatsoever. Holistic veterinarians use natural substances that restore the pet's body—most importantly, the pet's immune system—to its natural balance. When this can be accomplished, the dog's own immune system fights off the cancer—just as a strong immune system fights off cancer that invades our bodies every day. I find in that no miracle at all. I find instead sublime medical common sense, more common sense than in having your dog's body pumped full of poisonous drugs and hoping those drugs will kill only the cancer, not the dog. (By the way, surgery, radiation, and chemotherapy *weaken* the all-important immune system, rather than building it up. Might that be a reason orthodox medicine doesn't have a lot of success in treating cancer?)

As a matter of fact, over the years many holistic veterinarians and M.D.s have stressed to me the following idea, as once expressed by H. H. Robertson, D.V. M.: "*I* don't cure the cancer. Actually, I don't cure *anything*. All I do is run tests to see where the animal's body chemistry is—and then bring the chemistry back to where it should be. It's the animal's body that actually does the healing."

I have stressed that in treating cancer the immune system must be strengthened. The therapy used by the doctors Goldstein actually injects a total cancer-fighting immune system *into* the body. That sounds like magic, doesn't it? Trust me that it won't sound at all mystical when I explain it a little later on.

You probably won't ever need the information in this chapter if you are starting off with a puppy who is brand-new to the world and raise him as holistic veterinarians have detailed in chapters 2 through 4. (See, for instance, this chapter's covering quote from Michael W. Lemmon, D.V. M. This same sentiment was volunteered to me by many holistic veterinarians in reference not only to cancer but to other disorders.) The cancer rampage did not exist among our pets' ancestors, as it did not exist among our own ancestors, when we all ate nonpoisonous foods and didn't vaccinate. Indeed, cancer is still virtually unknown in the wild. Dr. Robertson, who has a rural practice and treats animals roaming free, once told me: "I have seen noncancerous tumors in deer, in coyotes, and in foxes— but even these are rare."

The initial diagnosis of cancer is very often a much more definitive death sentence for dogs and cats than it is for humans. Why? For one thing, traditional therapy is very expensive. In 1981, just one *week's* treatment and hospitalization for a pet often amounted to $1,000 to $2,000.

The orthodox centers I contacted for this new edition were loath to give estimated costs, saying so much depended on the type of cancer, the stage, and so on. Let's assume, though, that the top estimate seventeen years later is still $2,000 a week, even though we know that assumption is probably wrong. And let's compare that to today's costs for the very sophisticated natural therapy used today by the brothers Goldstein. That nontoxic therapy—which saves up to 60 percent of dogs and cats deemed late terminal by orthodox medicine—has a top estimated cost of $1,500, not for a *week* of therapy, but for *three months*. And often animals who respond positively to the therapy don't need to be in treatment that long.

Not only is traditional therapy expensive, it can be extremely painful and traumatic for the pet. And it often doesn't work. As John E. Craige, V.M.D., pointed out in 1981, all of this often results in owners opting, sorrowfully, for putting the animal to sleep once the word *cancer* is pronounced by the doctor. "The orthodox approach to cancer is seldom even used in veterinary medicine," he said. The veterinarian added that "the fact that orthodox cancer treatment is often not even tried by owners should give [conventional] veterinarians more of a rationale for trying alternative therapy than many [conventional] M.D.s may feel they have."

Dr. Robert Goldstein, who told me he became a holistic cancer specialist "out of necessity," once worked for one of this country's most prestigious orthodox veterinary centers, where he used standard treatments for cancer, including the newer orthodox treatment, chemical immunotherapy. "These therapies—when they worked—prolonged the animal's life but didn't induce a remission," he said. "Commonly, we told the pet owner that the prognosis without treatment was that their dog had two to three months to live. With chemotherapy, the owner could expect six months to a year."

Two Basic Problems in Treating Cancer Holistically: Neither One Lies in the Cancer Itself

Since the two basic problems reported in 1981 by holistic veterinarians came from owner skepticism, I feel confident this section is less important now because the public has been educating itself on alternative techniques and turning increasingly to their use.

However, I know that there are still some skeptics around, and that anyone who doubts the value of natural therapies at all is *particularly* skeptical that they can help treat cancer.

Problem number one, as Richard J. Kearns, D.V.M., expressed it years ago, was that "we almost always get the animals after they've been through everything else—the surgery, the radiation, the chemotherapy." As mentioned earlier, all these undermine the immune system, rather than build it up. "When everything else has failed, when the cancer has had time to spread, when the animal is terminal, *then* we get a chance to help it," he said.

Problem number two was expressed by S. Allen Price, D.V.M. (who echoed that he seldom got to use natural therapy on a pet "until the owners realize it's either try natural therapy, or the pet will *surely* die"). Dr. Price stated: "Even once they've agreed to try natural therapy, all they have to do is read somewhere in a newspaper that no natural therapy can possibly work for cancer; and they're on the phone saying, 'Absolutely. I see it here, right here in the newspaper: Only drugs and surgery can help cancer.' And the totally frustrating thing is that so often these are people whose pets were given up to die because the drugs and surgery couldn't work; and they can see that their pets are doing well on the natural therapy. But they read a paragraph in a newspaper . . ."

Dr. Price continued: "For instance, I've got two people right now who are driving me wild over a couple of dogs with tumors of the cranial cavity. The only thing orthodox veterinary medicine offered was to try to cauterize the tumors. Not only is this type of operation dangerous, but it certainly would never have corrected the tumor. The most it would have done was to reduce its size, not eliminate it. With the more natural treatment, the dogs are functioning well and are not even showing any problems at all. The only problems the dogs are having now is that their owners keep reading things in newspapers, and keep thinking they should take the dogs off the therapy that's keeping them alive and functioning."

Dr. Price summarized: "The disease of cancer worries me to death—not because of the cancer itself, but because so often you can't fight the owner's skepticism so you can cure the animal."

One basic misunderstanding some people have is that if they choose an alternative therapy for cancer, they will have to deprive their animal (or themselves) of orthodox therapy. As we have just covered, most holistic veterinarians don't get to see a dog until orthodox therapy has been tried and has failed. (Some thirty years as a medical writer convince me that the same is true of holistic M.D.s treating cancer in humans.)

Also, remember that, as I said in the introduction, holistic veterinarians have received the same degrees in orthodox veterinary medicine as have strictly orthodox veterinarians. And they will use conventional techniques when it is to the patient's advantage. For instance, holistic doctors tell me that if the tumor is pressing on a vital part of the animal's body, or is in any other way impeding the functioning of the body, they will remove it surgically. In this way, the animal can be functioning again while the more natural, metabolic approach has time to rebuild the immune system. In the same way, holistic veterinarians will sometimes use a drug to help the dog with cancer. However, they never use conventional techniques as the only therapy. The major treatment is always a metabolic approach, which can help do away with the usual side effects of drugs and surgery while at the same time getting at the actual cause of the cancer: a damaged immune system.

Injecting Your Dog with a New Immune System Designed Specifically to Fight Cancer

Although the above heading sounds like something from a science fiction novel, it is accurate. And these new immune systems have been given successfully to dogs and cats for seventeen years (as of 1998) by Drs. Robert and Marty Goldstein. This treatment, called Immuno-Augmentative Therapy (IAT), has also been given for even more years to human cancer victims lucky enough to have learned about it. The doctors Goldstein quoted in this section have worked closely with the original researcher for close to two decades to develop the same kind of success for dogs and cats that the therapy has shown for humans with cancer.

In a nutshell (we'll go into detail later), IAT uses a new technique to isolate components of the immune system designed by nature specifically to kill cancer. These components, isolated from the serum of healthy donors, are then given by injection to the cancer-stricken animal. Thus, the dog or cat almost instantly has within his body a complete *strong* immune system designed specifically to kill cancer.

In an interview, Dr. Robert Goldstein told me that he and his veterinarian brother, Marty, have treated approximately three thousand dogs and cats with the IAT treatment. All the animals had been diagnosed (most of them by other veterinarians) as having terminal cancer: three to six months to live.

"When we get them early in the terminal stage—when they are supposed to have six months left—we get into remission 50 to 60 percent of them," Dr. Goldstein told me. "Our success drops below that for those in the late terminal stage, although we can save about 25 percent of those animals." The veterinarian specifies that the 50 to 60 percent success rate means that those animals go into remission and stay in remission until they eventually die of natural causes ("old age"), an accident, or another disease unsuccessfully treated.

Since the diagnosis of terminal cancer is supposed to mean that nothing in the world can save the animal, you can see why Dr. Goldstein commented that he thought those results were "pretty good." (He doesn't consider them nearly good enough, however. As I write this, he is close to concluding further research to *prevent* cancer, which I will talk about soon.)

I pointed out parenthetically earlier that most of the dogs and cats treated by the Drs. Goldstein were not diagnosed by *them* as having terminal cancer, or as having cancer at all. I wanted to point that out early because there has been a tradition of staunchly orthodox doctors feeling they can discredit doctors with a natural cancer therapy by saying: "These quacks just *told* the patients they had cancer so they could bilk them of their money." Although there certainly may be quackery in treating cancer, I've researched several major natural cancer therapies over more than three decades, and I haven't found one of the doctors whose patients weren't diagnosed by orthodox physicians. I also haven't found any doctor leading a major natural cancer therapy who didn't charge a lot less than the going rate for conventional therapy.

Dr. Goldstein told me: "Sometimes we'll diagnose the dog in our own clinic, but usually another veterinarian—often from the other end of the country—calls me on the phone for help. The animal has been diagnosed by traditional methods, X ray and biopsy. Most often, we never even see the animal. I guide the treatment by phone, using the blood samples and test results that have been sent me by the cooperating veterinarian."

As you can see from that, if you and your dog don't live near Dr. Goldstein, or the very few other veterinarians who presently use this cutting-edge therapy, you certainly don't need to despair of getting this treatment for your dog.

Immuno-Augmentative Therapy, since it naturally restores the immune system's ability to do what nature intended it to do, has no toxic effects. Another plus of IAT is that pet owners can usually administer it at home.

How expensive is IAT? We have already said that, as of late 1998, if the animal needed the maximum three months on the IAT program the cost was about $1,500. "The *complete* program," Dr. Goldstein said, "including IAT, nutritional supplements, and the bionutritional analysis that tells us specifically what each dog needs in the way of nutrients, will run $2,000 to $3,000 over three months." He added that "when the program is successful, it usually brings the dog into remission in three months or less."

Can IAT work for all *forms* of cancer? "Yes," Dr. Goldstein said. "Although, like any other cancer therapy, orthodox or holistic, IAT has a higher success rate with some forms of cancer than with others."

By the way, Dr. Goldstein has been working with animal cancer since the early 1970s, when he developed a freezing technique (cryosurgery) to treat malignancies in animals that couldn't be helped by drugs or surgery. In particular, cryosurgery saves many animals with oral tumors from being euthanized, as they would have been before Dr. Goldstein developed animal cryosurgery. The technique kills tumors through a sort of controlled frostbite, while most of the nearby healthy tissue is unharmed.

Another of the many case histories Dr. Goldstein sent me was of Sam, a ten-year-old golden retriever with malignant melanoma. Before starting IAT, Sam had had three operations, on his gum, throat, and a lymph node. Dr. Goldstein wrote that Sam "presented very ill. He could barely walk." The lymph node that had been operated on was still very enlarged. (Lymph nodes provide the route by which cancer spreads to distant areas of the body.)

As if all this weren't enough for Sam to bear, he also suffered from chronic colitis, pancreatitis, prostatitis, and hypothyroidism. And radiographs showed that Sam's spine was "markedly filled with arthritis."

Dr. Goldstein wrote me of Sam's condition almost three years later, long after common sense might have told us Sam would have left this world. There was "no clinical evidence of cancer." But what about those other five serious medical disorders? Dr. Goldstein remarked further that Sam "is the picture of health."

If you wonder how one therapy can help a dog with six different severe health conditions, remember that IAT—like all holistic therapies—attacks what is biochemically off base within the body. It attacks not individual symptoms, but what is *causing* the symptoms.

Technical Information about How and Why IAT Works

If you tend to blanch when you feel it's important that you understand technical medical information, as I do when someone tries to explain computer technology to me, trust me that you can skip over this section entirely without missing any *practical* information that can help your dog. I write the following mainly for medical professionals who want to learn a bit more about IAT and for lay readers who might like to believe that this therapy can help their dog but are skeptical because I haven't given much of a biochemical rationale as to how IAT works.

Antibodies in the immune system are the "fellows" responsible for identifying and destroying invaders (antigens) that threaten the body they must protect. Specific antibodies are responsible for the "search-and-destroy mission" of specific antigens. Thus, if a measle virus enters your body, the "measle virus antibody" goes into action, while other antibodies relax and take it easy. About forty years ago, Lawrence Burton, Ph.D., stated that an antibody existed that defended the body against cancer cells. Even though his theory was consistent with the accepted antibody-antigen relationships of the time, his idea was not accepted by mainstream medicine—as many new ideas (such as penicillin) have historically not been accepted for many years. As Dr. Goldstein pointed out, "More recent developments related to the well-publicized 'monoclonal antibody' theory seem to affirm" Dr. Burton's discovery from four decades ago.

(Although Dr. Burton's therapy is not in use in mainstream medicine, the U.S. Patent and Trademark Office supported the theories and progress of his research by granting him a series of patents for his techniques. Dr. Goldstein also pointed out that Dr. Burton and his staff of M.D.s well proved both the effectiveness and the safety of IAT in mice before using it with humans.)

To get back to the immune system: Let's assume that cancer cells are trying to overwhelm a *healthy* immune system. (Keep in mind that where I'm going with the following is an explanation of how IAT gets the immune system back into this healthy state so it can naturally do its job of destroying the cancer invaders.) The tumor antibodies (IgA, IgG, and IgM) learn of the presence of tumor cells by a protein produced by the cancer cells themselves. These traitors are known as tumor complement factor, or TCF.

So right now we have the TCF traitors telling the body's tumor antibodies of their own invasion, and the immune system's tumor antibodies take up the challenge. But if the antibodies do their job too well and destroy too many cancer cells at a time, the person's liver may become overburdened. The liver is the major organ through which all poisons leaving the body must be filtered. If this organ receives too many poisons all at once, the person will die.

So a healthy immune system protects the body by producing blocking protein factors that lessen the rate at which the antibodies can kill the tumors.

The important balance of tumor kill rate is also maintained by another component of blood, called deblocking protein factor, which neutralizes the blocking protein factor if it goes overboard in its job of preventing tumor antibodies of overkill.

To review briefly: When our immune systems are healthy, they fight off cancer cells as a matter of course. First, those traitors tell the tumor-killing antibodies that they have a job to do. If the antibodies are too gung ho in rushing to destroy the invaders, the blocking protein factor stops the antibodies from "winning the battle but losing the war" for the body's liver and thus for the body. But if the blocking protein factor also becomes overzealous—preventing the antibodies from doing their job when the liver *can* filter out the cancer cells without killing the body—along comes the deblocking protein factor to take care of *that* problem.

When the immune system is *not* healthy, however, it may have an oversupply of blocking protein factor, along with undersupplies of deblocking protein factors and tumor complement factors. In other words, the tumor-fighting antibodies are being prevented from doing their job when they *shouldn't* be prevented, and they aren't getting strong enough information in the first place that they have a job to *do*. The immune system of the dog (or cat or human) is now helpless to stop the cancer from advancing uncontrolled throughout the body. We are now talking about an animal, or a person, who is sure to die from cancer. Sure to die, that is, if we can't find a way to get all those cancer-fighting factors of the immune system working naturally again.

Immuno-Augmentative Therapy has found a way to do just that. The methods of isolating these factors and extracting them from the serum are detailed in U.S. patents officially granted to Dr. Burton and his colleagues. The tumor antibodies and the factor that neutralizes the blocking protein that prevents antibodies from doing their job fully are extracted from the serum of animals with an immune system that is well equipped to fight cancer and are given to afflicted animals by injection.

The tumor complement factor is extracted from the serum of patients with cancer. Why put blood from someone with cancer into the body of an animal already diagnosed as dying from the disease? Isn't that like giving a blood transfusion tainted with the HIV virus to a person already dying from AIDS? First of all, you're not putting whole blood into the sick animal; you're giving him only the extracted immune factors. Second, this specific immune factor, which alerts the antibodies that they have a battle to fight, enters the body "on the back of " cancer cells—so this factor is not found in animals who don't have cancer.

If any readers who aren't medical professionals are still with me, you must have been following very closely. So you may see that we have a fourth factor that I haven't mentioned sharing with the sick dog. That's the blocking protein factor, the one that prevents the antibodies from killing too many cancer cells all at once. While this factor, too, can be isolated and extracted from serum, it's obviously not the first substance that a dog very ill with cancer needs.

With IAT, every time the animal is tested to determine improvement, measurements are made (by spectrophotometry) from blood samples to determine not only the combined readings of the four immune system factors we've been talking about, but also the readings of each individual factor. Further therapy is modified accordingly. Thus—fulfilling a major goal of holistic veterinarians—each animal's therapy is tailored specifically to what the individual dog's body needs at any given time.

The results of these measurements are combined with conventional measurements of tumor regression, such as biopsy and X rays.

What about This Therapy for Humans?

As I said earlier, IAT was originally developed for humans, and it continues to help people diagnosed as having terminal cancer. For more information on IAT for humans, call 242-352-7455.

Bio Nutritional Analysis

Dr. Goldstein stressed to me that the Bio Nutritional Analysis (BNA) is crucial to the success of IAT. This analysis tells veterinarians the current nutritional status of each animal's body, as well as the balance and effectiveness of the glands of the immune system. Thus, Dr. Goldstein wrote me, BNA eliminates "the trial-and-error approach" to choosing further treatment.

The analysis also prevents the danger of overloading the body with toxins if the cancer cells are broken down too fast. (I mention that problem elsewhere in this chapter.)

Dr. Goldstein pointed out that BNA uses standard routine blood tests, a fact that he believes will satisfy skeptics. He noted that BNA can be used to guide any holistic program for balancing and strengthening the immune system.

The veterinarian wrote me that further information on BNA and IAT is available for veterinarians and lay people at 800-670-0830.

What May Be on the Horizon for Truly Conquering Cancer?

When I talked to Dr. Goldstein in late 1997, he was in the process of setting up research grants at universities to study, along stringent scientific lines, work he has developed to *prevent* cancer. Despite the work he has already done to cure so many animals diagnosed as "incurable," he remains dissatisfied: "I don't want to keep battling this disease once it has taken over the animal," he told me, "and I don't want other doctors to have to keep battling it in humans."

Saying that he wished he could tell me more about his research— "because I think it's very exciting"—he added that, as a man of science, he couldn't overstep himself before his work was scientifically well proven. "But," he said, "you can quote me on this: I believe we are very close to *the* answer on cancer—and it is in prevention. And, although you certainly can help prevent cancer with good diet, genetics plays a gigantic role."

Giving a bit more of a hint about his research, Dr. Goldstein commented that "there are specific animal breeds like golden retrievers that are number one for getting cancer. Now, why are they number one? Because we've overbred them, and we've bred them wrong." Dr. Goldstein isn't advocating that we stop breeding golden retrievers, of course. "But let's find out what the specific genetic problem is—and we can breed cancer *out* of the line, just as we bred it *into* the line." He added that "enlightened breeders have already bred hip dysplasia out of the golden retriever line. But most breeders don't pay attention—so hip dysplasia continues to be, unnecessarily, a major problem for these dogs."

Since there may be a long interval between my writing of this book and your reading of it, you might want to keep an eye out for a book by Dr. Marty Goldstein, who as I write this chapter is preparing a book that will cover IAT. Dr. Robert Goldstein is also writing a book for veterinarians on nutritional therapies.

A final note: As I was finishing my editing on this section, I happened into the living room where my husband, Joe, was watching television. On the screen were a dog, a woman, and Dr. Marty Goldstein. "Oh," I said, "that's Marty!" Then my attention went to the dog, a beautiful animal whose sprightliness was infectious. Entranced, I watched the dog amusing himself while his owner and Dr. Goldstein talked to the host. "Why is the dog on the show?" I eventually asked.

"Snoopy's there," said Joe, "because he had terminal spinal cancer some years ago."

Nutritional Therapies for Cancer

As I write this, I know of only four veterinarians who use the cutting-edge Immuno-Augmentative Therapy directly, although other holistic veterinarians will often consult with those four and use this therapy under their guidance. Far more commonly used at this point are a variety of nutrients as well as certain acupuncture and homeopathic techniques that are known to help give strength to the immune system. As always, the specific therapy will be tailored to the individual dog, but you can get a good idea of some of the nutrients commonly used by looking at other sections of this chapter. A following section also tells *why* some of the nutrients strengthen the immune system.

To give you an idea of how well nutritional therapies for cancer have withstood the test of time, I'd like to tell you about Rush, a male German shepherd that was eight and a half years old in 1981. Robin M. Woodley, D.V. M., told me about Rush for the first edition of this book, when holistic veterinary medicine was primitive compared to today. One fact that was unusual was that Dr. Woodley, who cured Rush of terminal cancer using nutritional therapy, considered herself at the time basically an orthodox veterinarian. You'll notice the other unusual fact about this case on your own.

One day Rush's owner saw a raised nodule on her pet's head. Within the next few days, four more such nodules had developed on both the head and forelimbs. Whatever it was, it was spreading rapidly. An operation removed the lumps, but a biopsy revealed malignant histiocytoma, a rare type of cancer in dogs. Even though the tumors had been removed, several more new ones developed *within only a week after the operation*. As you might expect, at this point a prestigious university medical school said that nothing could be done; no further treatment should even be tried.

"Every specialist I contacted had only condolences to offer as 'help' for Rush," Dr. Woodley wrote me. Why condolences? Rush was Dr. Woodley's own dog.

The veterinarian gave her Rush 10 grams of vitamin C daily, administered orally and divided into two doses. In only two weeks, all the lumps—which had previously been spreading so fast—had disappeared. Rush was maintained on vitamins C, A, D, E, and the B complex. Ten months later, Dr. Woodley wrote me, Rush was still in excellent health, and there was no sign of cancer.

But then fate took a cruel turn for the now healthy Rush. He died of complications from a myelogram, a rather risky orthodox diagnostic test.

Dr. Lemmon's recent statement on the covering page of this chapter indicates the first two concerns he has in treating any case of cancer: stopping the use of excess conventional vaccines, as covered in chapter 3, and changing the diet to the dog's natural raw-food diet as detailed in chapters 2 and 4. When an owner can't or won't follow that diet, Dr. Lemmon urges at least a top-grade prepared food (again, see chapter 2) and prescribes enzymes because only raw foods contain these nutrients, which are essential for every biochemical reaction in the body. Dr. Lemmon has the owner give the enzymes with meals, to help the dog digest the food, as well as between meals.

If the dog is on a natural diet, the veterinarian prescribes enzymes to be taken only between meals. "I use Intenzyme from a company called Biotics, or S22 from Tyler," Dr. Lemmon said. "I've seen results with either one of those in reducing tumors of various different types of cancers."

Dr. Robertson, who reported a very high success rate with cancer in 1981, told me about his use of the enzyme bromelain, which helps dissolve the fibrous coating that forms around a long-standing tumor. This "coat" acts as a protective shield for the tumor so that the immune system, even as it gains health with other nutritional therapy, cannot get at the tumor to dissolve it.

Very recently, Dr. Lemmon told me that he uses bromelain by itself "if it's a good-quality bromelain." Bromelain is also in the Intenzyme product he mentioned a bit earlier.

"One of the things that I've been using for the last six months that has been helpful for some of the cancers we've been working with, and for immune problems including leukemia," Dr. Lemmon added, "is a probiotic by the name of Nature's Biotics. Or I'll use a similar probiotic formulation, Pet Defense."

Dr. Lemmon, as well as other holistic veterinarians, will also sometimes use raw glandular extracts corresponding to the organ system that's affected with the cancer. Obviously, if a glandular system is hit by cancer, it is weakened; and the raw extracts of that particular system can help to strengthen it.

If you give your dog the natural diet that her holistic veterinarian will almost certainly (if not certainly) recommend, you will not only increase her chances of successfully battling the cancer, you will lessen her suffering from pain. How so? There is very little salt in the dog's natural diet. As Dr. Price once explained, "Excessive sodium [salt] attaches with water around cells, forming sodium hydroxide, a very irritating substance."

As you might expect, one major reason holistic veterinarians will vary their therapy depends on the stage and the type of the cancer. "For instance," Dr. Lemmon said, "if the tumor is very large, I might suggest surgery to go along with holistic therapy."

A Warning Against a Therapy That Works Very Fast to Get Rid of Tumors

On occasion, a natural therapy for cancer can work *too* well, if administered by a doctor who is not very experienced in that particular therapy. In 1981, when I researched the first edition, some holistic veterinarians were reporting very good results with laetrile (otherwise known as vitamin B_{17} or amygdalin). Drs. Robert and Marty Goldstein reported, however, that they had found that laetrile in heavily toxic patients can cause "depression, vomiting, and a downhill course." They felt that these effects might be due to "too rapid [a] breakdown of tumor cells, further overloading the body with toxins." They stressed that in treating cancer, one should not become involved solely in watching tumors shrink, but should keep a close check on what changes may be occurring in the animal's overall body chemistry. "It is possible to have a shrunken tumor and a dead animal," they told me. (Earlier, we discussed how the

Immuno-Augmentative Therapy, which the doctors Goldstein now use, protects against this problem.)

On the other hand, the doctors pointed out that "it is very common initially in treatment for the tumor to increase in size due to an accumulation of toxin from the detoxifying process."

If your veterinarian is not highly experienced in treating cancer holistically, discuss the previous two points with him or her.

Some Technical Information on Why Certain Nutrients Are Used to Fight Cancer

I said in the introduction that I would occasionally interrupt the basically practical thrust of this book to point out that holistic veterinarians haven't built their therapies out of thin air, or even just empirical evidence. If you're not interested in technical information, go ahead and skip this section. You won't miss anything of practical help for your dog.

Jack Long, V. M.D., sent me short summaries of some of the biochemical reasons a number of the vitamins and minerals are used to treat cancer. I'll give just a sampling of that information here. In all cases, Dr. Long's references are to effects of the nutrients on workings of the immune system. However, these nutrients have other benefits, too. For instance, the four nutrients mentioned below after vitamin A are B vitamins. As Dr. Kearns has stressed, "The B vitamins enhance appetite, increase the feeling of well-being, detoxify the liver, protect the nervous system, *plus.*"

- Thymus extracts: As long ago as 1975, it was shown that crude extracts of thymus increased cell-mediated immunity in children. Since then, more effective extracts of thymus have been developed, and doctors specializing in holistic medicine have kept up with the new developments.
- Vitamin A helps to prevent abnormal atrophy of the thymus gland.
- Animals denied B_2 have a smaller thymus and fewer antibodies.

- Vitamin B_6 is necessary for antibodies and cell-mediated responses.
- People with folic acid deficiencies have an impaired ability to form white blood cells.
- Pantothenic acid helps produce antibodies.
- Vitamin C increases the ability of white blood cells to get to, engulf, and destroy antigens; it also increases the production of Interferon. The thymus needs vitamin C to produce its hormones.
- At lower levels of intake, vitamin E assists healthy immune responses. At higher levels, it fights *inappropriate* immune responses.
- The mineral calcium is essential for the destruction of foreign substances after they are engulfed by white blood cells.
- Cobalt helps the white blood cells to swallow and destroy the toxins.
- Manganese serves the same function as cobalt.
- Selenium in modest excess of what a healthy body needs stimulates antibody production.
- As reported by the Memorial Sloan-Kettering Cancer Center (a world-famous *orthodox* cancer center), zinc is essential for maintaining normal T-lymphocytes and other functions of the immune system.

Steps You Can Take Yourself to Help Your Dog Beat Cancer

I am definitely *not* telling you that you can use the suggestions in this section to cure your dog of cancer by yourself. You can use them primarily to give him a nutritional support that will help strengthen his immune system while at the same time offsetting some of the harmful effects of conventional cancer therapy. If your dog is being treated directly by a holistic veterinarian, show the suggestions in the rest of this chapter to your dog's doctor rather than proceeding to follow them on your own. This will serve two important purposes: First, the veterinarian may see that certain factors will duplicate or even overload your dog with something he or she is prescribing. Second, if the veterinarian doesn't have the extensive experience in treating cancer that Dr. Robert Goldstein does, he or she may look into something new that will help other dogs in the future, or may opt to consult with Dr. Goldstein to get further details to help your dog.

Dr. Goldstein sent me the following nutritional cocktail as printed in *Love of Animals*, a newsletter he puts out with his wife, Susan, who edits it.* (Dr. Goldstein, who started out as an orthodox veterinarian, readily admits that Susan was ahead of him in pursuing alternative cancer therapies for humans, and it was at her urging that he started seeking alternative cancer therapies for dogs and cats.)

This nutritional cocktail, Dr. Goldstein wrote, "is a helpful adjunct to treatment for just about any debilitating, degenerative, or chronic disease or condition. You can use it for any of the following diseases: cancer, liver and kidney disease, arthritis, skin problems, lupus, Lyme disease, inflammatory bowel disease, degenerative conditions of the pancreas, feline leukemia, feline AIDS."

In a 1995 issue of the newsletter, Dr. Goldstein reported that his dog, Leigh, who had once been crippled, "used to lap up a full bowl" of the cocktail every morning. (Leigh's recovery not only from crippling hip dysplasia but also from chronic skin and ear problems is recounted in chapter 5.)

Dr. Goldstein stressed that the ingredients in the cocktail must be organic: free of pesticides and other chemicals. "You certainly don't want a sick animal to get any more of these chemicals!" he exclaimed. Organic foods are most easily obtained in health food stores. But thanks to the public's new awareness, many supermarkets have organic food sections.

Dr. Goldstein calls the following "the radiation cocktail," because he learned about it from people on IAT therapy "who used it to counteract the negative side effects of prior radiation and chemotherapies." He explains that the recipe "provides ample digestible

* To subscribe to this newsletter, call 800-211-6365.

proteins, which help the body to manufacture more of the immuno-proteins necessary to fight disease. The beta-carotene gives the cocktail anticancer properties. Chlorophyll purifies the body. Aloe vera and vitamin E are renowned healers. Plus, this drink is teeming with life-force enzymes."

The Radiation Cocktail

In a blender, gently mix the following on the lowest speed possible. Because only the fresh drink with freshly extracted juices gives you the live enzymes, make a couple days' supply of the base and add the fresh juices just before feeding. Force-feed animals who are off their feed, but don't overfeed and cause vomiting. The ingredients are available at any good health food store.

Base:
¼ cup distilled or filtered pure water
1 tbsp. aloe vera juice
1 tbsp. powdered dulse or kelp
1 tbsp. nutritional yeast (unprocessed yeast containing the B vitamins)
1 tsp. organic apple cider vinegar (detoxifies the body)
½ tsp. ground rosemary (a natural preservative)
400 IU vitamin E (open a capsule and add its contents)
You can make up to a week's worth of this base at a time and keep it
    refrigerated.

Fresh Juices:
½ cup organic carrot juice (freshly extracted)
½ cup raw organic calves liver (fresh and blended) or 2 organic, raw egg yolks
    (no whites)
1 tbsp. parsley juice (freshly extracted)
These should be made fresh daily and added to the base just before feeding.
    Blend together on the lowest speed.
Dosage: For a dog up to 12 lbs: 2–3 tbsp., two to three times daily. Increase
    proportionately according to dog's weight.

You have already read that stopping vaccinations is a major concern of Dr. Lemmon in battling cancer. Dr. Goldstein said: "Vaccination-induced weakness of the immune system can lay the groundwork for cancer." He further stated: "I have treated scores of dogs and cats with cancer whom I know had had their immune systems weakened by annual vaccinations."

Dr. Goldstein adds that once a dog is diagnosed with cancer, "he should *never* be vaccinated. I have seen dogs go out of remission after getting a vaccine."

As I write in chapter 3, holistic doctors have a homeopathic remedy to do away with the negative effects of standard vaccinations. Dr. Goldstein said that "the homeopathic remedy *Thuja occidentallis* 30C removes the immune-suppressing effects of vaccinations." You can call a holistic veterinarian (see the list at the back of this book for those trained in homeopathy), and he or she will send this remedy to you.

The veterinarian recommends a product called Essiac, which contains a number of herbs combined synergistically to be "a potent tonic and detoxifier." He stated: "I never use Essiac by itself for cancer patients, but it works beautifully in combination with other remedies."

Dr. Goldstein noted that you can find Essiac at human health food stores, or you can call Essiac International at 800-668-4559 for further information. He advised: "Follow the instructions closely for how to make up the remedy. After the tea is made and the herbs strained out, dilute the Essiac with equal parts of distilled water." Dr. Goldstein recommended giving a dog weighing up to 25 pounds one teaspoon twice a day, either one hour before or after food. If your dog weighs 25 to 50 pounds, give her 2 teaspoons twice daily; if she weighs over 50 pounds, she should get 1 tablespoon twice a day.

Noting that vitamin C works directly on strengthening the immune system, Dr. Goldstein recommended the newer form of this vitamin, Ester-C, over the ascorbic acid and sodium ascorbate forms.

The following boxed information gives Dr. Goldstein's further recommendations for nutritional support for your dog with cancer.

Additional Nutritional Support for Cancer Patients

Give all supplements at mealtimes unless otherwise noted.

- **Vitamin E (the mixed tocopherols form):** 400 IU daily for a dog weighing up to 50 pounds, 800 IU daily for a dog weighing over that
- **Daily Health Nuggets:** Follow package directions (to order this product, formulated by Dr. Goldstein, call 800-711-2292)
- **Beta-carotene:** 10,000 IU to 25,000 IU daily, according to dog's weight (see above, under vitamin E)
- **Garlic tablets (Garlicin or Kyolic):** One tablet daily for the smaller dog, two to three twice daily for the larger animal
- **Selenium:** 50 mcg to 100 mcg daily. Don't confuse this with 50 or 100 mg, a much higher amount that can cause a lot more harm than good
- **Pancreatin:** One to two tablets daily, according to weight
- **Coenzyme Q10:** 50 mg a day for a small, 100 mg daily for a medium, 200 mg for a large, and 300 mg for a giant dog
- **Astragalus capsules:** Half a pill twice daily for the smaller dog, two pills twice daily for the larger
- **AOX/PLX:** One to two tablets twice daily, according to weight. (This is a high-dose antioxidant formula in an herbal base. Dr. Goldstein stated: "I love this product, but it is hard to find." You can order it from the Animal Health Line at 203-222-0260.)

Whenever you give your dog supplements, the liquid or powdered form should be used, rather than tablets. If those forms are hard to find, the tablets should be crushed (making them, of course, into a powder). Dogs have short digestive systems, and as Dr. Price has warned, a whole tablet sometimes goes through the dog's body so fast that "it comes out still a whole tablet." Obviously, the animal's body has not been able to utilize any nutrients in the tablet. Other veterinarians have warned that a small animal can choke on a whole tablet.

If you're working with a holistic veterinarian, remember to discuss all of Dr. Goldstein's recommendations to avoid duplication or overloading.

Summary

In this chapter I gave a number of case histories of dogs with diagnosed terminal cancer who responded well to holistic therapies. You may have thought that I had to search far and wide to get those case histories. Actually, the reverse is true: I received more histories of terminal cancer than I did of any other single disorder, and it was with regret that I had to leave most of them out because of lack of space. I will end this chapter, though, with two more. Donald, a dalmatian, was fourteen when he started IAT therapy. He had a history of skin allergies, chronic diarrhea, and severe hemorrhagic urination. Orthodox tests led to a diagnosis of cancer: transitional cell carcinoma—inoperable. With IAT therapy, Donald gained clinical remission within six weeks. He died of old age, still with no evidence of clinical cancer.

Amber is a golden retriever mix diagnosed with squamous cell carcinoma. Dr. Robert Goldstein, who sent me this case history, commented that this is a very invasive form of cancer. She had surgery before Dr. Goldstein saw her, but the veterinarians also recommended an extended hospital stay with both radiation and chemotherapy. If this were done, they said, Amber might live another six to nine months.

"Amber responded almost immediately" to holistic therapy, Dr. Goldstein wrote in a 1996 issue of his newsletter, *Love of Animals*. "She started eating voraciously. To [her owners'] delight, she even started barking again!" Her hair became healthier looking, and "as the months went by, all appearance of cancer and its effects disappeared. Where the cancerous growth once invaded, there now was healthy pink tissue." When Dr. Goldstein wrote this, Amber had already lived past the outer limit of her prognosis and was "a happy, energetic dog whose immune system shows no sign of cancer.'"

Amber's people, who had sought alternative care because they knew what radiation and chemotherapy would do to her quality of life in the remaining months orthodox therapy held out for her, wrote Dr. Goldstein: "Her quality of life is better than it was before she had the cancer."

I deeply hope the information in this chapter gives your companion years more to enjoy her life with you (and vice versa)—and that she gets to leave this world peacefully and without any suffering after a very long life. Or, as many holistic veterinarians have expressed to me as their goal, "when the dog herself has chosen to move on."

As mentioned, I have personal experience with return to full health from diagnosed terminal cancer in my little poodle, Shiki. My husband is alive and well a quarter of a century later than he "should be," according to orthodox specialists, of a disorder still classified as terminal even if found early. So I have been where you are now. Believe me, I know what you're feeling. And I wish you the same good fortune with alternative medicine that I have had.

But we have to face the fact that no doctor has yet found the secret to eternal life. If your dog doesn't respond to holistic therapy, you can comfort yourself that you tried the most advanced medical techniques to save her—and that maybe *she* made the final choice.

How to Reach Holistic Veterinarians Throughout the Country

This list gives names, addresses, and phone numbers of many holistic veterinarians across the country. They are listed according to the state in which they presently practice.

I am indebted to Carvel G. Tiekert, D.V. M., executive director of the American Holistic Veterinary Association (Maryland), for much of this information. Dr. Tiekert warns that, like any list of names and addresses, this information changes frequently. He suggests that you call the association for their list, which they update frequently.

The initials at the end of each lising indicate what modalities the doctor uses as this book goes to press. The explanation of the initials follows below.

Although only a relatively few veterinarians have listed themselves as doing phone consultations, many others offer this service as a matter of course.

MODALITIES

AC - Acupuncture
AC(IVAS) - Acupuncture
(International Veterinary Acupuncture
Society certified)
AK - Applied Kinesiology
BF - Bach Flower Remedies
BII - Biotron II
CH - Chinese Herbs
CM - Conventional Medicine
CN - Clinical Nutrition
CR - Chiropractic

CT - Color Therapy
EAV - Electroacupuncture (Voll)
GT - Glandular Therapy
H - Homeopathy
HC - Homeopathy Classical
HO - Homeopathy Other
IN - Interro
MT - Magnetic Therapy
NU - Nutrition
PMT - Pulsating Magnetic Therapy
WH - Western Herbs

ALABAMA

Mary Battistella, D.V.M.
2630 Dadeville Road
Alexander City, AL 35010
205-329-9900
AC(IVAS), CM

S. Allen Price, D.V.M.
1444 Montgomery Highway
Birmingham, AL 35216
205-822-0210
Small Animal
AC, BF, CN, HC, NU

ALASKA

Jeanne Olson, D.V.M.
1684 Palomino Drive
North Pole, AK 99705
907-488-2906
FAX: 907-488-2906
AC(IVAS), CM, CN, CR, EAV, H,
HC, NU

ARIZONA

James C. Armer, D.V.M.
2085 Mountain Road, Suite 1
Sedona, AZ 86336
520-204-1034
Small Animal
AC(IVAS), BF, CH, CM, CN, CR,
HO, NU, WH

Holly R. Keppel, D.V.M.
2641 E. 9th Street
Tucson, AZ 85716
520-297-3593
Small Animal, Exotic
HC, CM, CN

Deborah C. Mallu, D.V.M.
215 Disney Lane
Sedona, AZ 86336
520-282-5651
FAX: 520-282-3586
AC(IVAS), BF, BI, CH, CM, CN,
CT, GT, NU, WH, Hands-on
Healing, Animal
Communication

Judith A. Stolz, D.V.M.
6722 E. Avalon, Suite 3
Scottsdale, AZ 85251
602-899-1624
AC(IVAS), BF, CH, CM, CN, CT,
EAV, GT, HO, IN, MT, NU, WH

Norman Ward, D.V.M.
7030 E. Fifth Avenue, Suite 3
Scottsdale, AZ 85251
602-946-0663
Small Animal, Exotic
AC(IVAS), BF, CH, CM, CN, GT,
HC, HO, MT, NU, WH,
Homotoxicology

ARKANSAS

Pat Bradley, D.V.M.
Joy R. Dunn, D.V.M.
65 Sunny Gap Road
Conway, AR 72032
501-329-7727
FAX: 501-329-7727
Small Animal, Equine
HC, NU

CALIFORNIA

Robert A. Anderson, D.V.M.
1695 Clara Avenue
Fortuna, CA 95540
916-944-3749
BF, CM, H, HC

Marc Bittan, D.V.M.
11673 National Boulevard
Los Angeles, CA 90064
310-231-4415
FAX: 310-231-4418
Small Animal, Equine
AC, BF, CH, GT, HC, HO, NU

Linda C. Boggie, D.V.M.
Village Veterinary Hospital
3125 W. Benjamin Holt
Stockton, CA 95219
209-951-5180
FAX: 209-951-0732
AC, CH, CR, NU, WH

Pamela Bouchard, D.V.M.
39 Crestview Drive
San Rafael, CA 94903-2880
415-499-0909
AC(IVAS), BF, CH, CM, CN,
NU, WH

Kathleen M. Carson, D.V.M.
2103 Arlington Avenue
Hermosa Beach, CA 90501
310-372-8881
Small Animal
AC(IVAS), BF, CM, CT, HO,
Crystals, Therapeutic Touch

Douglas Coward, D.V.M.
25290 Marguerite Parkway
Mission Viejo, CA 92692
714-768-3651
Avian
CH, CM, CN, NU, WH

J. Lauren De Rock, D.V.M.
16311 Gustafson Avenue, #331
Patterson, CA 95363
209-664-1764
Equine
AC(IVAS)

W. Jean Dodds, D.V.M.
938 Stanford Street
Santa Monica, CA 90403
310-828-4804
FAX: 310-828-8251
CM Immunology and
Hematology, CN

William L. Farber, D.V.M.
2106 S. Sepulveda Boulevard
West Los Angeles, CA 91384
310-477-6735
Small Animal, Avian, Exotic
AC(IVAS), CH, CN, EAV, NU

Kevin M. Fenton, D.V.M.
78-359 Highway 111
La Quinta, CA 92253
619-564-1154
Small Animal, Equine, Exotic
AC, CH, CR

Stanley Goldfarb, D.V.M.
P. O. Box 150149
San Rafael, CA 94915-0149
415-459-2195
BF, BI, CH, CN, CR, CT, EAV, GT,
HC, IN, NU, WH

David A. Gordon, D.V.M.
22421 El Toro Road, Suite B
Lake Forest, CA 92630
714-770-1808
FAX: 714-770-8984
Small Animal
AC, CH, CM, CN, CR, NU, WH

Darren Hawks, D.V.M., DACVIM
1360 S. DeAnza Boulevard
San Jose, CA 95129
408-996-1155
FAX: 408-996-9434
Small Animal, Equine
BF, CM, CR, HC, HO, NU, WH,
Reiki

Henry W. Kostecki, D.V.M.
964 Rubicon Trail
South Lake Tahoe, CA 96150
916-541-3551
AC, BF, CH, CM, CN, CR, GT,
H, HC, NU, WH

Monica A. Laflin, D.V.M.
2159 San Elijo Avenue
Cardiff, CA 92007
760-436-3215
FAX: 760-436-4126
Small Animal, Avian, Exotic
AC(IVAS), AK, CN, CH, CR, AVCA
certified, NU

Margaret M. Larned, D.V.M.
3433 State Street, Suite D
Santa Barbara, CA 93105
805-569-5997
FAX: 805-569-5728
Small Animal, Avian
CM, HO, WH, Intuitive
Diagnostics Pendulum Dowsing

Douglas Lemire, V.M.D.
P. O. Box 40521
Santa Barbara, CA 93140
805-565-3985
AC(IVAS), BF, CH, CN, GT, HO,
NU, WH

John B. Limehouse, D.V.M.
Priscilla A. Taylor, D.V.M.
10742 Riverside Drive
N. Hollywood, CA 91602
818-761-0787
AC(IVAS), BF, BI, CH, CM, CN,
CR, CT, EAV, GT, H, HC, HO,
IN, NU, PMT, WH

Jack M. Long, V.M.D.
5033 Gravenstein Highway North
Sebastopol, CA 95472
707-823-7312
AC, CM, CN, CR, GT, H, HC,
NU, WH

Don E. Lundholm, D.V.M.
10130 Adams Avenue
Huntington Beach, CA 92646
714-964-1605
AC, BI, CN, CM, EAV, H, HC

Adrienne Moore, D.V.M.
Fallbrook, CA 92028
619-723-6633
BF, H

Manjit S. Nagi, D.V.M.
2335 "F" Street
Livingston, CA 95334
209-394-8556
FAX: 209-394-8250
Small Animal
H, HC, HO

Ken Ninomiya, D.V.M.
3624 Via Pacifica Walk
Oxnard, CA 93035
805-984-6293
FAX: 805-984-6293
Small Animal
AC(IVAS), CM, CN, HC, NU,
Network Chiropractic

Richard Palmquist, D.V.M.
721 Centinela Avenue
Inglewood, CA 90302
310-673-1910
Small Animal
AC, CM, GT, HO, NU

Kerry Parker, D.V.M.
Vallejo, CA
707-426-2174

Henry Pasternak, D.V.M.
526 Palisades Drive
Pacific Palisades, CA 90272
310-454-2917
AC(IVAS), CH, CM, CN, GT, NU,
WH, Ozone

David W. Penney, D.V.M.
Irving Street Veterinary
1434 Irving Street
San Francisco, CA 94122
415-664-0191
FAX: 415-664-6708
510-652-1003
Small Animal, Avian, Exotic
AC(IVAS), BF, CH, CM, CN,
CR, GT, HC, NU

Nancy Scanlan, D.V.M.
13624 Moorpark Street
Sherman Oaks, CA 91423
818-784-9977
FAX: 909-597-8933
Small Animal
AC(IVAS), BF, CH, CM, CN,
CR, HO, NU, WH

Cheryl Schwartz, D.V.M.
3619 California Street
San Francisco, CA 94118
415-387-6844
Small Animal
AC(IVAS), H

Robert Smatt, D.V.M.
5621 Balboa Avenue
San Diego, CA 92111
619-278-1575
AC(IVAS), BF, CH, CM, CN,
CR, GT, H, NU, MT, WH

Roger W. Valentine, D.V.M.
1637 16th Street
Santa Monica, CA 90404-3801
310-450-CATS
FAX: 310-392-7369
Feline
AC, AK, BF, CH, CM, CN, CR,
EAV, HO, NU, Allergy
Elimination Technique, House
Calls, Cat Products and Foods

Thomas Van Cise, D.V.M.
1560 Hamner Avenue
Norco, CA 91760
909-737-1242
Small Animal, Avian, Exotic
AC(IVAS), CH, CM, CR, CT,
HO, WH, Acuscope, Reiki,
Auricular Medicine, Low Level
Laser Therapy

Neal K. Weiner, D.V.M.
P. O. Box 628
316 Texas Avenue
Lewiston, CA 96052
916-778-3109
Small Animal
BF, CM, CN, CR, GT, HO, NU,
WH, Reflexology

Beth Wildermann, D.V.M.
17333 Bear Creek Road
Boulder Creek, CA 95006
408-354-1576
CM, GT, H, HC, NU, Reiki

COLORADO

Rachel Blackmer, D.V.M.
P. O. Box 841
Conifer, CO 80433
303-838-7698
FAX: 303-838-7698
Small Animal, Equine, Exotic
AC(IVAS), BF, CR, CT, HC,
Reiki, Pranamonics

Ron Carsten, D.V.M.
1602 Grand Avenue
Glenwood Springs, CO 81601
970-945-0125
AC, H, NU, Osteopathic Manip,
Meridian Therapy

Jay Clapper, D.V.M.
7700 W. 101st Avenue
Broomfield, CO 80021
303-469-7387
H, NU

Linda East, D.V.M.
311 S. Pennsylvania
Denver, CO 80209
303-733-2728
BF, CN, HC

Jan Facinelli, D.V.M.
5015 Raleigh
Denver, CO 80212
303-458-5428
AC(IVAS), BF, CH, CM, CN, CR,
GT, H, HC, NU, WH

David Fong, D.V.M.
P. O. Box 440410
Aurora, CO 80044
303-693-9314
AC, BF, H, NU, Contact Reflex
Analysis, House Call, CR, Reiki

Holly S. Foster, D.V.M.
7187 E. Wyoming Place
Denver, CO 80224
303-759-4540
AC, BF, Housecall Only

H. C. Gurney, Jr. D.V.M.
26497 Conifer Road
Conifer, CO 80433
303-674-0280
AC, BF, CH, CM, CN, CT, EAV,
GT, H, NU, MT, WH,
Immunology

Jean Hofve, D.V.M.
334 S. Pennsylvania Street
Denver, CO 80209
303-733-2728
303-733-3466
FAX: 303-733-2858
Small Animal (Feline)
BF, HC, NU

David H. Jaggar, MRCVS, DC
5139 Sugar Loaf Road
Boulder, CO 80302-9217
303-682-1167
FAX: 303-682-7168
Small Animal, Equine, Farm
Animal
AC(IVAS), CH, CR, NU

David McCluggage, D.V.M.
9390 Rogers Road
Longmont, CO 80503
303-702-1986
FAX: 303-702-9602
Small Animal, Avian, Exotic
AC(IVAS), BF, CH, CN, GT, HC,
NU, WH, Reiki

Rhonda L. Rodman, D.V.M.
7910 W. 20th Avenue
Lakewood, CO 80215
303-202-0420
FAX: 303-202-0420
Small Animal, Equine
AC(IVAS), BF, CN, CR, HC,
MT, PMT

Judith Miller Shoemaker, D.V.M.
2002-B W. 120th Avenue
Westminster, CO 80234
303-438-0439
FAX: 303-460-7622
H, NU, (Clinical)

Barbara S. Shor, D.V.M.
30884 Kings Valley Drive
Conifer, CO 80403
303-838-3419
FAX: 303-838-4244
BF

Robert J. Silver, D.V.M.
4660 Table Mesa Drive
Boulder, CO 80303
303-494-7877
FAX: 303-494-4496
Small Animal
AC(IVAS), BF, CH, CN,
CR, GT, HO, MT, NU, WH,
Therapeutic Touch, Crystal
Healing, Human Animal Bond

Elayne Williams, D.V.M.
2633 S. College
Ft. Collins, CO 80525
970-226-4620
Small Animal, Avian, Exotic
BF, CH, CN, GT, HC

CONNECTICUT

Theresa M. Digiulio, V.M.D.
356 Talcott Hill Road
Coventry, CT 06238
860-677-4638
AC, CM

Marcie Fallek, D.V.M.
248 Alden Street
Fairfield, CT 06430
203-254-8642
Small Animal
AC(IVAS), BF, CM, GT, HC,
NU, WH

Jeff Feinman, D.V.M.
73 Lyons Plain Road
Weston, CT 06883-2901
203-222-7979
FAX: 203-227-3231
Small Animal
AC, BF, BI, CH, CM, CN, CR,
GT, HO, IN, WH

Robert S. Goldstein, V.M.D.
606 Post Road East
Northern Skies Animal Clinic
Westport, CT 06880
203-222-0260
FAX: 203-227-8094
Small Animal
AC, BF, CH, CN, CR, GT, HO,
MT, NU, WH, Immuno-
Augmentative Therapy (IAT) for
Cancer, Bio Nutritional Analysis
of Blood

Allen M. Schoen, D.V.M.
15 Sunset Terrace
Sherman, CT 06784
860-354-2287
FAX: 860-350-3482
AC(IVAS), BI, CH, CM, CN,
CR, GT, H, HC, HO, NU,
MT, WH

Stephen Tobin, D.V.M.
26 Pleasant Street
Meriden, CT 06450
203-238-9863
FAX: 203-237-2334
CN, H, HC, WH

Neil C. Wolff, D.V.M.
530 E. Putnam Avenue
Greenwich, CT 06830
203-869-7755
AC(IVAS), BF, CH, CM, H, HC,
HO, NU, Laser AC

DELAWARE

Shelley R. Epstein, V.M.D.
828 Philadelphia Pike
Wilmington, DE 19809
302-762-2694
FAX: 302-762-1620
Small Animal, Exotic
CM, CN, HC

Greig Howie, D.V.M.
21 Muirfield Court
Dover, DE 19901
302-734-8425
FAX: 302-674-3099
Telephone Consultations
AC(IVAS), BF, CH, CM, CN,
GT, H, HC, WH

Lorraine Parris, D.V.M.
Wilmington, DE 19804
302-998-8851
AC(IVAS)

FLORIDA

Larry A. Bernstein, V.M.D.
751 NE 168th Street
North Miami Beach, FL 33162-2427
305-652-5372
FAX: 305-653-7244
Small Animal, Equine, Exotic
AC(IVAS), BF, CH, CN, CR, HC,
NU, WH

Beth Brown, D.V.M.
Braden River Animal Hospital
5012 State Road 64 East
Bradenton, FL 34208
941-366-4623
FAX: 941-746-0515
Small Animal, Equine
AC(IVAS), BF, CH, CM, CN,
CR, GT, HC, HO

Maurice F. Casey III, D.V.M.
Marianna Animal Hospital
Marianna, FL 32446-3445
904-482-3520
AC(IVAS)

Betsy Coville, D.V.M.
510 Stratfield Drive
Lutz, FL 33549
813-949-1818
Small Animal, Farm Animal,
Avian, Exotic
AC(IVAS), BF, CH, HC, WH

Joseph Demers, D.V.M.
496 N. Harbor City Boulevard
Melbourne, FL 32935
407-752-0140
FAX: 407-752-0150
Small Animal
AC(IVAS), BF, CH, CN, GT, HC

Laura Earle, D.V.M.
545 Gus Hipp Boulevard
Rockledge, FL 32955
407-632-3800
FAX: 407-632-2366
Small Animal, Avian, Exotic
CM, CN, CR, HC, NU

Lisa R. Edwards, D.V.M.
545 Gus Hipp Boulevard
Rockledge, FL 32955
407-632-3800
FAX: 407-632-2366
Small Animal, Equine
AC(IVAS), BF, CM, CN, CR,
GT, HC, NU, Neuroemotional
Technique

Brenda J. Ernest, D.V.M.
1795 10th Avenue
Vero Beach, FL 32960
561-562-0666
CM, H, HC, NU, WH

Peggy Fleming, D.V.M.
21412 Field of Dreams Lane
Dade City, FL 33525
352-583-2400
FAX: 352-583-4007
Equine
AC(IVAS), BF, CH, CN, CR,
EAV, GT, HC, HO, MT, NU,
PMT, WH

Mary Foster, D.V.M.
Alachua, FL 32615
904-462-7017
AC(IVAS)

John Fudens, D.V.M.
Affinity Holistic Clinic
1171 Lakeview Road
Clearwater, FL 34616
813-446-3603
Small Animal, Equine
AC, CH, CN, HC, NU, MT, WH,
Gemmotherapy,
Organotherapy, Radionic
Analysis
Phone Consultations

John C. Haromy, D.V.M.
3631 Highway 60 East
Lake Wales, FL 33853
941-676-5922
FAX: 941-676-7342
Small Animal
AC(IVAS), CM, CN, CT, HC,
NU, MT

Ronald A. Johnson, D.V.M.
680 Tennis Club Drive
Fort Lauderdale, FL 33311
954-731-2000
Small Animal
CH, CM, CN, HO, MT, WH

Robert Katz, D.V.M.
Arthur Young, D.V.M.
3003 S. Federal Highway
Stuart, FL 34994
561-287-2242
FAX: 561-287-0089
Small Animal, Exotic, Avian
AC(IVAS), BF, CH, CM, CN,
EAV, GT, HC, NU, WH

Lucille Kohut, D.V.M.
6465 142nd Avenue, North, #BB104
Clearwater, FL 34620
813-524-1190
FAX: 813-524-1190
Small Animal, Equine, Avian,
Exotic
HC, NU

Anne Lampru, D.V.M.
9409 Tillotson Court
Odessa, FL 33556
813-933-6609
FAX: 813-933-1103
Small Animal, Avian, Exotic
AC(IVAS), BF, CH, CM, CN,
GT, HO, NU

Jeff Saunders, D.V.M.
7200 U.S. Highway 27 North
Sebring, FL 33870
813-382-9400
Small Animal, Equine, Exotic
AC, CH, CM, CN, HC, NU, WH

Russell Swift, D.V.M.
7154 N. University Drive, Suite 720
Tamarac, FL 33321
954-720-0794
Small Animal, Avian, Exotic
BF, GT, HC, NU, WH,
Telephone Consultations,
Product Development,
Marketing

Gerald A. Wessner, V.M.D.
Belleview Holistic Veterinary Clinic
11409 SE U.S. Highway 301
Belleview, FL 34420
352-245-2025
Small Animal, Equine
CN, EAV, GT, HO, NU

Pamela Wood-Krzeminski, D.V.M.
5142 Glencove Lane
West Palm Beach, FL 33415
561-964-8553
AC(IVAS), CM, CR, H, HC, HO,
NU, WH

GEORGIA

Mary Brennan, D.V.M.
965 Bobcat Court
Marietta, GA 30067
770-612-0318
FAX: 770-916-9809
*AC(IVAS), BF, CH, CN, CR, CT,
GT, H, HC, HO, MT, WH,
Physical Exercise Therapy*

Heidi S. Newell, D.V.M.
3270 Summer View Drive
Alpharetta, GA 30202
779-752-7237
*Small Animal
BF, CM, CN, NU, WH*

Howard L. Rand, D.V.M.
2000 Bill Murdock Road
Marietta, GA 30062
770-973-4133
AC(IVAS), CM, EAV, H, HO

Michelle Tilghman, D.V.M.
1975 Glenn Club Drive
Stone Mountain, GA 30087
770-498-5956
FAX: 770-498-3458
*AC(IVAS), BF, BI, CM, CN, GT,
H, HO, NU, WH*

Susan Wynn, D.V.M.
1080 N. Cobb Parkway
Marietta, GA 30062
770-424-6303
FAX: 770-426-4257
*AC(IVAS), BF, CH, CM, CN,
HC, HO, NU, WH*

HAWAII

Ihor Basko, D.V.M.
P. O. Box 159
Kapaa, HI 96746
808-828-1330
FAX: 808-822-2452
*Small Animal, Equine, Farm
Animal, Avian
AC(IVAS), BF, CH, CM, CN, CR,
CT, GT, HC, HO, NU, PMT, WH,
Laser Therapy Massage*
Phone consultations worldwide at 808-
828-1330 or E-mail at
drbwavevet@hawaiian.net

IDAHO

Ronald L. Hamm, D.V.M.
Grace, ID 83241
208-427-6233
801-750-7610
AC(IVAS)

Debra J. Mack, D.V.M.
3660 Flint Drive
Eagle, ID 83616-4534
208-322-4449
FAX: 208-322-4612
*Small Animal
AC, BF, CM, CN, HO, NU, MT, WH*

Heather K. Mack, V.M.D.
P. O.Box 597
Mountain Home, ID 83647
208-366-7992
*Small Animal, Equine
AC, BF, CH, CM, CR, HC, WH*

ILLINOIS

Annie Logan, D.V.M.
34W 856 Country Club Road
St. Charles, IL 60174
630-513-7199
FAX: 630-377-8898
*Small Animal, Equine
AC(IVAS), AK, CH, CR, EAV*

Deborah M. Mitchell, D.V.M.
2237 W. Schaumburg Road
Schaumburg, IL 60172
847-891-8944
FAX: 847-891-9040
Small Animal
AC(IVAS), BF, CH, CM, CN,
GT, H, HO, HC, NU, WH,
Massage/Touch Therapy

Ellen M. Paul, D.V.M.
908 E. Main
Urbana, IL 61801
217-344-1017
FAX: 217-344-0654
AC(IVAS), BF, CH, CM, GT, NU, WH

Herbert W. Preiser, D.V.M.
2975 Milwaukee Avenue
Northbrook, IL 60062
847-827-5218
FAX: 847-827-7176
Small Animal
AC, BF, CM, CN, CR, HC, NU, WH

Ray Sytek, D.V.M.
1211-11th Street
Rockford, IL 61104
815-963-9685
FAX: 815-963-8192
CR(AVCA), EAV,
Orthomolecular Medicine

Judith Rae Swanson, D.V.M.
1465 W. Catalpa Avenue
Chicago, IL 60640
773-561-4526
AC(IVAS), BF, CM, CN, H, HC
(rare), HO (acute), NU

Sharon L. Willoughby, D.V.M.
P. O. Box 249
Port Byron, IL 61275
309-658-2920
FAX: 309-658-2622
Equine, Canine
CR

INDIANA

Carolyn S. Blakey, D.V.M.
1821 W. Main Street
Richmond, IN 47374
317-966-0015
FAX: 317-935-9043
Small Animal, Exotic
AC(IVAS), BF, CM, CN, GT, HO,
NU, WH

Mark P. Haverkos, D.V.M.
Box 119
Oldenburg, IN 47036
812-934-2410
AC, CH, CM, CR, EAV, H, HC,
NU, WH, Network Chiropractic

IOWA

Richard J. Holliday, D.V.M.
3 Allamakee Street
Waukon, IA 52172
319-568-3401
Dairy Cattle Specialist
AC(IVAS), Colustrum Therapy

Charles L. McDaniel, D.V.M.
2804 68th Street
Des Moines, IA 50322-3469
515-278-9032
Small Animal, Equine, Farm
Animal
AC(IVAS), CR

William Pollak, D.V.M.
1115 E. Madison Avenue
Fairfield, IA 52556
515-472-6983
CH, CM, CN, CR, NU, WH,
Ayurvedic Medicine

KANSAS

Jeffrey F. Van Petten, D.V.M.
RR 1, Box 98
Meriden, KS 66512
913-484-3358
FAX: 913-484-3230
Small Animal, Equine, Farm Animal
AC(IVAS), CM, CR, EAC, MT

Yashema, D.V.M.
Box 206
Neodesha, KS 66757-0206
316-325-2758
Small Animal, Equine, Farm Animal, Avian, Exotic
Communication with Animals

KENTUCKY

Frances E. Baker, D.V.M.
303 Stoner Avenue
Paris, KY 40361
606-987-0856
FAX: 606-987-1971
Small Animal
AC(IVAS), BF, CM, EAV, WH

Elizabeth (Betty) Boswell, D.V.M.
5607 Oxford Court, #862
Louisville, KY 40291
502-459-4506
AC, CH, CM, CN, EAV, NU,
Physical Therapy

Earl Sutherland, D.V.M.
P. O. Box 12009
Lexington, KY 40579
606-281-1183
AC(IVAS), CR

LOUISIANA

Mary Finley, D.V.M.
P. O. Box 234
Leonville, LA 70551
318-879-2020
Small Animal, Avian, Exotic
AC(IVAS), CH, CM, WH

Casey Lestrade, D.V.M.
P. O. Box 339
#4 Westbank Expressway
Westwego, LA 70094
504-436-7911
FAX: 504-436-7911
Small Animal, Avian, Exotic
AC, AC(IVAS)

Lowell K. Roger, D.V.M.
539 Bonnabel Boulevard
Metairie, LA 70005
504-832-5113
FAX: 504-832-5115
Equine
AC(IVAS), HC

Adriana Sagrera, D.V.M.
802 Octavia Street
New Orleans, LA 70115
504-899-9510
FAX: 504-529-7183
Small Animal, Avian, Exotic
BF, CR, HO, MT

MAINE

Lynda J. R. Bond, D.V.M.
Vet Centre of Cape Elizabeth
207 Ocean House Road
Cape Elizabeth, ME 04107
207-799-2162
FAX: 207-799-1794
Small Animal, Exotic
AC, CH, EAC, MT

Sandra Haggett, V.M.D.
21 Federal Street
Bar Harbor, ME 04609
207-288-5733
FAX: 207-288-5147
Small Animal
AC(IVAS), CH

Mary Orff, D.V.M.
Limerick Mills Animal Hospital
Route 11, P. O. Box 537
Limerick, ME 04048
207-793-4493
FAX: 207-793-2968
Small Animal
BF, CH, CM, HO, NU, WH

MARYLAND

Grace L. Calabrese, D.V.M.
P. O. Box 245
Phoenix, MD 21131-0245
410-557-6040
Small Animal, Equine
AC, BF, CH, CN, HC, NU, Reiki

Christina B. Chambreau, D.V.M.
908 Cold Bottom Road
Sparks, MD 21152
410-771-4968
F, H, HC, NU

Cindy Dahle, D.V.M.
150 Kent Landing
Stevensville, MD 21666
410-643-7888
FAX: 410-604-0081
Small Animal
AC(IVAS), CH, CM, CN, WH

John A. Eagling, D.V.M.
11843 Ocean Gateway
Ocean City, MD 21842
410-213-1170
AC, CM

F. L. Earl, D.V.M.
2613 Hughes Road
Adelphi, MD 20783
301-434-1811
CM, CN, NU

Linda Gray, D.V.M.
1200 W. Old Liberty Road
Eldersburg, MD 21784
410-795-6106
Small Animal, Equine, Avian,
Exotic
AC, CH, CM, HC, NU, WH, Reiki,
Massage, Chiro, Magnets

Wendy Jensen, D.V.M.
7764 Chatfield Lane
Ellicott City, MD 21043
410-379-0671
Small Animal, Farm Animal,
Avian, Exotic
GT, HC, NU, Reiki

Monique Maniet, D.V.M.
4820 Moorland Lane
Bethesda, MD 20814
301-656-2882
FAX: 301-656-5033
Small Animal
AC(IVAS), BF, CH, CM, CN,
GT, H, HC, NU, WH

Francine K. Rattner, V.M.D.
85 W. Central Avenue
Edgewater, MD 21037
410-956-2932
FAX: 410-956-3755
Small Animal, Exotic
BF, CM, HC, NU

Shearon C. Smith, D.V.M.
3217 Henson Avenue
Annapolis, MD 21403
410-571-9661
301-261-8488
Small Animal
CH, CM, CN, HC, NU, WH,
Grievance Counseling

Carvel G. Tiekert, D.V.M.
2214 Old Emmorton Road
Bel Air, MD 21015
410-569-7777
FAX: 410-569-2346
Small Animal, Equine
AC(IVAS), BF, BI, CM, CN, CR,
GL, H, HC, PMT, NU, AK,
Acupuncture, Chiropractic

MASSACHUSETTS

Bud Allen, M.S., D.V.M.
99 Main Street
Haydenville, MA 01039
413-268-8387
FAX: 413-268-3899
Small Animal, Equine, Avian,
Exotic
AC(IVAS), AK, CR

Constance Breese, D.V.M.
P. O. Box 1709
Edgartown, MA 02539
508-627-3623

Randy Caviness, D.V.M., C.V.A.
35 Militia Circle
Stow, MA 01775
508-733-1337
Small Animal, Equine
AC(IVAS), CH, CM, CN, EAV,
GT, NU, WH

Sarah L. Cochran, D.V.M.
75 Locust Street
Uxbridge, MA 01569
508-278-6511
FAX: 508-278-7356
Equine
AC(IVAS)

Brian Corwin, D.V.M.
96 Inverness Lane
Longmeadow, MA 01106
413-565-5104
FAX: 413-565-5104
888-567-3840
Small Animal
AC(IVAS), BF, CH, CM, CN,
GT, HC, NU, WH,
Homotoxicology, Dr. Reckewee

Nancy Crowley, D.V.M.
120 Canal Street
Salem, MA 01970
508-741-2300
FAX: 508-744-4578
Small Animal
BF, CM, CN, H, HC, NU

Walter C. Jaworski, D.V.M.
87 Old Wendell Road
Northfield, MA 01360
413-498-0174
Small Animal
GT, HC, NU

Robin Karlin, D.V.M.
99 Main Street
Haydenville, MA 01039
413-268-8387
FAX: 413-268-3899
Small Animal, Equine, Avian,
Exotic
BF, CM, HC, HO

Jeffrey Levy, D.V.M.
RR 01, Box 178-G
Williamsburg, MA 01096
413-268-3000
H, HC, NU

Robert G. Sidorsky, D.V.M.
Rt. 2
Shelburne Falls, MA 01370
413-625-9517
CM, CN, H, NU, WH

MICHIGAN

Grace Chang, D.V.M.
20158 Maplewood Street
Livonia, MI 48152-2021
248-356-0822
FAX: 248-356-0826
Small Animal
AC

Lynne Friday, D.V.M.
5346 Main Street
Lexington, MI 48450
810-359-8828
AC, AK, CR, CM, HO

Albert W. Lynch, D.V.M.
7966 U.S. 31 South
Grawn, MI 49637
616-276-6361
Small Animal
CM, CN, NU, WH, Super Blue-
Green Algae

H. D. Sheridan, D.V.M.
16025 68th Avenue
Coopersville, MI 49404
616-837-8151
AC(IVAS), CM, H, HO

John M. Simon, D.V.M.
410 N. Woodward
Royal Oak, MI 48067
810-545-6630
AC, AK, BF, CH, CM, CN, CR, EAV,
GT, HO, MT, NU, Mega
Therapy

Michael H. Stajich, D.V.M.
Ann Arbor, MI 49404
313-434-5800
AC(IVAS)

Russell W. Wagner, D.V.M.
7045 Traverse Avenue
P. O. Box 242
Benzonia, MI 49616
616-882-9906
FAX: 616-882-4434
AC, CR, HO, Energy Sensory

MINNESOTA

Roger DeHaan, D.V.M.
RR 1, Box 47A
Frazee, MN 56544
218-846-9112(MWF 9–12)
Small Animal, Equine, Farm
AC(IVAS), BF, CH, CM, CN,
CR, GT, H, HC, HO, NU, MT,
WH, Telephone Consultation,
Neuromuscular Release,
Proliferative Therapy, Neural
Therapy, Applied Kinesiology,
Laser Therapy

Fred Pomeroy, D.V.M.
185 E. 7th
St. Paul, MN 55101
612-224-4815
Small Animal
AK, GT, Cont Reflex Analysis

Catherine Sayler, D.V.M.
2400 Stevens Avenue, South
Minneapolis, MN 55404
612-870-4778
AC(IVAS), BF, CH, CM, CN,
EAV, GT, H, HO, NU, WH

Charlie Westman, D.V.M.
2620 Kenzie Terrace, #228
St. Anthony, MN 55418
612-464-8542
Small Animal, Equine
AC, CN, CR, MT

William G. Winter, D.V.M.
3131 Hennepin Avenue South
Minneapolis, MN 55408
612-825-6859
FAX: 612-824-6436
AC, BF, CH, CM, CN, GL, H,
HC, HO, NU, WH, Massage
Therapy, Behavior Therapy

MISSISSIPPI

John R. Adams, D.V.M.
5854 Canton Park Drive
Jackson, MS 39211
601-977-9327
Small Animal, Avian, Exotic
CH, CM, CN, WH

MISSOURI

Christine J. Crosley, D.V.M.
2615 S. Big Bend Boulevard
St. Louis, MO 63143
314-781-1738
FAX: 314-781-1702
Small Animal
BF, CM, CN, HC, WH

Randy Kidd, D.V.M.
911 W. 33rd Street
Kansas City, MO 64111
816-561-9011
FAX: 816-561-9011
Small Animal, Equine, Farm
Animal, Avian, Exotic
AC, BF, CM, CN, CR, HC, NU,
WH, Network CHIRO

Robert Schaeffer, Jr., D.V.M.
7001 Hampton Avenue
St. Louis, MO 63109
314-353-3444
Small Animal, Equine, Avian,
Exotic
AC(IVAS), BF, CH, CM, CN,
HC, NU, WH

MONTANA

John K. Harshman, D.V.M.
P. O. Box 371
Chinook, MT 59523
406-357-2936
FAX: 406-357-3367
Small Animal, Equine, Farm
Animal, Avian, Exotic
BF, GT, HO, NU

NEBRASKA

Joseph E. Landholm, D.V.M.
Lincoln, NE 68510-4972
402-483-4862
AC(IVAS)

Diane Simmons, D.V.M.
707 Tara Plaza
Papillion, NE 68046
402-593-6556
FAX: 402-593-8810
Small Animal, Equine
AC(IVAS), CH, CN, CR, EAC,
HO, NU, WH

NEVADA

Amy K. Mason, D.V.M.
P. O. Box 20283
Carson City, NV 89721
702-884-4362
Small Animal, Equine, Farm
Animal
AC, BF, CM, CN, CR, NU

Joanne Stefanatos, D.V.M.
1325 Vegas Valley Drive
Las Vegas, NV 89109
702-735-7184
FAX: 702-732-4266
AC(IVAS), BF, CH, CM, CN, CR,
CT, EAV, GT, H, HO, IN, MT,
NU, PMT, WH, Chelation
Therapy, Neural Therapy

NEW HAMPSHIRE

Katherine Evans, D.V.M.
38 Ham Road
Raymond, NH 03077
603-225-9680
AC(IVAS), CH, CM, WH

Gretchen E. Ham, D.V.M.
Derry, NH 03038-1949
603-329-6689
AC(IVAS)

George Tarkleson, D.V.M.
123 Main
Colebrook, NH 03576
603-237-8871
FAX: 603-237-8248
*Small Animal, Equine, Farm
Animal
HC, NU*

NEW JERSEY

Gerald Buchoff, D.V.M.
9018 Kennedy Boulevard
North Bergen, NJ 07047
201-868-3753
Fax: 201-868-0453
*Small Animal
AC(IVAS), BF, CH, CN, CR, GT,
HC, WH*

Mark D. Newkirk, D.V.M.
9200 Ventnor Avenue
Margate, NJ 08402
609-823-3031
FAX: 609-822-9152
*Small Animal, Avian, Exotic
AC(IVAS), BF, CR, WH,
Immuno-Augmentative Therapy
for Cancer, Metabolic Nutrition
Analysis*

Charles T. Schenck, D.V.M.
777 Helmetta Boulevard
East Brunswick, NJ 08816
908-257-8882
AC(IVAS), BF, CM, CN, HO, IT

Brian T. Voynick, D.V.M.
1202 Sussex Turnpike
Randolph, NJ 07869
201-895-4999
FAX: 973-895-4948
*Small Animal
AC(IVAS), EAV, WH,
Moxabustion*

Gloria B. Weintrub, V.M.D.
190 Rt. 70
Medford, NJ 08055
609-953-3502
FAX: 609-953-5907
*Small Animal
AC(IVAS), BF, CH, CM, CN,
CR, GT, HO, IN*

NEW MEXICO

B. Dee Blanco, D.V.M.
P. O. Box 5865
Santa Fe, NM 87502-5865
505-473-1012
*Small Animal
AC(IVAS), BF, CN, GT, HC,
NU, WH*

Mona Ann Boudreaux, D.V.M.
3200 Coors, Suite D
Albuquerque, NM 87107
505-836-1736
FAX: 505-836-1736
*Small Animal
AC(IVAS), BF, CH, CM, CR,
GT, HO, NU*

Gigi Gaulin, D.V.M.
Rt. 2, Box 135
San Juan Pueble, NM 87566
505-852-0213
Small Animal
AC, BF, CH, HC, NU

Jody Kincaid, D.V.M.
901 E. Franklin
Anthony, NM 88021
915-886-4558
Small Animal, Equine
AC, CH, CM, HO, NU, WH,
35% H_2O_2 Therapy

Sharon Reamer, D.V.M.
2501 E. 20th, Suite A6
Farmington, NM 87401
505-327-2031
Small Animal, Avian, Exotic
BF, CM, CN, EAV, HC

Annet L. Sheffield, D.V.M.
8200 Montgomery NE #230
Albuquerque, NM 87109
505-292-3666
FAX: 505-332-8187
Small Animal

NEW YORK

Diane C. Abbysinian, D.V.M.
250 Central Park Avenue
White Plains, NY 10606-1218
914-949-8860
FAX: 914-949-3478
Small Animal
AC, CH, CN, CR, CT, MT, NU,
Acupressure, Reike

Peter L. Brown, D.V.M.
112 W. Lake Road
Penn Yan, NY 14527
315-536-2771
Small Animal, Equine, Exotic
AC, BF, CH, CM, CN, HC, HO,
NU, MT, WH

Beverly Cappel-King, D.V.M.
11 S. Main Street
Chestnut Ridge, NY 10977
914-356-3838
Immuno-Augmentative Therapy
(Cancer)

Marcie Fallek, D.V.M.
451 E. 83rd Street, Apt. 5B
New York, NY 10028
212-330-7061
Small Animal
AC(IVAS), BF, CM, GT, HC,
NU, WH

Mary Finger, D.V.M.
East Village Vet
241 Eldridge Street
New York, NY 10002
212-674-8640
CM, CN, H, NU, WH

Martin Goldstein, D.V.M.
Rob Witel, D.V.M.
400 Smithridge Road
South Salem, NY 10590
914-533-6066
AC(IVAS), BF, CH, CM, CN,
CR, GT, H, HC, HO, NU, MT,
WH, Immuno-Augmentative
Therapy (Cancer), Ozone
Therapy, Metabolic Nutritional
Analysis (MNA)

Mark E. Haimann, D.V.M.
1 Bay Club Drive, Apt. W19J
Bayside, NY 11360
718-631-1396
CH, CN, H, HC, NU, WH

Richard J. Joseph, D.V.M.
Animal Medical Center
New York, NY 10021
212-838-8100
AC(IVAS) Neurology

Steven Kasanofsky, D.V.M.
250 W. 100th Street
New York, NY 10025
212-865-2224
FAX: 212-787-1993
Small Animal
AC, CN

Cynthia Lankenau, D.V.M.
3380 Maple Road
Wilson, NY 14172
716-751-3885
Small Animal, Equine, Farm
Animal, Avian
AC(IVAS), BF, CH, CR, GT, HC,
HO, NU, WH, Reiki

John A. Ober, D.V.M.
West Main Street
Westfield, NY 14787
716-326-3933
Small Animal (Split shift)
AC(IVAS), CH, CR, HO, WH

John and Sarah Ober, D.V.M.
P. O. Box 5
90 Main Street
Candor, NY 13743
607-659-4220
FAX: 607-659-7387
Small Animal
AC, CR, HC

Margaret B. Ohlinger, D.V.M.
3800 County Route 6
Alpine, NY 14805
607-274-8090
Small Animal, Equine, Farm
Animal
AC, CM, CR, HC

Lisa G. Potkewitz, D.V.M.
Foothills Veterinary Services
P. O. Box 3040
Saratoga Springs, NY 12866
518-587-5228
Small Animal, Farm Animal
CN, NU, WH, Anthroposophy
Biodynamic Farming
Preservation of Rare Farm
Breeds

Iris Prestas, D.V.M.
90 Main Street
Candor, NY 13743
607-659-4220
CM, H, HC, NU, WH

Phillip Racyln, D.V.M.
219 W. 79th Street
New York, NY 10024
212-787-1993
FAX: 212-787-1397
Small Animal
AC, BF, CH, CM, CN, GT, HO,
NU, WH

Craig H. Russell, D.V.M.
P. O. Box 396
Pleasant Street
Westport, NY 12993
518-962-8228
FAX: 518-962-8308
Small Animal
CM, CN, NU, WH

John F. Sangiorgio, D.V.M.
12930 Clove Road
Staten Island, NY 10301
718-720-4211
FAX: 718-720-4212
Small Animal, Equine
CH, CR, CM, CN, HC, NU, MT,
PMT, WH

Ron Scharf, D.V.M.
2764 Troy Schenectady Road
Niskayuna, NY 12309
518-785-9731
AC(IVAS), CM

Alisa Sheade-Koenig, D.V.M.
653 South Street
East Aurora, NY 14052
716-687-1808
Small Animal, Equine
HC, NU, WH

Ivan Szilvassy, D.V.M.
98 Norman Avenue
Brooklyn, NY 11222
718-389-8866
CH, CN, H, HC, MT, NU, WH,
Reflexology

Patrick Tersigni, V.M.D.
Hemmer Road, Rt. 1
Wayland, NY 14572
716-728-5562
CR, Radiance Technique (AKA-
Real Reiki)

Michele A. Yasson, D.V.M.
1101 Rt. 32
Rosendale, NY 12472
914-658-3923
Has office in New York City
Tuesdays at 47 E. 30th
AC(IVAS), BF, CN, HC, NU

NORTH CAROLINA

Ann Davis, D.V.M.
3741 High Point Road
Greensboro, NC 27407
910-299-5431
FAX: 910-299-5441
Small Animal
BF, CH, HC, NU, WH

Kim V. Hombs, D.V.M.
6520 McMahon Drive
Charlotte, NC 28226
704-542-2000
FAX: 704-542-2000
Small Animal
AC, AC(IVAS), BF, CH, CM,
CN, HO

John H. Koontz, D.V.M.
4306 Roxboro Road
Durham, NC 27704
919-471-1579
Equine
AC, CN, CT, HC

Charles E. Loops, D.V.M.
Rt. 2, Box 568
Pittsboro, NC 27312
919-542-0442
H, HC, Telephone Consultations

William M. Martin, D.V.M.
6795 Hendersonville Road
Fletcher, NC 28732
704-684-4244
AC(IVAS), CM

James Miller, D.V.M.
493 Warrior Mountain Road
Saluda, NC 28773
704-749-2233
AC, BF, IN, MT

Adele C. Monroe, D.V.M.
4122 Pecan Drive
Stem, NC 27581
919-693-0442
Small Animal
CN, CR, HC, NU, WH, Flower
Essence Therapy, Reiki

Kathy Radford, D.V.M.
4740 High Point Road
Greensboro, NC 27407
910-294-1944
FAX: 910-297-1040
Small Animal
BF, CH, CM, CN, HC, NU, WH

James E. Schacht, D.V.M.
6400 E. Independence Boulevard
Charlotte, NC 28212
704-535-6688
Avian, Exotic
AC(IVAS), BF, CH, HC

OHIO

Pamela Fisher, D.V.M.
5250 Pinedrive Circle NW
North Canton, OH 44720
330-494-7387
FAX: 330-494-8179
Small Animal
CH, CM, CN, GT, HO, NU, WH

Donn W. Griffith, D.V.M.
3859 W. Dublin-Granville Road
Dublin, OH 43017
614-889-2556
FAX: 614-761-3623
AC(IVAS), BF, BI, CH, CM, CN,
CR, CT, EAV, GT, H, HC, HO,
NU, MT, WH, Osteopathic,
Radionics, Counseling,
Prepurchase Exotic Animals

Ronald L. McNutt, D.V.M.
Lima, OH 45805
419-331-1456
AC(IVAS)

George D. Norris, D.V.M.
5756 N. High Street
Worthington, OH 43085
614-885-0333
AC(IVAS), BF, CM, CN, H, HC,
NU, MT, PMT

OKLAHOMA

George A. Carley, D.V.M.
Hunters Glen Vet Hosp
9150 S. Braden
Tulsa, OK 74137
918-493-3332
Small Animal, Exotic
AC(IVAS), CM, CN, HC, N, WH

Nita McNeill, D.V.M.
130 E. Highway 152
Mustang, OK 73064
405-376-4556
AC, BF, CM, CN, CR, EAV,
NU, Bio Acidative Medicine

OREGON

R. H. Anderson, D.V.M.
1590 E. Ellendale
Dallas, OR 97338
503-623-8318
AC(IVAS), CM, CN, CR, EAV,
H, IN, MT, NU

Jeffrey Judkins, D.V.M.
Bob Ulbrich, V.M.D.
1431 SE 23rd
Portland, OR 97214
503-233-2332
Small Animal, Avian, Exotic
AC(IVAS), BF, CH, CM, CN,
GT, HC, WH

Donna Starita Mehan, D.V.M.
27728 SE Haley Road
Boring, OR 97009
503-663-7277
FAX: 503-663-9393
Small Animal, Equine, Farm
Animal
BF, CH, CM, CN, CR, CT, EAV,
GT, HO, NU, MT, WH,
Ridionics, Crystal Healing

Richard Pitcairn, D.V.M.
1283 Lincoln Street
Eugene, OR 97401
541-342-7665
FAX: 503-344-5356
Small Animal
BF, CN, H, HC, NU

Jim Simpson, D.V.M.
19073 Beavercreek Road
Oregon City, OR 97045
503-650-1667
FAX: 503-650-1667
Small Animal
AC, BF, CH, CM, CN, CR,
GT, HC, HO, WH

Bob Ulbrich, V.M.D.
2227 SW Primrose Street
Portland, OR 97219
503-233-2332
Small Animal
BF, CH, GT, HC, NU, Pranic
Healing

PENNSYLVANIA

Susan Beal, D.V.M.
Glen Dupree, D.V.M.
East Main Street
Big Run, PA 15716
814-427-5004
FAX: 814-427-5929
Small Animal, Equine, Farm
Animal, Avian, Exotic
AC, BF, CN, CR, GT, HO,
MT, NU, WH, Magnetic Therapy

Elizabeth E. Burke, D.V.M.
929 Northampton Street
Easton, PA 18042
610-559-0728
Small Animal
BF, HC

John C. Harthorn, D.V.M.
2176 Brush Run Road
Avella, PA 15312
412-345-3350
FAX: 412-345-3706
Equine
AC(IVAS), CR, HC, WH

Carlos F. Jimenez, D.V.M.
All Creatures Mobile Vet
St. Peters, PA 19470
610-469-1119
AC(IVAS)

Deva Kaur Khalsa, V.M.D.
1724 Yardley-Langhorne Road
Yardley, PA 19067-5517
215-493-0621
Small Animal
AC(IVAS), AK, BF, CH, CM, CN,
CR, EAV, GT, HO, IN, MT, NU,
WH, Phone Consultations,
Ozone, NAET, Allergy
Elimination Technique

Douglas E. Knueven, D.V.M.
357 State Street
Beaver, PA 15009
412-774-8047
FAX: 412-774-5774
Small Animal
AC(IVAS), BF, CM, HC

Marjorie M. Lewter, D.V.M.
RR 2, Box 155F
Ulster, PA 18850
717-596-3757
Small Animal, Equine, Farm
Animal
AC, AC(IVAS), BF, CH, CN,
HO, WH

Sally Myton, V.M.D.
999 Killarney Drive
Pittsburgh, PA 15234
412-884-2434
FAX: 412-884-5222
Small Animal
BF, CM, H, HO, NU

C. Edgar Sheaffer, V.M.D.
P. O. Box 353
47 N. Railroad Street
Palmyra, PA 17078-0353
717-838-9563
FAX: 717-838-0377
Small Animal, Equine, Farm
Animal
CM, HC

Meredith Snader, V.M.D.
2140 Conestoga Road
Chester Springs, PA 19425
610-827-7742
FAX: 610-827-1366
Equine
AC(IVAS), CH, CR, HO

Michael S. Tierney, V.M.D.
428 Brownsburg Road
Upper Makefield
Newtown, PA 18940
215-598-3951
FAX: 215-598-3746
Small Animal, Equine, Farm
Animal, Avian, Exotic
AC(IVAS), BF, CH, CM, CN,
CR, GT, HC, NU

Jeanne F. Wordley, V.M.D.
402 W. 3rd Street
Media, PA 19063-2601
610-566-9019
Small Animal
AC(IVAS), CH, CM, NU

Susan Yatsky, V.M.D.
341 W. Butler Avenue
New Britain, PA 18901
215-340-0345
AC, CH, CM, CN, GL, HO, NU

RHODE ISLAND

Elizabeth Campbell, D.V.M.
Wolfrock Animal Health Center
710 S. County Trail
Exeter, RI 02822
401-294-0102
Small Animal, Farm Animal,
Exotic
AC, BF, CH, CM, EAV, HO,
NU, WH

SOUTH CAROLINA

Jeanne R. Fowler, D.V.M.
409 Old Buncombe Road
Travelers Rest, SC 29690
864-834-7334
AC, CN, CM, GT, H, HC

Stanley Gorlitsky, D.V.M.
461 Coleman Boulevard
Mt. Pleasant, SC 29464
803-881-9915
AC(IVAS), BF, CH, CM, CN,
GT, H, HC, HO, MT, WH

TENNESSEE

Sandra Priest, D.V.M.
600 Bennington Circle
Knoxville, TN 37909
423-690-3863
FAX: 423-690-3863
Small Animal
BF, CR (AVCA certified), GT,
HC, NU, WH, Reiki

TEXAS

James K. Bielfeldt, D.V.M.
305 Fawn Drive
San Antonio, TX 78231
210-696-1700, 210-696-3753
Small Animal
AC, EAV

Nancy A. Bozeman, D.V.M.
5721 SW Green Oaks Boulevard
Arlington, TX 76017
817-572-2400
AC(IVAS), BF, CM, CN, CR,
GT, H, HC, HO, NU, WH

Paul R. Bruton, D.V.M.
1615 E. Southlake Boulevard
Southlake, TX 76092
817-481-1382
Small Animal, Equine
AC(IVAS), CM, CR, EAV, NU

Jackie Cole, D.V.M.
3802 Cove View
Galveston, TX 77554
409-740-0808
Small Animal
AC(IVAS), CM, EAV

Patricia A. Cooper, D.V.M.
1951 Lexington
Houston, TX 77098
713-520-5588
FAX: 713-523-8345
Small Animal
BF, CN, HO, NU

Jerry B. Dittrich, D.V.M.
9009 Highway 377 South
Benbrook, TX 76126
817-249-2744
FAX: 817-249-0714
Small Animal, Equine, Farm,
Avian, Exotic
AC(IVAS), CH, CM, CN, CR,
EAC, GT, H, NU

William Falconer, D.V.M.
8005 N. Madrone Trail
Austin, TX 78737
512-288-5400
FAX: 512-288-5402
Small Animal, Avian
BF, GT, HC, NU

Thomas L. Granger, D.V.M.
380 North LHS Drive
Lumberton, TX 77656
409-755-7216
Small Animal
AC(IVAS), CH, CM, EAC, WH,
Reiki

S. J. Gravel, D.V.M.
Rt. 2, Box 140
Lockhart, TX 78644
512-398-3719
Small Animal
AC(IVAS), CH, CM, EAV, WH

Shawn Messonnier, D.V.M.
2145 W. Park Boulevard
Plano, TX 75075
972-867-8800
FAX: 214-985-9216
Small Animal, Avian, Exotic
AC, CM, NU, Dietary
Supplement, Allergy and
Arthritis Treatment

Norman C. Ralston, D.V.M.
12500 Lake June Road
Mesquite, TX 75180
214-286-6407
AC(IVAS), BF, CR, EAV, H, MT,
Proliferant, Neural Therapy

Brian A. Reeves, D.V.M.
2711 University Boulevard
Tyler, TX 75701-7465
903-566-2011
AC(IVAS)

Anna Maria Scholey, D.V.M.
2922 Mill Trail
Carrollton, TX 75007
972-245-1123
FAX: 972-245-1123
Small Animal
AC(IVAS), BF, EAV, GT, HC,
MT, NU, Reiki

Betsy Walker-Harrison, D.V.M.
100 Park Road South
Wimberley, TX 78676
210-935-2596
Small Animal
BF, CN, GT, HC, WH,
Telephone Consultations

Madalyn Ward, D.V.M.
Rt. 6, Box 47-H
Austin, TX 78737
512-288-0428
Equine
CN, CR, HC

UTAH

Kimberly Henneman, D.V.M.
150 Starview Drive
Park City, UT 84098
801-647-0807
FAX: 801-647-2985
Small Animal, Equine, Exotic
AC(IVAS), BF, CM, CR, ElecAC,
H, MT, N, WH

Shannon Hines, D.V.M.
3305 S. Orchard Drive
Bountiful, UT 84010
801-296-1230
FAX: 801-298-8445
Small Animal
CM, H, MT

VERMONT

David T. Lamb, D.V.M.
Justin Morrill Highway
South Stafford, VT 05070
802-765-4400
AC, CM, CR

George Glanzberg, V.M.D.
RR 1, Box 373
North Bennington, VT 05257
802-442-8714
CM, CN, H, HC, NU

Alaire Smith-Miller, D.V.M.
RR 1, Box 636
Wilmouth Hill Road
Cuttingsville, VT 05738
802-747-4076
Small Animal, Equine, Avian
AC, BF, CM, CN, HC, MT, NU

William K. Kruesi, D.V.M.
Nickwackett Animal Hospital
RR 3, Box 3113
Pittsford, VT 05763
802-483-9318
Small Animal
CM, CN, HC, NU, WH

VIRGINIA

Nino Aloro, D.V.M.
2212 Laskin Road
Virginia Beach, VA 23454
757-340-5040
FAX: 757-340-5043
Small Animal
CH, CM, CN, NU, WH

Cheryl A. Caputo, D.V.M.
P. O. Box 240
430 Roanoke Road
Daleville, VA 24083
540-992-4550
FAX: 540-992-1822
Small Animal
AK, BF, CM, CN, GT, HC, MST,
NU, WH

Stephen Dill, D.V.M.
Rt. 2, Box 156
Barboursville, VA 22923
804-985-4795
Equine
AC(IVAS), CM, CR, HC

Joyce C. Harman, MRCVS
P. O. Box 488
Washington, VA 22747-0008
540-675-1855
FAX: 540-675-1447
AC(IVAS), BF, CH, CN, Network
CR, H, HC, HO, NU

Jordan A. Kocen, D.V.M.
6136 Brandon Avenue
Springfield, VA 22150
703-569-0300
FAX: 703-866-4962
AC(IVAS), CH, HC

Carol A. Lundquist, D.V.M.
P. O. Box 394
Washington, VA 22747
540-675-2273
FAX: 540-675-2040
Equine
AC, AK, BF, CH, CN, CR, HC,
HO, LM, MT, NU, WH

Maureen McIntyre, D.V.M.
6540 Megills Court
Clifton, VA 20124
703-449-9144
Small Animal, Equine
AC(IVAS), CR, EAV

Martin Schulman, V.M.D.
RR 1, Box 20
Crozet, VA 22932
804-823-4300
FAX: 804-823-6436
Small Animal
CH, CN, GT, NU, WH

Anita Walton, D.V.M.
P. O. Box 488
Locust Grove, VA 22508-0488
703-972-3869
FAX: 703-972-9216
Small Animal
AC(IVAS), BF, CM, CN, GT,
HC, NU, WH

WASHINGTON

Junia Childs, D.V.M.
Holistic Veterinary Medicine
and Acupuncture
722 16th Avenue West
Kirkland, WA 98033
425-889-9498
Small Animal
Traditional Chinese Medicine
AC, BF, CH, H, NU, WH
Telephone Consultations

Kerry Fisher, D.V.M.
11901 N. Division
Spokane, WA 99218
509-468-0443
FAX: 509-468-0452
Small Animal
AC, CH, CN, CR, MT, WH, Pain
Management

Michael Flaherty, D.V.M.
6741 Beach Drive SW
Seattle, WA 98136
425-745-6745
Small Animal, Exotic
CM, CN, CT, NU, Home
Euthanasia Consultations

Eric P. Hartmann, D.V.M.
704 E. Thomas Street, #107
Seattle, WA 98102-5434
206-781-6709
Small Animal
AC(IVAS), BF, CH, CN, GT, HC,
HO, NU, WH

Lee Herzig, D.V.M.
8306 Stringtown Road East
Eatonville, WA 98328
360-832-6500
FAX: 360-832-6252
Small Animal
AC(IVAS), CM, CN, CR, GT, WH

Pamela Jen, D.V.M.
21416 NE 10th Avenue
Ridgefield, WA 98642-9459
360-887-0714
Small Animal
AC(IVAS), BF, CH, CM, CN, CR
Network, HO, NU, WH, Qi
Gong, Massage TX,
Physical TX

Donna Kelleher, D.V.M.
6741 Beach Drive SW
Seattle, WA 98136
206-935-3041
Small Animal
AC(IVAS), CH, CM, CN, EAV,
GT, WH

Michael W. Lemmon, D.V.M.
P. O. Box 2085
Renton, WA 98056
206-226-8418
AC, BF, CH, CM, CN, CR, GL,
H, HC, MT, NU, PMT, WH

Steve Marsden, D.V.M.
7302 NE 43rd Way
Vancouver, WA 98662
503-255-7355
Small Animal, Exotic
AC, BF, CH, CM, CN, EAV, GT,
HC, NU, WH, Naturopathic
Medicine

Patti Schaefer, D.V.M.
3430 Pacific Avenue, Suite #6355
Olympia, WA 98501
360-923-5759
206-370-1350
Small Animal
AC, BF, CH, CM, CN, HC, NU

Larry Siegler, D.V.M.
8015 165th Avenue NE
Redmond, WA 98052
425-885-5400
FAX: 425-869-2304
Small Animal
AC(IVAS), BF, CH, CM, CN,
HC, NU, WH

Tevinder Sodhi, D.V.M.
6501 196th Street SW, #F
Lynnwood, WA 98036
Bellevue, WA 98004
206-771-6300
FAX: 206-771-6300
206-455-8900
FAX: 206-455-9946
Small Animal, Exotic
BF, CN, HC, HO, Ayuvveda

Douglas R. Yearout, D.V.M.
9004 Vernon Road
Everett, WA 98205
425-334-8171
FAX: 425-334-1136
Small Animal, Avian, Exotic
Wildlife Rehab
AC, AK, AR, AY, BF, CH, CM,
CN, CR, EAV, GT, HC, LM,
MT, NU, RI, WH

H. Jonathan Wright, D.V.M.
7327 S. Cedar Road
Spokane, WA 99224
509-443-0803
Small Animal
BF, GT, H, HO, NU, Reiki
Telephone Consultations
House Calls

WEST VIRGINIA

Jane Laura Doyle, D.V.M.
P. O. Box 568
Berkeley Springs, WV 25411
304-258-5819
AC(IVAS), BF, CH, CM, CN, CR,
EAV, H, HC, HO, NU, WH

WISCONSIN

Marta Engel, D.V.M.
Rt. 1, Box 1198
Soldiers Grove, WI 54655
608-734-3711
FAX: 608-734-3306
Small Animal, Equine, Farm
Animal
CM, H, HC, NU

Maria H. Glinski, D.V.M.
1405 W. Silver Spring Drive
Glendale, WI 53209
414-228-7655
FAX: 414-228-1072
Small Animal
AC(IVAS), BF, CH, CM, CN,
CR, EAV, GT, HC, HO, LM,
MT, NU, WH

Mike Kohn, D.V.M.
1014 Williamson
Madison, WI 53703
608-255-1239
Small Animal
AC(IVAS), BF, HC, NU, WH

Pedro Luis Rivera, D.V.M.
9824 Durand Avenue
Sturtevant, WI 53177
414-886-1100
FAX: 414-886-6460
Small Animal, Equine, Farm
Animal, Avian, Exotic
BF, CH, CM, CN, CR, CT, GT,
HC, HO, NU, WH, Massage
Therapy, Acupressure

Deborah L. Schroeder, D.V.M.
1440 E. Washington Avenue
Madison, WI 53703
608-255-2977
AC(IVAS), BF, CH, CM, CN

WYOMING

Vicki Burton, D.V.M.
812 S. 13th Street
Laramie, WY 82070
307-742-2488
Small Animal, Equine
AC(IVAS), BF, CH, WH

Stephen M. Kerr, D.V.M.
RR #2, Box 326
Torrington, WY 82240
307-532-7704
FAX: 307-532-4736
Small Animal, Equine, Farm
Animal, Avian, Exotic
AC, BF, CH, CM, CN, CR, EAV,
HC, WH

Index

About the Author

PAT LAZARUS has been a respected investigative medical journalist since the late 1970s, publishing some four hundred articles in magazines for the public and in technical publications written for doctors. These articles have disseminated little-known successful orthodox and natural treatments for humans. Her first book, *Keep Your Pet Healthy the Natural Way*, one of the very first books written on holistic care for animals, was widely acclaimed, remained in print for almost two decades, and is often considered the classic book in the field of natural care for dogs and cats. This present book greatly expands and completely updates the earlier book and focuses only on dogs. Its companion book, *Keep Your Cat Healthy the Natural Way*, also updates the earlier book and focuses only on cats.

A fourth book, *Healing the Mind the Natural Way*, compiled the work of a number of psychiatrists who use nutritional therapy and other natural techniques to treat emotional and mental disorders in humans.

Pat, who greatly respects orthodox techniques such as drugs and surgery—particularly in emergency situations—has come by her particular passion for natural therapies by a personal route. She, her husband, and many of her own animal companions have used nutritional therapy, acupuncture, homeopathy, and/or glandular therapy to recover easily from problems diagnosed by orthodox doctors as needing dangerous major surgery or potent drugs—or as being untreatable or downright terminal.